ENDLESS WAR

Books by Ralph Peters

Nonfiction

Looking for Trouble
Wars of Blood and Faith
New Glory
Never Quit the Fight
Beyond Baghdad
Beyond Terror
Fighting for the Future

Fiction

The War After Armageddon
Traitor
The Devil's Garden
Twilight of Heroes
The Perfect Soldier
Flames of Heaven
The War in 2020
Red Army
Bravo Romeo

Writing as Owen Parry

Fiction

Rebels of Babylon
Bold Sons of Erin
Honor's Kingdom (Hammett Award)
Call Each River Jordan
Shadows of Glory
Faded Coat of Blue (Herodotus Award)
Our Simple Gifts
Strike the Harp

ENDLESS WAR

Middle-Eastern Islam vs. Western Civilization

Ralph Peters

STACKPOLE
BOOKS

Published by
STACKPOLE BOOKS
5067 Ritter Road
Mechanicsburg, PA 17055
www.stackpolebooks.com

Printed in the United States

First edition

10 9 8 7 6 5 4 3 2

Library of Congress Cataloging-in-Publication Data

Peters, Ralph, 1952–
  Endless war : Middle-Eastern Islam vs. Western Civilization / Ralph
Peters.
    p. cm.
  ISBN-13: 978-0-8117-0550-9 (hardcover)
  ISBN-10: 0-8117-0550-1 (hardcover)
  1. Comparative civilization. 2. Civilization, Western. 3. Civilization,
Islamic. 4. Islam and world politics. 5. East and West. 6. Violence—
Religious aspects. 7. Terrorism—Religious aspects. I. Title.
  CB251.P484 2010
  909'.09821—dc22
                                    2009031232

To Friend Peters, an uncle I never met,
gassed on the Western Front in 1918.

And to John Parfitt and Robert Parfitt, uncles wounded
a day apart in the final push to the Rhine in 1945.

Their country called. They answered.

May they rest in peace.

———————————

"Search into the essence of each matter, whether of
doctrine, practice or belief."

—Marcus Aurelius,
Meditations

CONTENTS

Introduction

History and Hysteria

The citizens of the United States do not stand apart from history. We are in it and of it. Many of our ancestors came here hoping to escape it, but history is a pack of bloodhounds. Desperate to put those persistent dogs off the scent, we embrace fantasies in preference to facts. When the baying grows too near, we succumb to superstitious rituals, chanting that peace is the natural order of things and behaving as if violence were a spook we might drive away with Ivy-League fetishes and bouts of self-flagellation.

History so threatens us that its serious instruction has been stripped from our schools, replaced by narratives meant to correct the social views of children. Teachers know little; children learn less; and myths flourish. At the university level, the discipline of history has been perverted and the historian abandons his duty to society like a medieval doctor fleeing the plague. Careers are made by decades of concentration on dental hygiene in a hamlet in twelfth-century Languedoc, rather than in a struggle to comprehend the human excesses that haunt the centuries. The effect of character upon events is downplayed, while religion is regarded with nostrils pinched shut. Above all, the study of warfare—that infernally addictive human activity—is shunned in horror.

Once cherished, history is currently viewed as onerous—unless employed for social engineering. The results are political leaders who cannot weigh the consequences of their actions; journalists who confuse the exciting with the significant; military officers who view their profession through peepholes; and impatient citizens easily misled. In place of history, we get hysterical headlines.

A solid grounding in history won't provide us with maps to the future, but helps us frame risks and analyze behaviors. It may not hand us a repair manual, but offers a dashboard full of warning lights. It gives us the context essential to understanding the events of our time in their gravity and fullness. Above all, history that adheres to facts inoculates the citizen against lies.

A paradox of today's American society is that our best-educated citizens have the least sense of historical reality. When genial professors play pretend, students are only too glad to play along, and when the man or woman behind the podium absolves them of the responsibilities of service, translating their timidity into imagined courage and assuring them that "war doesn't change anything," how many students feel compelled to question the dispensation? The clever subversive panders to the young.

But in the real world—in which even academics perish—war often changes everything. The blood-drunk killer is rarely disarmed by the man who lives in books—or by the eternal adolescent clinging to the lie that all men want peace.

History isn't comforting, and therein lies its public-relations problem. Recent bursts of violence notwithstanding, we Americans have been blessed to live in such deep peace, prosperity, and comfort for so long that we find humankind's record unbearable: We want no part of it. For the man or woman whose notion of tragedy is a cancelled vacation, the mad butchery splashing history with blood is socially unacceptable.

But we're a species that fights when sufficiently frustrated. And under the brutal pressures of globalization, human frustrations will increase throughout our lifetimes. We face an era of endless war, relieved only by interludes of exhaustion.

We may wish it otherwise—and I do—but history insists that we're murderous animals, and the worst among us feel most alive when inflicting pain on others. We cry that "All men want peace," but some do not (few "peace activists" would care for a police-free world). One of our most-dangerous illusions holds that the "rights" of monsters in human form must be protected. And so, in our crusades to save terrorists and mass murderers from punishment, we condemn the billions who do want peace to suffer the rule of the gun: When we elevate the cause of the killers above the security of the citizenry, we are guilty of a profoundly perverse elitism. Yesteryear's fairy tales warned us not to trust the wolves, but today's well-brought-up children are expected to consider the wolf's needs and discontents.

Sometimes, though, the wolf still needs to be killed.

To study what men have done is to see ourselves as we are: History's mirror disintegrates our makeup. With its casualty lists, litany of atrocities, and suggestions that heroism, too, may require violence, history shows us "the skull beneath the skin." And no matter how firmly we shut our eyes, the skull will still be there.

In selecting the essays, articles, and columns for this collection, I found myself drawn to those most deeply rooted in history. My own view of the world has always been shaped by what knowledge of the past I could assemble, but I've never felt so frustrated as I do now by the historical illiteracy of those who make policy, mold opinions, and vote. Listening to a talking head or reading a newspaper column, I all too often want to bellow, "Read some [expletive deleted] history, for God's sake. . . ." But when we have a vice president who believes that Franklin Delano Roosevelt communicated with the American people via television during the Depression and a president who insists that

Islam played a major role in our country's early development, one can hardly fault the average citizen for lacking a historical perspective on casualty rates.

So I have chosen to begin this book with articles that highlight the cringe-inducing fact that the Muslim and Christian worlds have been at war ever since a visionary merchant in Arabia composed the Koran (what a splendidly charismatic man Mohammed must have been!). Of course, we pretend otherwise—frantically so. We leap to sanitized judgments about the roots of our present conflicts, while denying that religion has even a tangential influence on human behavior. We are even less honest about the power of faith than about the allure of war. And the history of religion's influence on human affairs is strictly avoided—unless an anecdote or two can be used to deride Christianity. In an astonishing corruption of the historical facts, we ascribe a level of tolerance to Islam—a religion spread and maintained by the sword—that makes murderous caliphs sound like the merry leaders of hippie communes. After fighting in the Middle East for nearly a decade, we still don't know how we got there.

Would it have influenced anyone's thinking about Iraq had they known that the last mass slaughter of local Christians occurred as recently as 1933, or that, in bygone centuries, Saddam Hussein's hometown was passionately Christian? Perhaps not. But the knowledge couldn't hurt.

We've barely escaped a century in which Turkish Muslims delighted in the massacre of a million and a half Christian Armenians; when six million Jews were slaughtered because they were Jews; when at least a million human beings died as British India divided because they were either Hindus, Muslims, or Sikhs; in which Christians and Muslims continued to struggle atrociously on the African frontier of these two militant faiths; and in which—little more than a decade ago—thousands of men and boys were executed at Srebrenica because they were Muslims (it mattered not a whit that they drank alcohol and ate pork—to their Christian Serb executioners, they were *Muslims*).

We pretend that every next genocide, pogrom, or massacre is an aberration that will not happen again. But history insists that *faiths fight*. Mocking their god's better-natured instructions and their holy texts, men find infinite excuses to slaughter their neighbors. Blubbering that "Islam's a religion of peace," or that any religion is inherently peaceful, won't save a single life. Religion as practiced on this earth is what men and women make it. All too often, we make a bloody mess.

As a religious believer, I am ashamed. As a citizen, I am wary. As a human being, I am fascinated.

The conviction prevails in privileged circles that, if we study history without first reshaping it to our contemporary prejudices, history will corrupt us. May I suggest that the opposite is true?

Some of the pieces in this book engage history more obviously than do others. But every line is shaped by a sense of the past. I have sometimes changed my mind, but I have never changed the facts.

Those who deny history die of myth.

—Ralph Peters
June 1, 2009

PART I

The War We Pretend Away

Crescent Triumphant!

Armchair General

July 2008

Despite lashing out intermittently with terror, the Islamic world has been thrust onto the strategic defensive over the last three centuries. Superior Western militaries shattered one Muslim army after another, and since the failed siege of Vienna in 1683, victories for the jihadis of Islam have been ever fewer and humiliations ever more frequent. It was not always so.

During the first thousand years of military competition between the cross and the crescent, Muslim standards waved in triumph over countless battlefields as the *ghazis* who followed Mohammed's revelation annihilated Christian armies and devoured "infidel" states, ultimately dominating half of the territory we now include in Europe. Arab cavalry raided north of the Pyrenees, and Muslim emirs ruled the Iberian Peninsula for centuries. In a later wave of Muslim conquests, the Turks rampaged across the Balkans, their janissaries failing them only at the plague-haunted gates of Vienna. Tatars thrust deep into Poland, Arabs mastered Sicily, and the Greeks lost their independence for half a millennium.

This greatest of struggles between civilizations produced history's longest military confrontation: The identities of emperors, kings, sultans, and despots changed, as did the composition of their armies, but the thirteen-hundred-year contest for hegemony

over the Middle East, North Africa, and Europe never really ceased
(nor has it now). The intervals of peace were simply fits of exhaustion.

So many campaigns, battles, and skirmishes were fought that
the majority of their names and details are lost. Historians argue
over whether or not certain legendary battles really took place,
and we shall never hear the names or tales of the commanders
and common soldiers on both sides who died in forgotten
clashes in Anatolia or Spain, on the Great Steppes or on Mediterranean islands. Those warriors of contending faiths left behind
numberless ghosts in the gleaming mail of Byzantine knights and
the carnival colors of Ottoman sipahis, in the tunics with crosses
on their breasts and the robes of Arab raiders.

A handful of the greatest battles and sieges remain familiar
in name, if not in their details: Roncesvalles and Granada, the
conquest—and loss—of Jerusalem, the fall of Constantinople to
Mehmet the Conqueror, and the following century's Turkish disaster at Lepanto. Not least, we recall the day when the tide
turned forever as the Polish *husaria* gutted an Ottoman army
outside Vienna's walls in the most influential cavalry charge in
history. Thereafter, Muslim reverses multiplied: Clive—that
neglected British genius—exposed the Indian Mughal's decayed
might at Plassey, Napoleon smashed Egyptian Mamelukes with
ease, and Russia's Skobelev clutched Central Asia for his czar.
For every grisly Gandamak suffered by John Bull, the soldiers of
the Queen won a dozen Omdurmans. One after another, Muslim states and empires disappeared, from Timbuktu to Delhi. By
the dawn of the last century, only the hollow Ottoman realm
remained. It soon fell.

But what of those earlier centuries and other battles—the
decisive combats that nearly won the whole world for Islam? This
article sketches five of the greatest triumphs of Islamic armies.
There were many more. When the call of the *muezzin* sounds in
the cities of Europe today, the faith of Mohammed belongs to
refugees and immigrants, not conquerors. If not for the valor of
forgotten heroes, it might have been a very different case.

THE DAY GOD TURNED AWAY—MANZIKERT, 1071

The Byzantine Empire was far better than its repute. Our prejudice has been shaped by one-sided historical writing and, above all, by Edward Gibbon's peculiar bigotry—he lionized the Arabs, whom he romanticized, and Islam, which he misunderstood, while treating Constantinople, the city that saved the Christian world, as Sodom without Lot. Gibbon's peerless work, *The Decline and Fall of the Roman Empire*, remains worth reading in full as a work of literature, but the farther he strays from the Appian Way, the worse his judgment.

As the first Muslim armies exploded out of the Arabian Peninsula, blazing with zeal for holy war, their ferocity seemed irresistible. Visigothic Spain collapsed at the first push, and even Constantinople's empire found itself on a desperate defensive as one province after another fell. Yet the armies of Byzantium held their lines at last; much was lost, but the Arabs could not conquer Anatolia. Four centuries of struggle shifted the empire's borders back and forth, but rugged Byzantine infantrymen stood firm behind their shields and blocked the key invasion route to Europe.

But empires tire. By the middle of the eleventh century, the tastes of the imperial court had grown impossibly lavish, its bureaucracy hopelessly ponderous, and its military fatally weak. When court officials faced declining revenues, they starved their crucial navy, scrapping the hulls that had ruled the eastern waters. Ill equipped, poorly trained, and badly led, the shrunken standing army went unpaid. Vanity replaced essential capabilities.

As a result of one of the court's intricate succession struggles, a capable general, Romanus Diogenes, abruptly found himself atop the empire (as well as atop the empress, who had chosen him). Ever quick to denigrate the Byzantines, even Gibbon had praise for Romanus: "[I]n the camp, he was the emperor of the Romans [Byzantines], and he sustained that character with feeble resources and invincible courage. By his spirit and success, the soldiers were taught to act, the subjects to hope, and the enemies to fear."

This characterization must be kept in mind, since Romanus IV was destined to lose one of history's decisive battles.

Even talented generals make mistakes. Faced with a threat from the Seljuk Turks, who had just destroyed the Armenian kingdom and its brilliant capital, Ani, Romanus declined a diplomatic solution and trusted in his sword arm. Setting off across Anatolia with, at a sound estimate, the 70,000 men the empire still could muster, the emperor wrong-footed himself from the start by overextending his supply lines. He also had to accept a court rival, Andronicus Ducas, as a subordinate commander as his weary soldiers passed Lake Van and marched deep into Armenia.

The army under Romanus was weaker than the numbers suggest, since ideals of service had faded and mercenaries filled out his order of battle beside allies whose allegiances were doubtful. Byzantine infantryman and cavalry drawn from the landed gentry still formed the core of the army, but the core had gone rotten.

The emperor's opponent, Alp Arslan, was recognized as a clever raider, but the Byzantines failed to grasp that, in the course of his conquests, the Seljuk sultan had built a superb field army. In the past, nomadic Turks had broken under the shock of Byzantium's armored troops. But the patterns of warfare were changing.

The immediate goal of Romanus was the recapture of the fortress of Manzikert, which his army achieved with ease. But the emperor had made a fateful error by splitting his force and sending half of his soldiers off on a wild-goose chase under Joseph Tarchaniotes, whose loyalties veered toward the Ducas clan and its claims to the imperial throne. Accounts conflict as to whether Tarchaniotes was defeated elsewhere or fought at all, but he certainly made no effort to return to Romanus's side.

The old, victorious Byzantine military machine had always sent scouts and spies in advance of its march, yet Romanus, despite his experience, failed to do so. Perhaps it was overconfidence, or the old soldier might have been distracted by the intrigues in his own camp. Whatever the reason, he was surprised when, the day after he retook Manzikert, a foraging party was ambushed by Seljuk horsemen.

Assuming he faced yet another raiding party, the emperor further weakened his force by sending out a detachment under a trusted subordinate to deal with the Seljuks. Within hours, the detachment's commander, Bryennius, sent back a plea for reinforcements. Amid growing confusion, Romanus dispatched under the Armenian Basilacius a larger detachment, which soon blundered into a major Turkish force—just as Bryennius returned to camp with his party's survivors. The emperor sent Bryennius back into the melee, which raged beyond the line of sight from his camp, with an entire wing of the army.

Alp Arslan's forces nearly overwhelmed the Byzantines. Basilacius was captured and his detachment was destroyed. Bryennius, a reliable soldier, managed to withdraw his embattled wing in fighting formation but suffered multiple wounds along the way.

The Turks understood the psychology of warfare better than the Byzantines did. All night, Seljuk archers kept up harassing fire against the emperor's camp, while small parties of warriors probed the imperial defenses. These actions were intended more to deny their enemies rest than to inflict real damage.

The damage would come the next day. Yet Byzantium still had the power to awe its opponents, and Alp Arslan considered himself the underdog. After all, he was only a few generations removed from the steppes, while his enemy represented an empire that claimed fifteen hundred years of history, with its roots in the soil of Rome. The sultan proposed a truce to Romanus one last time, but the emperor dismissed the idea. Alp Arslan then robed himself in white. If he fell, his battle dress would serve as his shroud.

On Friday, August 26, 1071, what remained of the Byzantine army marched out across a broken plain bordered by low hills, determined to crush the Seljuk threat forever. As always, the infantry heart of the army formed the center, with cavalry guarding the flanks and a large reserve and rear guard moving behind. Tragically for the empire, that reserve moved only at the command of Andronicus Ducas, whose family despised Romanus.

On the skillet of a plain in Asia Minor, the Christians plodded toward their fate. The sultan let them come on, while pestering them from the flanks. Mounted archers danced in to loose a few volleys before galloping off again, letting the Byzantines exhaust themselves as they sprinted to respond.

The emperor's army was no longer the disciplined force of bygone centuries, or even of the emperor's own youth. Attempting to defend itself on the cheap, the empire got what it paid for. The Seljuk army stretched across the horizon, but kept receding, a mirage in the thickening dust. The Byzantine wings began to break down as frustrated cavalrymen broke ranks to chase their antagonists. The sun began to decline, but the emperor pushed on, determined to drag the sultan into a battle.

Too late, pride gave way to soldierly sense. Romanus realized that he had moved too far from his camp and the protective walls of Manzikert. He gave the order to turn the imperial standards—the signal for the army to reverse its line of march.

Alp Arslan saw that his hour had come. As the Byzantines' battle order grew confused, he launched his entire army in an attack.

Untrained in Byzantine military procedures, the mercenary forces failed to understand that the reversed standards simply signaled a disciplined withdrawal. They assumed a general retreat had begun, and they ran. The Seljuk cavalry spotted the widening gaps in the line of march and poured between them.

Even then, disaster might have been averted. But Ducas, who should have brought the reserve to the aid of his emperor, started a rumor that the battle was over and the emperor was defeated. He then ordered the reserves and rear guard back to camp.

Deep in the fray, Romanus fought ferociously, surrounded by his personal guard and the last good Byzantine cohorts. The left wing of his army disintegrated, and the right wing, which attempted to rescue the emperor, was struck in the rear. The famous fighting order of the Byzantine infantry gave way to a muddle of individual combats. Those who ran were slain like game, while those who fought on toppled from their wounds. The empire's hirelings had deserted, its allies fled headlong, and the flower of its nobility, massed in reserve, abandoned the emperor. The long neglect of the military had proved fatal.

Romanus fought on horseback until his mount was killed. Then he fought on foot until wounds left him unable to grip his sword. At last, he was taken prisoner.

Paraded before Alp Arslan the next morning, Romanus IV Diogenes no longer looked like the ruler of an empire. In bloody rags and wearing chains, he was ordered to prostrate himself on the ground, at which point Sultan Alp Arslan lowered his foot onto the emperor's neck in a symbolic gesture of triumph.

He allowed Romanus to live and even treated him kindly after his ceremonial humiliation. Wise enough to see that despite his victory he'd conquered an army, not yet an empire, the sultan didn't even move against the fortress of Manzikert. He allowed the emperor to ransom himself under the terms of a dictated peace treaty, preferring Romanus's continued rule to that of an unknown who might seek military revenge.

The court factions who had deserted Romanus on the battlefield deserted him again. Upon his return, his rivals seized him and put out his eyes. The old soldier died in misery and shame. The emperors who grasped the throne thereafter found themselves caught between the frenzied Crusaders erupting from the West and ever more invaders from the East. Political tacticians, they never grasped how profoundly their strategic environment had changed.

The empire didn't disappear after Manzikert, but it became an invalid, never to regain its full strength. The Fourth Crusade would give it a near-fatal blow, doing as much damage to Christianity's eastern bulwark as the Seljuks had done. Yet somehow, the shrinking empire held on through twilight centuries, until Mehmet the Conqueror broke its walls (1453). Even in its crippled form, Byzantium's mere presence saved Europe from becoming a Muslim fief.

As for Manzikert, the precise location of the battlefield remains in dispute. On a visit to Turkey, I found that several local sites fit the descriptions in the old chronicles. Details of the battle have been argued over, too, along with the degree of internal treachery. However, Manzikert's reality wasn't about a patch of dirt but rather the destruction—forever—of the Byzantine Empire's strategic capacity to regain its former glory.

ALLAH'S VENGEANCE—HATTIN, 1187

Today, an Israeli highway follows the route a great Crusader army took to its stunning defeat at the Horns of Hattin. Erupting from a ridge just west of the Sea of Galilee, the horns look more like bumps than anything devilish, but for the exhausted and dehydrated knights and foot soldiers who perished on the surrounding slopes, the experience was as close to hell as the earth could offer.

By 1187, transplanted European nobles had ruled the littoral from Antioch to Jerusalem for almost a hundred years. But the fire of the Crusades had turned to embers as the rival lords of patchwork fiefs quarreled among themselves, losing their sense of purpose along with their military discipline. The East corrupted many of those whose ancestors had marched from Europe to save the Holy Land from the infidel, while the famous military orders, the Templars and Hospitalers, spent as much time feuding as they did fighting the Saracens.

Saladin, the ethnic Kurd who would lead Arab armies to glory, is remembered for his courtesy to his enemies (although he could be savage when brutality seemed the wiser policy), but the details of his generalship go ignored. A brilliant campaigner, Saladin understood how to shape a battle in the field by playing on his enemy's psychology—which is what he did at the Horns of Hattin.

Already a force to be reckoned with, Saladin had attempted to reach a political accommodation with King Guy of Jerusalem—but the king could not control his feudal underlings, a number of whom were little more than bandits. After suffering raids on peaceful caravans—including one that carried a family member— Saladin accepted that only war might win him a measure of peace.

When his army crossed the Jordan on July 1, 1187, Saladin viewed the campaign as a punitive expedition intended to teach his enemies to respect their own agreements. He soon achieved success beyond his hopes.

King Guy had gathered an army near Acre—the entire strength of his realm, augmented by local mercenaries, for a total of twelve hundred knights, ten times as many foot soldiers, and a mass of native cavalry. Guy and his nobles were still arguing over strategy when the news startled them that Saladin, ever swift, had taken Tiberias on the western side of the Sea of Galilee, although the Countess of Galilee still held out in her lakeshore castle.

Count Raymond of Tripoli, who possessed a better grasp of Arab strategy and tactics than his peers, had argued for days that a defensive stance was best, forcing Saladin to extend his lines of communication and fight—if he still wished to do so—on ground of the Christians' choice. In a pattern that would prevail for more than 300 years, Saladin's rivals pushed for a bold thrust to drive the Saracens from the kingdom.

The situation was complicated by the fact that the besieged countess was Raymond's wife. Even so, Raymond kept his head as others raged. He understood what Saladin was doing. His army could have stormed the castle; instead, the Arabs allowed a

messenger to escape with a plea for rescue. Saladin was using the
countess as bait.

It worked. Even though Raymond, who knew the ground and
the difficulties of campaigning over waterless stretches in the summer heat, continued to argue for caution, he was overruled by
lords and knights aflame with chivalric visions—not only the need
to rescue the countess, but the quest for individual martial glory.

The Crusaders marched east. When they paused briefly at
the old Roman city of Sephoria—which managed to survive a
succession of occupiers—Raymond argued for a defense of the
local heights, where water was plentiful, forcing Saladin to come
to them.

The hotheads shamed King Guy into rushing ahead. The
army's men marched for Tiberias, counting on rumored wells to
sustain them as they crossed the arid terrain that separated them
from their enemies.

Saladin waited. The men in his army had plenty of local
wells to quench their thirst, as well as the entire Sea of Galilee.
And the Christians came on, drinking dry what wells there were,
and then going athirst beneath the punishing sun. Men who had
swaggered in the morning staggered into the afternoon. Horses
foamed, and then the foam dried and the mounts slowed under
their heavily armored burdens. Foot soldiers drifted away from
their bands in search of water, and haughty noblemen found
they couldn't command empty wells to produce a drink.

They crested a plateau and saw the Horns before them. The
great lake and its deep waters waited beyond the ridge.

Aware of the army's desperate situation, Count Raymond
counseled the king to press on, to reach water at any cost; otherwise, the army would be lost. But the Templars, long renowned
for their ferocity and discipline, had grown decadent. Bringing
up the rear, they complained that they could go no farther without rest. Fearing disaster, Raymond did his best (later, he would
be vilified for his efforts), selecting a campsite just below the
Horns. A last, longed-for well gave nothing but sand.

Scouts reported the condition of the Christians to their master, Saladin. He must have prayed his thanks for such a gift.

When darkness fell, Arab irregulars set fire to the brush surrounding the king's exhausted army, clogging the men's lungs with smoke and literally keeping things hot for the increasingly desperate Christian men-at-arms. At dawn, Saladin struck.

Christian discipline collapsed immediately. Maddened foot soldiers rushed toward the crest and the promised water beyond, only to find themselves corralled and slaughtered as the Saracens herded them back toward a brushfire. Mounted knights fought as best they could—even in that bitter hour, the Muslim cavalry found no easy victories. But courage was all that the Christian force had left. Fragmented, it fought in a maelstrom, without a plan to counter Saladin's trap. Count Raymond led his own knights in a classic charge of the sort the Crusaders had often employed against the lighter Saracen horsemen. Instead of suffering the weight of the attack, the Arab cavalry galloped off to each side, letting the armored attack spend its strength against empty fields. Afterward, Raymond and a few other lords who cracked the Arab lines discovered they couldn't fight their way back to rejoin the king, who was making a valiant last stand.

King Guy and his inner circle found themselves driven uphill against the Horns. Attempting to restore order to his forces, Guy managed to have the royal tent erected on the high ground as a rally point. Astonishing their enemies, the King and his men resisted ferociously, countercharging repeatedly. But at last their sword arms grew as tired as their throats were dry—and the heat accomplished what Arab arms alone could not. Baking inside their armor, knights collapsed, still untouched by a blade. The king himself fought on until he crumpled, physically unable to continue, probably a victim of heat exhaustion. The Arab *ghazis* closed in, vying to seize noble captives to deliver to their victorious lord.

Saladin's triumph was so complete that it led to the fall of Jerusalem. But first, Saladin revealed himself as a masterful politician as well as a skilled commander. Executing—by his own hand—a single Christian lord notorious for his crimes against Muslims, the greatest of all Kurds allowed the remainder of his grand haul of nobles to be ransomed. He realized that if alive, they would continue to feud—and he preferred the devils he knew. Meanwhile, the strength of the Kingdom of Jerusalem lay dead upon the battlefield, and the remains of the True Cross had been lost. The catastrophe at Hattin and the holy city's fall would inspire a rescue effort—the Third Crusade, with the colorful Richard Coeur de Lion, the Lionheart, leading the English contingent. But Jerusalem would never again be a Christian city. Outremer, the European name for the territories seized by the First Crusade, would live on for another century, shriveling with the decades, until the last cities of the coast fell to Arab arms. The disastrous Crusade against Egypt was only postscript. At Hattin, the Crusades passed their apogee and fell into a long, irreversible decline.

How did Saladin win? He understood his enemies and exploited what we today would call intelligence. He enforced unity of command and purpose. He never outran his logistics. His grasp of terrain was as acute as his sense of his enemy's psychology. While bold, he shunned overconfidence. More than just the robed-up "gentleman" beloved of Hollywood, Saladin was a brilliant commander who earned his success.

When I visited the battlefield of Hattin, the site struck me as bearing an uncanny resemblance to the scene of a much later disaster, the British debacle at Isandlwana in the 1879 Zulu War, and the course of the two battles were much the same. Perhaps the military professional's lesson from both tragedies is simply that the army that knows what it's doing will always defeat the army without a clue.

APOCALYPSE ON THE DANUBE—NICOPOLIS, 1396
As the Crusader presence ebbed from the eastern Mediterranean, a dynamic new force transformed the landscape of the

Muslim world: The Ottoman Turks shoved the Seljuks into history's shadows. Not yet able to take Constantinople—where the Byzantine Empire had been reduced to little more than a city-state—the Turks bypassed its walls and raced into the Balkans, pausing only when they reached the Danube and threats elsewhere diverted their sultan's armies.

Beyazit the Thunderbolt—a Turk born for war—renewed the westward advance, subduing Serbia and pushing his frontier toward the Christian bulwark of Hungary, where the young king Sigismund understood that he could not stop the Ottomans without allies. Sigismund pleaded for a new European crusade to defeat the Muslim invaders. From both of the schismatic popes to the intrigue-plagued court of Paris, Europe echoed the call. The king of France would send a contingent of illustrious noblemen, while the Duke of Burgundy—the "swing vote" of the Hundred Years' War, then in a lull—dispatched his son, the young, untried and still unknighted Jean de Nevers.

Proud beyond measure, the French and Burgundians formed the core of a force that included captains from Flanders, Poland, Bohemia, the Germanies, and, probably, England. As the reality of the Crusades faded into the past, romance replaced it. These assembled nobles of Western Europe assumed that, given their valor and sacred cause, they would not only defeat the Turks on the Danube with ease, but would stroll on to liberate Jerusalem—their grasp of geography was as weak as their naive zeal was strong.

If they lacked a sense of reality, the members of the great army that gathered in Hungary in 1396 didn't lack for luxuries. Instead of siege engines, the French and Burgundians brought with them bargeloads of fine wines and delicacies, along with sumptuous costumes, tents equipped like movable palaces, minstrels, great ladies, and more than a few prostitutes. Sigismund was appalled, especially when it became clear that his dynasty's experience in fighting the Turks counted for nothing. As had happened at Hattin (and would happen again and again), the chivalric ideal confounded the hopes of an army that may have numbered 100,000 men. Sigismund wanted to fight on his own frontiers, on advantageous ground, where he and his allies could set the terms of the campaign. But the Western nobles wanted to see action. Since Beyazit had not yet appeared, he must be a coward. The chivalry of Europe would march into his domain and conquer it.

What began as a crusade turned into an orgiastic procession of banquets, spectacles, looting, rape, and the massacre of Turkish frontier garrisons whose lives had been guaranteed in return for their surrender. Moving down the Danube past the Iron Gates and still without any sign of Beyazit, the Christian army recaptured a few minor fortresses and then came to a halt before the formidable citadel of Nicopolis, which controlled the Balkan passes as well as the route to the Black Sea.

Without siege equipment, the Christians could only flirt with the use of mines to weaken the walls. Frustrated, the army delayed its march in an attempt to starve out the garrison. Without even daily marches to give the soldiers purpose, camp life resembled a great fair more than it did a bivouac. Discipline—what there was of it—disintegrated, as the common soldiers aped the nonchalance and debauchery of their leaders.

The first rumors of approaching Turkish forces reached the camp, but the leaders of the great army—except for Sigismund—felt no apprehension. Who could defeat the greatest knights of Europe? Sigismund alone deployed scouting parties. One returned with a report that Beyazit had already crossed the Shipka Pass, one of history's great military conduits.

The French, Burgundians, and their hangers-on remained more concerned with festivities than preparations. Beyazit was about to validate his nickname.

The Sire de Courcy, one of the few French knights with military sense—as well as a great deal of experience—at last rode south with a thousand men to see for himself what might lie behind the rumors. De Courcy soon spotted the Turks, and a disastrous thing happened: He won a minor victory. After ambushing a Turkish advance party and nearly wiping it out, he returned to camp a hero—but his deed outraged all the noblemen who outranked him. Each of them believed that the "honor" of being first in battle belonged to them.

The Europeans were amateurs accustomed to fighting other amateurs. Beyazit led an army professional at its core and honed in far-flung campaigns. That base of regulars (to employ a modern term) was augmented by tens of thousands of auxiliaries and contingents from vassal states, including a force of Serbian knights whose perfectly timed arrival would deliver the *coup de grace* against their fellow Christians.

In a classic illustration of the power of national myth to trump historical fact, today's Serbs still mourn their people's defeat by the Turks at Kosovo Field in 1389 and portray it as a catastrophe for the Christian world. They never mention their role as Ottoman allies at the far greater disaster of Nicopolis a mere seven years later.

In what should have by now become a recognized pattern, Beyazit combined a strategic offensive with an initial tactical defensive, baiting a trap much as Alp Arslan and Saladin had done before him. Choosing his ground, Beyazit insured that only a fraction of his army could be observed by the Christians—whose revels had ended at last.

Like Count Raymond before Hattin, King Sigismund knew his enemy's practices and tried to reason with his fractious allies. With the French knights impatient to launch a headlong charge (as they had done so fatally at Crecy and would do yet again at Agincourt) and seize as much personal glory as each man could, Sigismund tried to explain that the Turks always placed their least valuable elements out front as wastage to blunt an opponent's attack and exhaust his forces before launching their own enveloping counterattack with elite troops held in reserve.

The Sire de Courcy sided with Sigismund, but his counsel was dismissed as the treachery of a man who had already staked his claim to glory and wished to deprive others of greater fame. The French and Burgundian knights rode forward in a headlong charge.

Smashing through the sultan's auxiliaries only heightened the confidence of the knights. They plunged uphill into the Turkish infantry, dismounting to fight on foot when a palisade of stakes gutted their horses.

Then the arrows began to fall among them. Separated from the mass of the Western infantry, the knights soon felt the weight of Turkish numbers. But the one thing the French and Burgundians didn't lack was courage. Burdened by their armor, they nonetheless fought their way to the top of the ridge, some on foot, others still on horseback, all increasingly weary.

Gaining the crest, they looked down and saw the main body of Beyazit's army, tens of thousands of his finest troops, superbly disciplined, trained and blooded, and still uncommitted to the battle the knights imagined they had nearly won.

Suddenly, Turkish cavalry swept behind the knights, as if drawn from the earth by a magic spell. Some of the knights and retainers broke and ran, but most fought on, determined to die well—and recognizing their folly at last.

With no one empowered as its supreme commander, the still-massive Western force succumbed to confusion and then to panic. Turkish warriors swept over the landscape. Amid the gory chaos, King Sigismund escaped across the Danube and lived to fight the Turks for years to come. The great lords of Europe, however, fell on the field or were captured. Beyazit the Thunderbolt had won a stunning victory.

Yet the Ottoman army had suffered, too. Chivalric valor had littered the field with as many dead Turks as Europeans. Enraged by his losses and no less by the reports of massacred Muslims (the most recent such atrocity had occurred just before the battle, when the last prisoners of the Christians were put to death), the sultan decided to teach his novice enemies a lesson they could take back to their homes—since even he preferred to let the noblest survivors be ransomed, including the wounded de Courcy, as well as Burgundy's son, the Count of Nevers.

As the next day dawned, the captive European nobles were lined up before Beyazit and forced to watch as their soldiers, naked and bound, were thrust forward and beheaded at their feet. As many as three thousand prisoners died in a morass of blood before Beyazit had enough and ordered a halt.

The great age of the Ottomans had begun. It would threaten the West's survival for another three hundred years and linger on in decline for an additional two centuries. For thirteen decades after the Battle of Nicopolis, Hungary held the line that Byzantium once manned as the Christian world's eastern border with Islam—until the crown of St. Stephen suffered its own irredeemable disaster.

But the Ottoman rise faced setbacks, too, even if the Turks proved fiercely resilient. Only a few years after Beyazit's triumph, a threat to the empire's other extreme drew him east. Another Turkic giant had arisen, this one strengthened by a Mongol legacy: the "world-bestrider," Timur the great, or Tamerlane. After Timur crushed the Ottoman army and took Beyazit prisoner (1402), he displayed his ragged captive in an open cage that was dragged behind his armies until the fallen sultan died of shame.

THE ECLIPSE—MOHACS, 1526

Almost five centuries after the worst debacle in Hungarian history, a citizen of Budapest down on his luck will still shrug and say, "Well, it was worse at Mohacs." The defeat of King Lajos by Suleiman the Magnificent on the Danube plain remains embedded in the national psyche even more powerfully than the more recent ordeal of Soviet oppression. The rainy battlefield of Mohacs was the graveyard of a nation.

By 1526, the Ottomans had reached beyond the Danube's Iron Gates to seize the crucial fortress-city of Belgrade, the last great bulwark protecting the Kingdom of Hungary. Faced with the difficulties of administering a far-flung empire, a succession of sultans preferred to reduce frontier states to vassalage rather than subject them to expensive occupations—the Sublime Porte in Istanbul needed tribute and allied troops more than it needed land. Even Suleiman, the greatest Ottoman ruler of all, offered Hungary's young king a peace treaty in lieu of war.

But King Lajos could not control his nobility. Some longed to fight, while others feared Habsburg encroachment from the West more than they did the Turk. In a scenario that too often had been the undoing of European military endeavors, internal divisions and rivalries delayed and ultimately prevented effective action. Out of patience with the recalcitrant Hungarians, Suleiman opened the campaigning season by marching northwest at the head of a force that may have amassed 100,000 combatants by the time it reached Belgrade. A warlike kingdom still, Hungary might have rallied a force adequate for the defense of its heartlands, had the king enjoyed the power to act decisively. But he needed the cooperation of dozens of great magnates and thousands of lesser aristocrats. Nor were the Hungarians certain where the Turks would strike. As a result, the crown's eastern army received its marching orders so late that it had no chance to join the royal forces in time to face Suleiman. Advised by veterans to conduct a defense in depth and draw the sultan on, Lajos ultimately deferred to the hotheads who were convinced—this will sound familiar—of their martial superiority over the Turks.

By 1526, the Ottoman Empire had reached its zenith. The sultan had the best-trained, best-equipped, and by far the best-disciplined army in the world, while the administrative resources of Suleiman's court remained superior to those of any European rival (that would alter in the coming decades). Most important, Suleiman enjoyed unquestioned authority: He was willing to hear advice, but once he made a decision, his army responded as a killing machine. At the Ottoman apogee, unity of command

and unity of purpose remained the empire's greatest military advantages.

In another echo of bygone disasters, Suleiman arrived in force before he was expected. Although outnumbered as much as three to one, the Hungarian king's army still managed to choose good defensive ground, with its lines anchored by Danube marshes on one flank and canalized terrain on the other, which would limit the sultan's ability to deploy his superior numbers simultaneously—at least, that was the theory. The Hungarians failed to take into account the march discipline and responsiveness of the Turks, whose campaign regimen would not be rivaled until the prime of the Duke of Marlborough almost two centuries later.

Still, the Hungarians had a fighting chance. Their tactical scheme was designed by a splendid soldier, Pal Tomori, and called for a spoiling attack on the Ottoman vanguard as it broke ranks to set up its tents on the afternoon before the conventions of the age dictated a battle. Under favorable conditions, the heavily armored European knights still had the power to devastate Ottoman formations. Pal Tomori's plan called for the piecemeal defeat of the Turks and relied on prompt execution.

At first, things appeared to move ahead as planned. An advance wing of the Turkish army clumsily worked its way down an escarpment onto the plain where the Hungarians had planned what today's soldiers would call a "kill zone." The Turks would be pressed against the steep slope, hindering the deployment of reinforcements.

When the Hungarians across the plain remained in their defensive positions, the first Turks on the field did as expected, laying aside their arms to set up camp in anticipation of a battle the next morning. Meanwhile, a Turkish flanking movement was detected and cavalry dispatched to counter it. A few raindrops fell.

Pal Tomori begged his king to give the order for the planned attack. But even at that critical moment, the Hungarian "command group" fell to bickering again. Time slipped away from the mortified Tomori, who feared the arrival of the Turkish main body. And the rain became an intermittent drizzle.

At last, the king made a decision: Attack! Within minutes, thousands of hooves pounded the earth in a terrifying spectacle, throwing up clots of mud behind a wall of armored horsemen. Bewildered, the Turks failed to rally as the chargers bearing the knights crashed into their midst. Hungary's chivalry seemed on the cusp of victory.

But the king's delay had robbed them of their chance. Rain began to turn the earth to muck, even as poorly disciplined Hungarian soldiers broke off their attack to loot the Turkish camp. And Suleiman had arrived on the scene, not only with his janissary shock troops, but bringing up the best handled artillery on the continent. Historians argue about the effect of the Turkish guns on the outcome, but contemporary sources credit them with breaking the final Hungarian charge.

The battle became a melee of the sort where numbers always tell. Suleiman was no coward, but he was wise enough to recognize that he was more valuable in command of his army than engaged in single combat. Hungarian arrows struck his breastplate, but the sultan calmly directed the commitment of his elite formations.

King Lajos himself led the charge of the Hungarian reserve wing, but by doing so he lost the last semblance of control over his army. No longer reeling, the Turks reformed under Suleiman's steadying hand. Once again, the Christian knights fought with such courage than even Ottoman chroniclers and Suleiman himself praised their valor. But just as the courage of future Muslim bands would count for nothing against Maxim guns, the heroism of the Hungarians and their too-few allies bought them only an epitaph. Drilled to function even in the rain, ranks of Turkish musketeers and the sultan's skilled artillerymen stunned their attackers with massed volleys. Masters at enveloping an enemy even in confined space, the Turkish cavalry swept in for the kill.

Pal Tomori died on the field. Bleeding from a head wound, King Lajos fled. He escaped the carnage, but as his mount splashed across a stream, it reared and threw him off. Encumbered by heavy armor and exhausted, he couldn't save himself. A close companion-at-arms drowned in a rescue attempt.

The rain-swept battlefield turned into a slaughterhouse. Only two thousand Hungarian prisoners were taken, all of whom were beheaded in front of the sultan, who ordered his men to pile up the skulls of Hungarian nobles killed in battle or executed (Suleiman understood the use of terror as a psychological weapon). At least ten thousand Hungarians—possibly double that number—died in combat. Fatally for the kingdom, it lost not only its king but almost thirty magnates (roughly equivalent to dukes), as well as over a thousand other noblemen. Hungary's entire leadership had been swept away.

Suleiman marched on to the twin cities of Buda and Pest, still separate on their opposite sides of the Danube. He burned both to the ground. Autumn, however, was progressing, which meant the end of the campaigning season. The sultan had not intended to conquer and occupy Hungary, only to force his peace terms upon its king. Personally, Suleiman regretted the death of young King Lajos, whom he would have preferred on a vassal's throne instead of in a grave.

But Hungary had fallen. The mighty Turkish columns would return when the sultan was ready to digest his conquest. In fifteen years, the Turks would reenter the fortress atop the Var in Buda to stay for five generations.

A century and a half later (1687), the great Habsburg commander Charles of Lorraine would follow up his reconquest of Buda and Pest by handing the Turks a crushing defeat in the field. Twenty thousand Ottoman soldiers would lie dead in the rain. At Mohacs.

THE BATTLE OF THE THREE KINGS—
ALCACER QUIBIR, 1578

By the second half of the sixteenth century, the West had begun to win. The give-and-take would continue for another hundred years before the Ottoman Empire was thrust onto its long strategic defensive, but European advances in fields as diverse as navigation, administration and banking, combined with the fantastic wealth from New World conquests and global trade, had allowed backward Europe to leap ahead of an Ottoman world that had locked itself into the airless rooms of the past, refusing to admit the light of a worrisome future. Nonetheless, the armies of Islam still had plenty of fight left in them—and Christian kings had not yet finished repeating the mistakes of their headstrong predecessors.

The tragic story of the battle of Alcacer Quibir (or Alcazarquivir) begins with the greatest Western victory over a Muslim force in more than four centuries. In 1571, the combined Spanish and Venetian fleets under Don Juan of Austria annihilated the Ottoman navy at Lepanto, off the coast of Greece. Although the sultan's empire still had deep reserves, the defeat was a shock that bravado could not erase. But if Lepanto marked a renewal of the struggle for the eastern Mediterranean, it had grave consequences for a Christian kingdom far to the west.

Portugal had established modern Europe's first great overseas empire, reaching around the southern tip of Africa and on to the East Indies. However, Portugal remained a small country, so poor in manpower it was never able to administer its distant colonies well and had to rely on its meager military and naval forces to hasten from Africa to India to the Spice Islands and back again in a never-ending struggle to maintain control of trading centers and sea-lanes under threat not only from local princes but also from envious European rivals.

The Portuguese empire was hollow inside. Soon its shell would break under the weight of hubris and folly. Born after his father's death, King Sebastian was crowned at the age of three and handed over to court Jesuits at the fevered dawn of the Counter-Reformation. He inherited a kingdom still gathering in the wealth of the world, and by the time he reached the verge of manhood, he was determined to turn his merchant empire into a crusader state. At twenty, he first led his forces against the edge of the Ottoman world in Morocco. Tragically, his minor foray succeeded. Coming three years after Lepanto, it left the twenty-year-old king dreaming of greater victories.

Sebastian drained his treasury to hire the mercenaries his population-poor realm required for foreign adventures. The wealth of the Indies enlarged his fleet, and loans made it larger still. Sebastian judged himself ready when the opportunity came to meddle in the confused affairs of Morocco, where Ottoman power seemed distant and opportunity immediate.

Begged for military support by Abu Abdallah, who had lost his throne to his uncle, Emir Abd al Malik, Sebastian ignored the advice of Philip II of Spain and landed a force of over twenty thousand men (a distressing portion of whom were noblemen) in a Portuguese-held enclave on the Moroccan coast. The usurper, Abd al Malik, tried to buy off Sebastian with an offer to cede territory, but the king was aflame with the longing to win a decisive victory for Christ (how he intended to handle his Moroccan allies after his triumph remains unclear, but no doubt his Jesuit tutors had an answer ready).

Abd al Malik's health was failing and Abu Abdallah might have regained his throne without a fight had he only possessed more patience. Given no choice but war, the sick emir managed to muster a powerful army, which included a contingent of Ottoman janissaries. The emir also possessed a secret weapon— a wing recruited from Moors whose families had been driven from Spain and Portugal and who viewed the coming battle as a grudge fight.

Despite his fleet of five hundred ships anchored offshore, King Sebastian lacked the logistical support to move deep and move fast—or the experience of the harsh conditions in the

Moroccan interior. His combined Portuguese, mercenary, and Moorish army didn't get far inland before it found itself facing the emir's horde across a river below the castle of Ksar al Kebir (the Arabic from which the Latinized names for the battle derive). On August 4, 1578, as Sebastian was delivering a speech to inspire his troops, the ailing emir attacked.

In the first shock of combat, the captain of the king's mercenaries fell. The Moorish children of exile fell upon the befuddled Christian ranks. The emir's cavalry galloped around the Portuguese flanks, drawing a curtain of dust around the battlefield. Moorish allies dissolved before Sebastian's eyes, and Abu Abdallah drowned in the river while trying to flee. The foreign mercenaries broke and ran. Only the Portuguese nobles, imbued with notions of chivalric heroism that more properly belonged to the Middle Ages, stood their ground. They won their share of glory, but lost Portugal.

Emulating so many fallen kings and princes before him, Sebastian led a forlorn-hope charge into the enemy's midst. He fell amid fighting so ferocious that his body was never identified (leading to an enduring myth that "Dom Sebastian" would return one day to rescue his suffering country). At least eight thousand Christian dead lay on the field, with a disproportionate number of casualties drawn from the Portuguese aristocracy, whose males of military age had been wiped out. Of the thousands of Portuguese prisoners, few returned. The luckiest were sold into slavery.

The ironic twist of the day came when the victorious emir died from the stress of fighting under the August sun. Whether his sudden collapse was from a heart attack or heat exhaustion, his death meant that both contenders for the Moroccan throne had perished.

Thus Alcacer Quibir became the Battle of Three (dead) Kings, Portugal's Mohacs. While Lisbon didn't face a Moorish or Ottoman invasion, it soon found itself absorbed into the Spanish empire of Philip II, whose dynastic claims were of adequate strength to overcome a dead king's army of ghosts. Taking advantage of Sebastian's folly, Philip invaded and assumed his throne as Philip I of Portugal. Sebastian's unfortunate country would be looted of its last wealth by its Christian neighbor, only regaining a fragile independence in the next century as the invalid pawn of the empires that had eclipsed it.

THE MILITARY LESSONS OF DEFEAT

Do these half-remembered battles and campaigns hold lessons for the wars we face today? Familiar with the enduring principles of war, readers will have drawn their own conclusions; but a few laws bear repeating, since we never quite seem to learn them:

Unity of command and unanimity of purpose are the keys to victory. If any worrisome similarity exists between the West of the late Middle Ages and Renaissance and the West of today with its response to Islamist violence, it's our lack of unity and penchant for quarreling for slight political gains. Although the violent minorities in the contemporary Muslim world do not pose the sort of threat Islam's great eastern armies of the past presented, the West's overwhelming military superiority is hobbled by the sort of command arrangements that, prevailing in Afghanistan and echoing Nicopolis, prevent a single commander from fully integrating and exploiting all of the forces nominally at his service. Arab and Ottoman armies won because they knew what they wanted to do, what they had to do, and who was responsible for doing it. Numbers, although they mattered, were secondary.

Discipline is more important than numbers—or even technology. This relates, of course, to unity of command and control, but one striking factor in the battles summarized above is that when armies clashed, the Christian forces tended to break down into factions or even individual combatants, while the Muslim forces did a better job of preserving unit integrity and continuing to operate in concert with an overarching plan.

Valor is no substitute for organization. This, too, relates to the matter of discipline, but goes beyond it. The situation five or six centuries ago was the opposite of that which we face today:

Ottoman organization had advanced beyond the administrative abilities of Western forces, which remained in thrall to local rivalries and destructive notions of chivalry that rendered vainglorious knights dysfunctional within the armies they joined for the campaigning season. Today, the West's forces are far better organized than those of the Muslim world and cannot be defeated on the battlefield—although they are vulnerable to failing political will.

Fanaticism provides motivation, but attention to detail wins campaigns. Today, secular historians play down the religious passions within Western crusading armies; but for all of their misbehaviors on the march, the knights who reached Jerusalem in 1099 or who died at Alcacer Quibir in 1578 firmly believed that they were doing God's work with their swords. Passion, however, is no substitute for logistics. At Hattin, the greatest army the Kingdom of Jerusalem had ever put into the field perished for lack of water, while the naive Crusaders who died at Nicopolis might have beaten Suleiman on a different field had they brought along siege equipment to reduce the fortress and not found themselves immobilized.

Knowledge of, and respect for, your enemy is essential. Consistently, the Muslim commanders of yesteryear better understood the psychology and inherent weaknesses of Western forces than Christian commanders grasped the nature and vulnerabilities of their opponents. Overconfidence is another consistent thread that runs from Manzikert to Alcacer Quibir. Ablaze with fervor, Christian knights could not imagine losing, while their Muslim opponents calmly shaped their plans to minimize their chances of suffering a defeat. Again and again, Arab, Seljuk, and Ottoman armies appeared before they were expected, employed tactics that amounted to battlefield judo, and adhered to their battle plans as the feeble schemes of their enemies collapsed.

The tactic of luring the enemy onward and then ambushing or enveloping him remains the preferred Middle Eastern battlefield stratagem. Drawn from nomadic warfare on the Asian steppes, the practice—employed two millennia ago against Rome's legions—is still in use in Iraq and Afghanistan today. And it's still effective. Faced with conventional armies, tribesmen of the distant past learned to use terrain and surprise against superior foes. Deeply ingrained in the culture, this is still the primary "trick" used by Iraqi insurgents, terrorist bands, or Taliban supporters, whether staging a small ambush to set up a greater one or appearing to withdraw to lure opponents into a bomb-riddled kill zone. A good rule for our officers at war in the Islamic world is always to ask themselves, "What does the enemy *want* me to do?"

At present, the fallen Muslim world cannot field great armies as it once did, nor does it present an existential danger to the West. Yet the deadly annoyances of the present are indisputably an extension of a competition that began in the seventh century. We would be fools to celebrate history's longest war, but we would be even greater fools not to attempt to understand it.

Crescent Descending

Armchair General

September 2008

The process of turning the tide against the conquering armies of Islam lasted over a thousand years. From the contest's earliest centuries, isolated Christian victories stemmed the jihadi onslaught at its farthest reaches; yet for most of this long struggle, Arab, Berber, Seljuk, or Ottoman armies held the initiative. While the *reconquista* crusade to free Spain of Moorish rule slowly progressed southward, Turkish triumphs devoured the Byzantine Empire and the Balkans, subsequently reaching the gates of Vienna more than once.

The last siege of Vienna is—rightly—viewed as a decisive turning point, a defeat after which the Ottomans never again threatened to conquer all of Europe, but declined into centuries of fighting bitter holding actions against the resurgent West. Yet Ottoman power was far from exhausted in 1683, and that year of victories for Austria, Poland, and allied German principalities was only the beginning of the offensive phase of a "long war" against jihadi terror—a series of harsh, atrocity-riddled campaigns that would only be settled by the Treaty of Karlowitz in 1699, with the sultan forced to sign away his claim to Hungary and a critical portion of the Balkan frontier.

Officially recorded as the Great Turkish War (1667–99), that long conflict wasn't an uninterrupted succession of imperial victories over the sultan's forces. Mirroring the give-and-take across centuries, the war was a microcosm of a greater struggle that had raged from Granada to the Ukraine. After a brilliant beginning culminating in the reconquest of Belgrade for Christianity, resurgent Ottoman forces retook that crucial fortress and plunged back into Hungary for another round of rapine, destruction, and slaughter.

Ever short of funds, the desperate court in Vienna had been fighting on two fronts—in the Balkans to the southeast, and in the West, against the armies of France's Louis XIV. By the time a respite arrived in the struggle over Savoy, a massive new Ottoman army, led by Sultan Mustapha II himself, had assembled for a campaign to reconquer Hungary. The Habsburg army that took the field to defend the empire consisted of a core of hardened veterans, but they would be outnumbered at least 3 to 1. Worse, the army lacked a dependable system of supply (mismanaged contracts left regiments short of food), its arms were barely adequate, and medical support hardly existed. All the Habsburg regiments had was an inextinguishable hatred of an enemy who continued to ravage Christian lands, carrying off slaves for the markets of Istanbul and the bazaars of Egypt and the Middle East.

And then they got a leader.

Best known to English-speakers as the battlefield ally of the Duke of Marlborough, Prince Eugene of Savoy helped England's greatest soldier maintain the balance of power in the cockpit of Europe. However, his greatest achievements were in the East, where his string of near-miraculous victories permanently shifted the balance of power against the Turk.

The unlikeliest of soldiers, Eugene was the son of one of Louis XIV's many lovers, although the Sun King didn't father the prince. Eugene's mother, unable to refrain from engaging in the intricate plots that festered at Versailles, fell into disfavor, and

Eugene, small in stature and feminine in appearance, was sexually abused by a cabal of older males at the court. The embarrassing reputation that resulted from the scandal kept him from the commission he wanted so badly and, with classic Gallic cynicism, his fate was decided for him: a career in the church.

But if Eugene lacked physical presence, he possessed a valiant character. When Louis aligned himself with the Turks during the last siege of Vienna, Eugene defied the laws of the court and escaped from France to join his Savoyard relatives in the defense of Christendom. Hoping to assume the command of a regiment formerly led by a cousin—who was killed at the head of his troops—young Eugene had to content himself with a staff position. But the relief of Vienna would mark the beginning of his rise as one of the greatest soldiers the world has known, a man who would frustrate the generals and marshals of the Sun King—who often must have regretted his misjudgment of the boy—and who would hand the Turks a succession of defeats that would deny them any future hope of regaining Hungary, the strategic pivot in the clash between Islam and Europe.

The greatest of Eugene's victories was his first as an independent commander.

THE BATTLE OF ZENTA, 1697
Today the mention of September 11 calls to mind the catastrophe in Manhattan, but for centuries it evoked one of the greatest Ottoman military disasters and the day when the Austrian-Habsburg army came of age.

In the summer of 1697, as Sultan Mustapha II led an army of more than a hundred thousand men up the Danube, determined to seize the chain of frontier fortresses protecting a weakened empire, Vienna sent its impoverished military all the support it could muster—no back pay, but an officer the troops had come to adore: Prince Eugene.

Eugene's previous commands had stretched from the regimental level up to posts as a deputy commander of field armies.

On every front, the prince gained a reputation for personal courage (suffering a series of wounds) and for caring for his soldiers (a quality he shared with his comrade John Churchill, later the Duke of Marlborough). In an age when foot soldiers were regarded as the scum of the earth, Eugene borrowed money, sinking deep into debt, to insure his soldiers were properly fed, clothed, and armed. He also organized the first decent medical services Habsburg troops had ever known.

The effect of his appointment was electric: A field army that had been nearly demoralized jumped to attention. Urgently, Eugene gathered the Austrian forces scattered on both sides of the Danube and, instead of adopting a defensive stance in the face of the greater than 2-to-1 odds favoring the sultan, immediately marched toward the enemy.

Well aware of Eugene's reputation and leading an army of uneven quality (from the elite janissaries down to fierce-but-erratic Tartar horsemen), the sultan broke off one siege after another, losing his bids to seize frontier fortresses before Eugene could arrive.

Eugene always moved more quickly than the sultan's counselors believed possible. With remarkable speed, he had organized a series of field depots, allowing his forces to maneuver with a lighter train, confident that supplies would be available wherever march and countermarch might take them.

After failing in repeated attempts to outwit Eugene, the sultan gave up. He chose to retreat across the Tisza (Tisa) River to winter his forces in today's Romania. But Eugene knew his man and knew his enemy: The little general was determined to fight. And when Eugene caught up with the sultan's horde, fortune *did* favor the bold.

Napoleon always wanted lucky generals, but the best generals make their own luck. Despite the sultan's attempts at deception and frantic efforts to elude Eugene, the prince stayed on the heels of the "Grand Turk." His reconnaissance efforts identified the approximate location where the Ottoman army would cross the Tisza. Finely judging the risks, Eugene split his army into twelve columns, six up and six back, to speed the march and converge on the Turks while their backs were to the river.

Meanwhile, the sultan not only had the advantage of numbers, his French engineers also had designed a portable bridging system that had no equal. Nor did the sultan intend to take chances. His grand vizier supervised the construction of massive, moated earthworks on the near side of the bridgehead. Should Eugene arrive before the crossing was completed, his troops would face a fortress whose redoubts were dense with artillery and whose defenders were stiffened by the janissaries in reserve.

Eugene galloped ahead of his hurrying troops, anxious to assess the situation for himself. An early skirmish nearly ended badly for an armed reconnaissance party, but the timely arrival of a cavalry contingent led not only to the rescue of the Austrian advance detachment but also to the capture of a high-ranking Turk—who proved wonderfully cooperative when threatened with beheading on the spot. As Eugene cantered up to survey the Turkish field fortifications, he already knew that the best Ottoman cavalry, the sultan's siege train and heavy guns, and Mustapha II himself had crossed the river—leaving behind the infantry and several thousand light cavalry.

Despite the sense of urgency invigorating the Austrians, Eugene's march columns made uneven progress in the heat and dust. Morning seeped into afternoon as the prince and his deputies sought to deploy an order of battle strong enough for an assault. With no obvious options for maneuver, this would be a frontal attack into the guns on the Turkish battlements, against startlingly high walls of the sort the Ottomans seemed able to summon out of the earth. Another general might have hesitated, but Eugene had a genius for judging the atmosphere on the day of battle. His soldiers *wanted* to fight, but the Turks didn't.

As sunset approached, Eugene's forces were ready at last. The order came down to advance. Eugene commanded in the center, while trusted deputies on each wing were empowered to grasp opportunities as they arose.

As the Austrians surged forward, Turkish guns tore into their ranks so fiercely that the right flank shifted to an oblique attack. But the Austrians could not be stopped. This was the chance they'd been waiting for—not just for that fateful campaign season, but for decades. Instead of faltering, they fixed bayonets and charged, shouting, "Long live Eugene!" In coats faded gray and torn ragged by hard campaigning, one infantry regiment after another swarmed through a dry moat and up the defensive walls, charging with such fury that even Eugene was astonished.

The Turks were sturdy defensive fighters, and at first they refused to break. Then a Turkish cavalry commander made a catastrophic mistake. Leading a charge against the Austrian left in an effort to break the lines of advancing regiments, a light-cavalry contingent was soon repelled by volley fire and a countercharge by Austrian cuirassiers. In their headlong retreat, the Turkish horsemen rode right into the river, seeming to gallop on the water's surface—revealing the presence of sandbars along the shore. The commanders of the Austrian left saw their chance. Maintaining the frontal pressure, they diverted regiment after regiment around the defensive works, splashing through the shallow water to take the Turks in the rear.

The Ottoman defenses crumbled. The Corps of Janissaries turned to face the Austrians sweeping up from the river, willing to die to keep the bridge open as long as possible. But a killing fury possessed Prince Eugene's soldiers as they closed on the Turkish infantry. Pouring over the walls and bringing up their guns through fallen sally ports, the Austrians took their revenge for the long series of Ottoman massacres, betrayed surrender terms, and slave raids. Pashas pleaded for their lives, promising magnificent ransoms, only to be bayoneted by common soldiers who would never hold a gold piece in their hands. Austrian artillery gained positions from which the Habsburg guns could sweep the bridge. Panicked Turks and their allies leapt into the water. Others tried to swim from shore to shore. On the far bank, the sultan could only watch in horror as his harem was captured, his grand vizier killed, and the agha of the janissaries fell beside his soldiers.

As darkness fell, four additional viziers and 27 pashas lay dead. The sultan's seal, seven great horsetail banners, 423 flags, 87 guns, and vast quantities of military supplies had fallen into Austrian hands. According to Eugene's biographer, Alexander Lernet Holenia, the startled Austrians even captured a train of camels.

But morning light truly told the tale. More than 20,000 Turks had been killed at Zenta, while another 10,000 drowned—the downstream banks of the river were lined with corpses for miles.

The Austrians lost just over 2,000 officers and men, killed and wounded. They'd lost more horses than soldiers.

The Ottoman Empire would fight on for just over two centuries, but it would never again seriously threaten the heart of Europe. The long, grim twilight of the sultans had begun.

THE SIEGE OF DELHI, 1857

The following decades and centuries saw the slow, bloody contraction of the caliphate in the west, north, and south. Generals as diverse as Napoleon and Russia's Suvorov shattered the lagging armies of the Sublime Porte, and even John Paul Jones, during his brief Russian service, took his turn at battering the Ottoman navy. By the mid-nineteenth century, Turkey had become the "Sick Man of Europe," and the great powers worried more about each other than they did about yesterday's scourge of the Christian West. England and France even sided with the Ottoman Empire in the Crimean War to check the expanding empire of the czars. In the same decade, however, Britain would face a new outbreak of jihad far to the east, during the Great Indian Mutiny (1857–58), an event often dramatized but little understood.

Students of history know that the introduction of bite-them-open rifle cartridges greased with pig or beef fat—offending both Muslims and Hindus—triggered a series of viral mutinies based on long-standing resentments and grievances against the

British presence in India. But the traditional accounts in the West missed two salient points as they portrayed doughty Brits fighting off blood-spattered fanatics intent on ravishing white women: First, for many of India's Muslims and supporters of the decayed Mughal dynasty, the insurrection rapidly became a jihad against the infidel; and second, for the British, too, this became a contest of religions, with many trappings of a traditional crusade as the scarlet- and khaki-clad soldiers of John Company (the Honorable East India Company) or the queen regained their equilibrium and launched campaigns of vengeance.

By 1857, the once-great Mughal dynasty had degenerated into nothing more than an impoverished court that barely held sway in Delhi's city-within-a-city behind the Red Fort's walls. Bloated princes bickered, bored wives schemed, and the aged Bahadur Shah Zafar II, destined to be the last of his line, lay on his couch composing poems for contests with Delhi's literati. Playing pretend, the British paid him a pension and went through the motions to honor him, but they controlled even his personal possessions. For his part, the "emperor" was no religious fanatic—he lacked the energy to be much of anything—but Indians (including Hindus) whose folktales told of bygone days of Mughal glory still looked to Zafar as a unifying figure.

When the first mutineers rode into Delhi early on May 11, 1857, Zafar was as surprised as the British—who were cut down within the Red Fort, in the streets, and in their offices and homes (if they had been foolish enough to live in the city instead of in the civil and military lines beyond the walls). Desperate for a leader, the mutineers commandeered the withered emperor . . . who may have caught a fleeting glimpse of past glories himself.

Overwhelmed and stunned, the British found that the local sepoy regiments were all too ready to join the mutineers, while British regulars were in short supply. Officers and their families fled the cantonments on Delhi Ridge, unable to cope with the sudden disintegration of their world and its good order. Survivors could thank the occasional loyal Indian, but more often

they lived only because the mutineers had no clear sense of what
to do next.

As the British reeled, mutineers from other garrisons poured
into Delhi. The standard telling of the tale pits them against the
thin red line that struggled back to Delhi Ridge after scorched,
cholera-nagged marches. A long summer of no-quarter assaults
and counterassaults finally led to the city's recapture—a saga rich
in skirmishes of the sort that would fill the pages of boy's books
for the next half-century. Now, thanks to the opening of Indian
archives and recent research (most notably, the brilliant work of
William Dalrymple, a splendid English writer whose heart lies in
India), we know far more of the Indian side of the story.

The great missing piece to the narrative was what happened
inside Delhi while Western eyes focused on the wretched camp on
Delhi Ridge. Court records reveal that, as the siege dragged on,
the mutineers increasingly lost heart—and influence. First, they
were a disaster for the city, looting with abandon and extorting
ransoms. Second, they could not cooperate successfully in an
active defense of the city—the lack of trained officers among
them told, and they could not overcome internal rivalries. The
mutineers' forays against the British lines failed miserably, despite
their far greater numbers. But the real revelation was who else
appeared in Delhi.

As the influence of the mutineers ebbed, Wahhabi fanatics
gained strength. The Mughal court had become—unintentionally—a rallying point for a passionate jihad. The Wahhabis of the
mid-nineteenth century applied the same fanaticism toward
their enemies, and even their fellow Muslims, as their twenty-
first-century successors do today. Historians may argue over the
economic causes of the mutiny or the structural problems of
colonialism, but the fighting in Delhi ultimately came down to a
jihad opposed by a crusade.

One key myth was reversed at Delhi, though. While today's al
Qa'eda terrorists generate propaganda about the purported rape
of Muslim women by American soldiers, throughout the mutiny

the galvanizing myth for the British wasn't the slaughter of women and children (for instance, the atrocity at Cawnpore) but the idea that, before being killed, the women had been molested. We forget how recently our own reactions resembled those of today's Muslims. While the Victorian-era British certainly didn't want to see their women harmed in any respect, a swift, clean death was immeasurably less alarming than a rape: The murder of a *memsahib* was one thing; the sexual violation of her was quite another.

The British were convinced that the women murdered in Delhi had been sexually tormented before their deaths. It simply wasn't true. While some suffered horribly, rape doesn't seem to have occurred to either the Hindu or Muslim mutineers, who would have viewed it as a pollution of themselves. But the vision of white women being ravaged by brown men excited a blood-lust in the British that had few, if any, parallels in their imperial history.

For many of the rich merchants or members of the native intelligentsia in Delhi, the siege was a disaster from start to finish. Those suspected of secret loyalty to the British were robbed or even killed. Then when the British returned, they took their turn at vengeance, indiscriminately slaughtering the native population and discounting old friendships—while indulging in a lucrative orgy of looting.

On September 14, 1857, after four months of misery in the summer heat and decimated by sickness, the British stormed the Kashmir Gate and established a foothold within the walls of Delhi. The fighting was savage, with neither side interested in taking prisoners. Many of the Hindu mutineers had left the city, but the Muslims who remained fought with abandon—not least the Wahhabi extremists, who had outperformed the sepoys in the failed attacks against the British positions over the months. Nonetheless, once the British penetrated the walls, the result was inevitable. The mutineers still had the numbers on their side, but internecine bickering and repeated combat failures had

disheartened them. Superior British organization and a ferocious spirit of vengeance soon told.

As the bloody days of street fighting passed, resistance crumbled. The king and his court fled, along with as many of the
inhabitants as could muster the resources to leave the city.
Princes hid amid old tombs, and the roads were packed with
refugees as members of the royal family plodded beside former
servants. Now it was the turn of the British to go on a killing
spree. And they did.

Officers who had lost their families felt no mercy toward anyone whose skin wasn't as pale as their own. Swashbuckling killers,
such as the dashing, psychopathic Captain William Hodson of
Hodson's Horse, reveled in the chance to exterminate any Indian
on whom the least suspicion fell. (Hodson personally oversaw the
cold-blooded execution of senior Mughal princes he had taken
captive, and he may have done the work himself.) Even Indians
who had actively spied for the British did not always escape the
fury of men from whom they expected gratitude.

Mosques were leveled. Broken in spirit, the half-senile
emperor was captured along the road. Some local lords got a
perfunctory hearing before they were executed, but the massacre was of a scope that never made the empire's official histo-
ries. Entire quarters of Delhi were depopulated, even leveled.
The city that had been the center of a vast empire and a paragon
of culture lay in ruins.

Of course, Delhi had lain in ruins many times before. It's
one of those cities that always rises again. But 1857 saw the end
of Delhi as a Muslim capital. While the great mosque remains
active to this day, the Muslim center of gravity was hurled westward to where, ninety years later, it would settle behind the
newly created border of Pakistan. Four centuries of drama as
Islam conquered two-thirds of India, then lost it again, ended in
brutal urban warfare and its aftermath as the Great Indian
Mutiny bled to a close. The frontiers of the faith of Mohammed

---

had been thrust back decisively, never to recover. But the fanaticism would only intensify, and just as the stern Wahhabis soon alienated the civilized population of Delhi, a century and a half later their furious descendants would appall the Muslims of Anbar province in Iraq.

The struggle has never ceased.

THE SIEGE OF PLEVNA, 1877

As the Ottoman "Sick Man of Europe" struggled to maintain its shrinking empire, Imperial Russia replaced the Austrian Habsburgs as the Ottomans' nemesis. Throughout the nineteenth century, the forces of nationalism and pan-Slavism—the latter impassioned by its identification with the Orthodox Church—gnawed at the decaying Ottoman domains in Europe. As Turkish power grew hollow and fearful, its intolerance increased, and the sultan's Slav subjects suffered one stunning atrocity after another. With Russia championing the Slav cause and the Orthodox religion, by midcentury it appeared that only the concern of other European powers with maintaining a strategic balance kept the once-great empire alive. After the Crimean War (1853–56), the bankrupt sultan did manage, thanks to crippling loans, to rearm to the point where his new ironclads dominated the Black Sea. Yet it seemed to all that the Ottoman regime would not survive a major confrontation.

In 1877, that confrontation appeared to have arrived (in fact, the last sultans would rule for another four decades). Another round of Turkish atrocities in the Balkans in the wake of local revolts ignited a near hysteria in Russia. Nationalism married a sense of Christian brotherhood as the court of St. Petersburg embarked on a crusade that wore the trappings of a modern conflict between great powers. Russian enthusiasm for a war to liberate brother Slavs and co-religionists found its expression in military volunteers from the educated classes, an outpouring of martial music and literature, and an ambitious strategic war plan that would have gotten high marks in any staff college, but which soon ran into difficulties due to the inadequacy of Russian logistics, staff work, and leadership.

While a Russian corps in the East plunged through the Caucasus, two Russian armies and the czar's brother, Grand Duke Nicholas, swept across Romanian territory in an attack meant to reach Constantinople by the end of the campaigning season. Daring and good engineers got the Russians across the Danube. Nicopolis, the scene of a high-medieval Christian disaster, fell to the czar's forces. An audacious raiding party dashed through the Balkan passes, creating panic in Istanbul and, crucially, opening the door to Russian control of the vital Shipka Pass.

Then things began to go wrong. Russian zeal bumped up against Osman Pasha, who may have been the finest operational commander the Ottoman Empire produced in the nineteenth century. Instead of withdrawing south of the Balkan Range, Osman drew his forces into the town of Plevna (Pleven) and turned it into a sprawling fortress of interlocking earthworks— working at a speed that bewildered the overconfident Russians.

The Siege of Plevna ran from July 20 to December 10, 1877, and counts as one of the valiant defensive fights of the age. Usually divided into four Battles of Plevna, the siege was perfectly designed to reinforce Turkish strengths and expose Russian weaknesses. This time, the Turks were better armed, with steel guns from Krupps and—fatally for the Russians—new Peabody-Martini repeating rifles (according to some accounts, the Turks had Winchesters as well). While the Russians were armed with breechloaders, these were single-shot weapons made in Russia or "Berdankas" turned out by an American arms industry that had come of age during the Civil War (the Russo-Turkish War was the first foreign conflict in which both sides used American-made arms). In the global arms race that followed Robert E. Lee's surrender at Appomattox (1865), the Russians had bought too early—as the Italians and French would later do after the Great War—and they bought unwisely. Like many of their European counterparts, Russian generals and logisticians believed in the bayonet and maintained that repeating rifles would merely encourage soldiers to waste bullets.

Before the earthworks of Plevna, the Russians learned the power of the repeating rifle much as Americans had experienced the killing power of earlier rifled weapons on the third day at Gettysburg and at Cold Harbor. Throughout the siege, Russian battle casualties would dwarf those of the Turks.

Despite Prussian training missions, the Turkish military had fallen behind in the skills of modern offensive campaigning, but the ferocious determination of an armed and uniformed Anatolian peasant fighting behind breastworks prefigured the British Empire's tragedy at Gallipoli in 1915. At Plevna, a crusading Orthodox field force, Russian and Romanian, came up against a brilliantly commanded Ottoman garrison one-third its size but every bit as brave. Battle cries of "Allah!" and "Allah is great!" would resound a last time above the Danube's flood plain.

The Russians almost won at the outset. A blind attack on Plevna's unfinished defenses on July 20 foundered on a lack of confidence by the Russian commander, the unavailability of reinforcements, and—in a classic example of the fog of war—the Russians' failure to realize how close they had come to success before they simply withdrew. Osman Pasha gained the time to make a fortress materialize from the earth as if summoned by djinns from the Arabian Nights.

At the end of July, a massed Russian and Romanian force assaulted Plevna from three sides. Despite fatalistic courage and bold tactical leadership, the allies were repulsed with casualties four times as high as those of the Turkish defenders, setting a pattern for the remainder of the siege. Once again, the Russian attack wasn't hopeless, but this time the effort was doomed by staff work in a shambles, a failure to reinforce success, and an abysmal lack of coordination (the Russians were unaccountably slow to deploy their field telegraphs). Even General Mikhail Skobelov, younger than forty and already a legend after his magnificent performance in Central Asia, couldn't create a lasting penetration of the Turkish defenses.

In the lull that followed the bitter Russian and Romanian defeat, corpses festered and cholera—that bane of nineteenth-century armies—prowled the camps. But Plevna was too well garrisoned and too strategic in its location to be bypassed. And the contest for the prize of Plevna had now become a competition of national wills in the eyes of the world, thanks to the telegraph (journalists embraced it, even if generals didn't) and the proliferating media of the day.

On September 11—a fateful date throughout the long struggle between Muslims and the West—the Russians staged a better-planned, massive assault on Osman Pasha's works. Again, Skobelov led his portion of the attack from the front, galloping along the lines in his white tunic, virtually daring the Turks to kill him. This time, the "white general" and his soldiers successfully stormed two key redoubts, while the Romanians, still smarting from their long subjection as vassals of the sultan, seized the vital Grivitza fortification, an act of valor that "made" the Romanian military.

Once more, though, inept Russian staff work and poor coordination erased all but the Romanian gains. By the end of the two-day fight, the Russians had again lost four times the number of casualties suffered by the Turks. In the first three battles of Plevna, the Russians and Romanians had lost well over 30,000 men—not counting deaths from disease. And they weren't a mile closer to Constantinople.

The global media of the day made Osman Pasha a hero—a remarkable feat given that world opinion was overwhelmingly anti-Turkish at the war's outset, thanks to the publicity given to Ottoman atrocities in the Balkans. But the media have been influencing warfare far longer than we recognize, and journalists have rarely been shy about taking sides on a whim. The startled government in Istanbul found it had the first-ever Ottoman hero celebrated in Europe.

The Russians decided to starve Osman Pasha out and sealed the last approaches to Plevna. As autumn progressed, the Turkish soldiers were reduced to eating vermin, and their strength began to wane. Osman wanted to withdraw while he still had a chance and preserve his thirty-five thousand men to fight again. Unfortunately for its defenders, Plevna was no longer just a small, obscure city in the Balkans—it was a cause. National pride was engaged on both sides. Osman received the order to hold out to the end, while promises of a relief force proved as empty as the sultan's treasury.

As winter began to torment the hungry defenders, Osman Pasha realized it was only a matter of time. He also recognized, much more clearly than his superiors, safe in their offices, that his army was vital to the empire's dwindling hopes of preventing a Russian strategic victory south of the Balkans—and perhaps at Istanbul itself. Finally, he decided to break out on his own initiative.

On December 9, 1877, Osman set into motion a plan far better designed than any the Russians had brought to bear against him. Under the cover of a biting winter night, he conducted a successful river-crossing operation (of the Vit) and struck the unsuspecting Russians, bursting into their fieldworks. But the Russians now had over a hundred thousand men surrounding Plevna. The Turkish attack, for all its desperation and all the calls on Allah for assistance, could not break completely through the layered Russian positions. Full daylight revealed a murderous brawl of point-blank shots, blood-greased bayonets, rifle butts slimed with brains, and pistols, knives, and fists.

A random bullet struck Osman Pasha's leg, and rumors flew through the Turkish ranks that their general had been killed. Panic erupted. Yet even then, enough Turkish units stood their ground to permit the bulk of Osman's forces to re-enter the Plevna defenses.

Carried from the battlefield, Osman Pasha knew the game was up. He surrendered the city a day later, asking only that his soldiers be treated honorably. They weren't—although Osman himself was feted by his captors. Driven into captivity through the winter snows and starved along the way, thousands of Turkish soldiers perished on their trek north. Within Plevna, vengeful Slavs—with the blessing of their clergy—massacred the Turkish wounded left behind. Centuries of pent-up rage exploded in atrocity.

Of course, the Balkan penchant for atrocity survives into our own time. But when Plevna fell, the Ottomans' European empire fell with it. In risk-it-all forced marches, Russian columns dashed through the Balkan passes in the dead of winter. Handily defeating the remaining Ottoman field forces, the Grand Duke's entourage ended the campaign less than a dozen miles from Istanbul, with British warships offshore to warn the Russians against dismantling the Ottoman Empire.

A crusade in all but name, the Russo-Turkish War of 1877–78 broke the last hold of Ottoman power in Europe, leaving only a few restive scraps to the sultan. After much squabbling between the great powers of the day, Romania's independence was confirmed (with Russia snatching Bessarabia from its helpless ally); a nascent Bulgarian state emerged; Serbia and Montenegro expanded; Austria-Hungary put down deeper, ill-fated roots in the Balkans; and newly free Christians prepared for war with each other. Osman Pasha gave the empire a last glimmer of pride, but the day when Turkish armies would strike fear into European hearts was over.

The next great jihad, like the very first, would burst out of the deserts of Arabia.

When Muslim Armies Won

Armed Forces Journal

September 2007

When terrorists or insurgents in Iraq detonate a roadside bomb to draw out our forces in response, or when they stage a small ambush to lure us into a larger one, they're pursuing a Middle Eastern way of war more than two millennia old, with roots in the techniques of tribes from the steppes. What's surprising isn't that the old lure-and-ambush technique is still in use, but that, after many centuries of Western experience with this particular hook, we remain prone to taking the bait.

While doing research for a history project, I was struck both by the enduring characteristics of jihadi warfare—even though yesteryear's triumphant Muslim armies have been replaced by terrorist cells and irregular bands—as well as the specific military lore the Islamic world lost. Much of what Arab, Seljuk, or Ottoman armies did in bygone campaigns to annihilate their enemies is now the intellectual inheritance of Western commanders—although cultural flaws that led medieval Christian armies to defeat remain with us as well.

The use of atrocities to break an enemy's will, the power of fanaticism and charismatic leaders, the value of surprise—even the need to defeat armored forces (in the form of mounted knights) were all there a thousand years ago. Lighter Muslim

47

forces dealt with heavy armor above Alexandria, at Nicopolis, and in countless other battles and skirmishes by drawing the armored vehicles of the day onto unfavorable ground where the knights could not maneuver or escape—much as our opponents attempt to do today in the alleys of Iraq.

UNITY OF COMMAND AND WILL

The greatest advantage the better Arab and all Seljuk or Ottoman armies enjoyed over their Byzantine or European enemies was unity of command—along with a strategic unity of purpose and will. In countless Crusade encounters and Balkan battles, what undid the Western forces (often equal in size to their opponents) was a consistent inability to accept and obey a single commander: When the going got tough, the tough went every which way. Patchwork Western armies behaved centrifugally, while the better Muslim forces acted centripetally.

In the West, centuries of feudalism and chivalric codes (the ruggedest form of rugged individualism) reinforced local and protonational rivalries: The French argued with each other; they argued with the Burgundians; the Burgundians and French quarreled with the English and Germans; no one from Flanders would obey a Hungarian king; nobody trusted the Venetians; and the Christian Byzantines were regarded as heretics—this was the situation not in royal or ducal courts but in war councils on the eve of battle.

Today, Western militaries recognize the importance of unified command—although national contingents in coalitions often stipulate limits on its use. Nonetheless, in serious combat, the quibbling tends to stop. And within twenty-first-century Western armies, chains of command are clear and acknowledged. The West's dilemmas today lie at the political level, where disunity and rivalries continue to hamper unified responses to Islamist threats as absurdly as they did in the Middle Ages—if with blessedly fewer consequences thus far. (From the early sixteenth century onward, the French generally aligned politically with the Ottomans to weaken the Habsburgs; *plus ça change*...)

For its part, the Muslim world has lost (or at least misplaced) this principle of unity of command for the direction of campaigns or even battles. Despots, such as Saddam Hussein, enforced a hollowed-out caricature of unity of command, but we are fortunate in the degree of inter- and intra-factional quibbling among our enemies in Iraq and elsewhere. Even charismatic figures such as Osama bin Laden enjoy a limited ability to command, because the cellular nature of terrorist forces, as well as geographic dispersion, makes him more of a figurehead and instigator than a field marshal. Arab terrorists praise him—then do whatever they want.

Even in the conventional-warfare realm, late-twentieth-century Arab armies were faction-ridden internally and suspicious of allies (whom they routinely tried to deceive, as in the 1967 and 1973 wars with Israel). This inability to pull together to achieve and sustain battlefield synergies has granted Western armies a signal advantage—and the one development in this sphere that should worry us has been Hezbollah's ability to combine a cellular organization with discipline and unity of purpose—enabled by Hassan Nasrullah's appreciation of the value of mission-type orders.

Terrorists do have a strategic unity of purpose—to kill as many Westerners, Israelis, and liberal Muslims as possible—but the diffuse, essentially anarchic manner in which the goal is pursued leaves it, to be frank, a dramatic annoyance, not an existential threat.

By contrast, yesteryear's Muslim armies were, indeed, existential threats to Europe, and given the long European genius for doing exactly the wrong thing in war, it should astonish us that the caliphate did not extend at least to the Shetland Islands.

When it comes to destructive rivalries and military incompetence, the Middle East and the West have changed places.

THE GREAT REVERSAL

Another factor that empowered Ottoman armies, especially, was their superior organization, from unit design to logistics. A comparatively sophisticated sense of logistical needs helped Saladin's Arab armies defeat overconfident Crusaders, but it was the Ottomans who first displayed a genius for organizing logistical feats that helped them crush European armies in battle—and take Constantinople. Whether hauling ships over hilltops, deploying disciplined artillery on the battlefield (a daunting undertaking in the days before true field guns), or sustaining enormous armies on the march, the Ottoman sultans in the century that included Mehmet the Conqueror and Suleiman the Magnificent harnessed the resources of their empires through effective administration and achieved logistical successes far grander than, and predating, those credited to Wallenstein a hundred years later. Suleiman's triumphant campaign that destroyed the Hungarian kingdom at the Battle of Mohacs was an organizational masterpiece.

In one of history's not fully explicable twists, the Ottoman Empire lost its suppleness by the second half of the sixteenth century, calcifying and falling behind a rapidly developing Europe. Ottoman organization was more effective in the fifteenth century than in the seventeenth (perhaps the empire's sprawl explains at least part of the decline). In a sense, the rise of Europe was the triumph of the clerks, as the once-lagging continent's accounting and organizational procedures improved exponentially as they were forced to cope with the opening of the New World. In 1526, the Ottomans fielded the best-organized, best-trained, and best-disciplined (and, arguably, the best-led) army in the world. A hundred years later, all of the Turkish gears were in reverse.

Today, logistics weaknesses plague all Muslim armies (a situation exacerbated by corruption), but terrorist organizations appear to have made an intellectual breakthrough, returning, in a sense, to their ancient nomadic roots, when traveling light and exploiting local resources was a life-and-death necessity. The ability of terrorists (and insurgents) to pluck the West's common technologies, from cell phones to passenger jets, from cars transformed into bombs to the internet, places them firmly in the raiding tradition of their ancestors, if in a postmodern form. This guerrilla force without a heavy logistics tail—but with great mobility—also represents a rejection of the Western way of war, to which Arab states had signed on in the 1800s. For two centuries and more, Muslim rulers attempted to copy the West's military forms, only to fail with 100 percent consistency. Now we may be witnessing, between Hezbollah and al Qa'eda, a new synthesis of tradition and technology suited to the cultural environment in which our enemies operate.

We're the masters of conventional logistics. Our enemies reject the conventions and pick up whatever they need at the local bazaar.

SURPRISE!

One lesson Middle Eastern Muslim forces, regular and irregular, have never forgotten is the value of surprise. Another legacy of their ancient raiding heritage, calculated surprises gave Arabs, especially, their few glimmers of triumph in recent decades, whether speaking of the opening phases of the Yom Kippur War in 1973, the attacks of September 11, 2001, or simply the detonation of an IED along a roadway in Iraq.

Surprise is almost always effective—initially. But there's a disconnect between the effects of surprise at the tactical vs. the operational or strategic level. It's extremely difficult to recover when surprised tactically (although our well-trained forces do as well as any troops could), and the surviving victims are usually left bloodied, furious, and frustrated. At the strategic or operational level, though, surprise lends only an initial advantage, as at Pearl Harbor or the Battle of the Bulge in our own military history, or, in the Arab case, the 1973 crossing of the Suez Canal or Saddam Hussein's invasion of Kuwait. Short, sharp tactical engagements can be decided by who shoots first (although, of course, that's not always the case). But at the levels of campaigns and wars, residual strength and resources tell, as long as the victim of the initial surprise doesn't simply surrender.

Today, surprise remains a primary tool in the Arab arsenal (as well as in other Muslim cultures), and the raid remains the model of Arab warfare. On the other hand, Muslim forces, regular or terrorist, in the greater Middle East tend to fare badly when they are themselves surprised. Although our disciplined forces can often recover, even at the tactical level, surprised Muslim forces usually fold, whether we speak of a successful dark-of-night raid in Iraq or the campaign against the Taliban in Afghanistan. Discipline and trust tell, and our troops are remarkably disciplined, and they trust each other and their leaders. Terrorist cells may have their peculiar forms of discipline, but, beyond that, Arab and other regional security forces and militaries are poorly disciplined in the conventional sense and are plagued by internal religious, tribal, and ethnic rivalries: When things go badly, the fingers (and sometimes the weapons) start pointing internally.

Of course, there are exceptions. The Egyptian infantry has sometimes proven remarkably tenacious on the defense, and the Jordanian military includes genuinely professional elements. But the Islamic art of war seemed to have died with the Ottoman Empire, with the region returning to either a reliance on mass (as in the Iranian Revolutionary Guard's wave attacks during the Iran-Iraq War) or postmodern forms of raids (the Madrid bombings or the attacks on police stations and recruiting centers in Iraq today).

In the past, surprise was connected to an instinct for choosing advantageous battlegrounds. That connection may remain, despite our superiority on most forms of terrain. The modern choice of terrain, the city, is really about the exploitation of masses of human beings (what I termed "human terrain" in an essay about urban operations a decade ago). Although urban warfare is a new phenomenon for Muslim warriors, they've taken to it with a facility that should worry us. We're familiar with the hackneyed phrase "the urban jungle," but the cities of the Middle East may have become urban steppes, where tribes of raiders appear out of nowhere to strike and disappear again.

A last advantage yesteryear's Arab and Turkic armies enjoyed over their Byzantine or European opponents was superior campaign intelligence. Although Byzantine armies deployed practiced scouts (and spies) and prized good intelligence during their centuries of glory, by the time of the Seljuk victory at Manzikert in 1071, the Byzantine military system was in decline and even the veteran emperor-general, Romulus IV, neglected to push scouting parties deep into enemy territory. The result was a disaster.

Acute intelligence is, of course, crucial to achieving surprise or luring an enemy onto a particular killing field. By the Ottoman era, the great sultans (and the grand viziers serving the lesser ones) exhibited a much more sophisticated understanding of the exploitable weaknesses, composition, order of march, and disposition of Western armies than the Europeans managed to achieve until the late seventeenth century. Careful to remain aware of the location and rate of advance of their antagonists, the Ottomans were able to move at much higher speeds (even with larger forces) and to fight effectively from the line of march (as at Mohacs in 1526).

Today, our enemies within the Muslim world, from the Nile to the Indus, display bifurcated capabilities in intelligence collection and, especially, analysis. At the tactical level, terrorists and insurgents are often quite good at identifying units and their behavior patterns, from the quirks of specific commanders to the movement discipline of a particular platoon. Obviously, they face an easier time of it than we do, because they generally operate in a familiar environment that's profoundly foreign (and often unwelcoming) to us. All things considered, it's impressive how much progress our tactical intelligence personnel have made since we arrived, goggle-eyed, in Iraq in 2003. But the home-court advantage still tells.

Terrorist intelligence performance at the strategic level is
another story entirely. Identifying targets isn't hard—the West
offers plenty—but Islamist terrorists become psychologically
imprisoned by their fervor, in their belief in the inevitability of
their triumph. While such emotional intensity gives them deep
reserves of will, it's disastrous when they make intelligence esti-
mates. The notion that the 9/11 attacks would bring the United
States to its knees, the conviction that Washington was too cowardly to send forces into Afghanistan, and the assumption that
Iraqis would embrace their medieval version of Islam have all
proven catastrophic for al Qa'eda—and it isn't just the terrorists
who get it wrong. Saddam was certain that we wouldn't invade in
2003, and the Turks utterly misjudged our conventional and
logistical capabilities, as well as our determination. The penchant for power fantasies that Fouad Adjami captured so suc-
cinctly in the title of his (splendid) book, *The Dream Palace of the
Arabs*, has left both Muslim terrorist cells and general staffs inept
at conducting strategic appreciations on the eve of war or in the
prelude to a major terrorist strike.

Certainly, our own strategic intelligence performance has
been mixed, at best (and occasionally susceptible to fantasies of
our own); nonetheless, our culture of empiricism, our functional
pragmatism, and our internal self-criticism win through in the end:
We may convince ourselves of stupid things, but we don't stay convinced when the evidence shows overwhelmingly that we were
wrong (certain political leaders excepted). Our enemies cling to
their fantasies with a positively Rumsfeldian obliviousness.

AND IN THE FUTURE

None of the observations above offers a checklist for defeating
our enemies. This brief historical analysis is meant only to provoke thought and, perhaps, an occasional shock of recognition.
Moreover, the insights on offer apply to the situation today. After
centuries of inertia and ineptitude, we're seeing the first glimmers of a new Islamic competence at alternative forms of war-

fare. The large field armies of the Middle East remain less than the sum of their ill-maintained parts, but innovative approaches to fielding combatant forces—exemplified on the high end by Hezbollah and on the lower by terrorist cells in Iraq—have posed unexpectedly solution-resistant challenges to English-speaking militaries, as well as to the Israeli Defense Force.

For centuries, Europe failed to adapt to the Muslim way of war, persistently clinging to doomed warfare techniques. Then the Islamic world took its turn at calcification, as a rejuvenated Europe leapt ahead for long centuries and, more recently, the United States fielded conventional forces impossible to defeat in a set-piece battle. Now, it appears that the Muslim world is adapting at last, pursuing innovative organizations, tactics and strategies, while brushing aside our insistence on the "laws of land warfare." We cling to the rules we know and value, while our enemies ignore them.

That's exactly what the Ottoman Empire did—by refusing to adapt to new battlefield conventions—as it slipped into its long decline and ultimate fall.

PART II

The Devils These Days

The World after the "Age of Ideology"

Unscripted address to the JINSA Policy Forum

January 24, 2007

I want to speak not just about Israel or the Middle East, but also about the global context. The United States, as powerful as it is and shall remain, exists in this context. Israel exists in the desperate, boundlessly frustrating context of the Middle East and, of course, in this partially and asymmetrically globalizing world.

I try to understand history, and I emphasize the word "understand," because in Washington there are all these misnamed think tanks, which don't think terribly much but produce a great deal of paper. The quest for general understanding exists only in pockets inside the Beltway, and much of it is tied up with policy beliefs and rhetoric. I always caution outsiders about this. Washington, for all its Ph.D.s and shining superficial brilliance, is not a thinking town; it is not an innovative town. In fact, I would argue that it is an extremely conservative town intellectually, no matter which side of the aisle you look at. And this ties directly to the problems we are having in Iraq and around the world today.

On the surface we're Democrats and Republicans—but I believe that our intellectual dysfunction stems from the fact that we are increasingly incestuous, at least educationally. The ruling elite, such as it is, is somewhat porous, but people get in by going to the same schools, they read the same books—fundamentally, they start from the same premises about the world. Washington's thought processes, regarding strategy or the challenges we face, are locked in the twentieth century and have not progressed beyond it, despite what happened in 2001. And neoconservatives, for all the mistakes they may have made, at least pushed America forward, pushed the Republican Party forward, to begin to engage in the world, pushed us toward the realization that we cannot all hide in a bunker in Kansas. But despite such exceptions, Washington's a reactionary town that cannot think beyond a European World Order. The State Department is a quintessential example of stalwart resistance to changing realities. You may disagree—and my thesis would be contradicted if many of you did not.

I take what the military would call a "GPS approach" to strategy—a Global Positioning System device. The first thing you have to understand about the historical moment is where you are. And I don't believe we do. Many Israelis understand it viscerally, but not necessarily consciously, because they are faced with intrusive reality so routinely.

So where are we in history? We're at the abrupt confluence of several powerful currents. Above all, we're at the end of the Age of Ideology. I cringe every time I hear President Bush say we're in a war of ideas. That is utterly wrong, and it's symptomatic of why we have such trouble fighting this war.

The United States military officer takes an oath to defend the Constitution of the United States. In most of the rest of the world, dying for a constitution would be regarded as a lunatic proposition. In Iraq, look at the challenges we're having getting people to fight for a rule-of-law democracy. It's just not part of their moral firmament.

We stand at the end of the Age of Ideology, which really was amazingly short. In historical terms—a blip. It dated formally from 1789 to 1991. You may argue that it started a few years earlier, but just leave it at that—the French Revolution to the collapse of the Soviet Empire in 1991. It was an aberration in human history. Future scholars will definitely deem it bizarre as well as deadly, not least because "reason" and "rationality" culminated in the Great European civil war from 1914 to 1945 that reached its apotheosis in the Holocaust and echoed in Srebrenica in the 1990s—whenever anyone tells me that today's Europeans are weak and defenseless, I remind them that Europe is the continent that perfected genocide and ethnic cleansing. And forget "Eurabia." Europeans will not "go gentle into that good night." They've simply enjoyed a golden age of peace under the American defense umbrella with Uncle Sam paying the bills. Now, the party's over, but they don't want it to end. Historically, when Europeans are sufficiently provoked, they react savagely. Europe's also, by the way, the continent that exported more death and destruction than any other.

Back to the end of the Age of Ideology, though: In many ways its demise is a blessing, the end of this bizarre human fascination with a lunatic notion that one man or a small cabal could sit down and design a better system of social, economic, and political organization than the vast human collective had done organically over the centuries. If you think about America, the Anglo-America tradition of government, it wasn't designed. We glibly reference the Magna Carta as the fountainhead, but, honestly, no one among our political ancestors sat down in the twelfth, thirteenth, or even eighteenth century, worked out a blueprint, and declared, "We need to do exactly this, this and this." We learned by doing, by trial and error, and for systems of government it appears to be the only method that results in a healthy state.

It really was an amazing achievement, the development of democracy as we know it, from which we all profited—eventually. It's also a very long and sometimes painful process. The important thing to understand is that the English-speaking world's evolution of democracy—whether a presidential or parliamentary system—was not the work of a lone genius sketching it all out from scratch. There was no five-year plan, no ten-year plan. It's too much to say that our system's an accident, but it evolved over a millennium. And then you come to 1789, and much of humanity falls for this trap of believing that an individual or a junta of intellectuals can design a social system that will work for all of humanity. And, of course, humanity always disappoints, whether it's under Marxism or National Socialism or fascism—the humans disappoint the system. Hitler, at the end of the war, wanted apocalyptic destruction because he felt the German people didn't deserve his great vision. What happened when people didn't live up to Stalin's vision? Or to Lenin's before that? When you try to impose an ideology arrogantly designed by man upon humankind, you're on the road to Auschwitz or the Gulag or Srebrenica or the killing fields of Cambodia.

Simultaneously, this now-defunct Age of Ideology was also the great age of nationalism. But what's increasingly missing from the equation in the European context—it's still robust elsewhere—is religion. In Europe, religion starts to fade, it starts draining away. Oh, you have the "muscular Christianity" of the Victorian era, but it's much more genteel than past forms of faith—it's certainly not a violently passionate faith. Passionate faith begins to disappear, or it's transmuted into ideologies or nationalism or a nationalist ideology such a national socialism. Basically, humanity takes a crazy detour through the Age of Ideology, slaughtering hundreds of millions of humans to perfect human societies. Good riddance.

Why does this matter to us today? It matters because our diplomats, our politicians, still think in terms of this Age of Ideology. Now, when you get to fighting insurgencies, instead of looking at Europe historically, we should be looking beyond Europe. This brief, dead Age of Ideology distorts our vision today, even though it's over, it's done. Oh, there are still echoes in Latin America and elsewhere, but it's essentially over for our strategic purposes. We have returned to the human historical mainstream—and that is rebellions, insurgencies, revolts, terrorist movements, wars based upon religion and ethnicity—wars of faith and blood.

The good news, such as it is, is that hyper-charged religious zealots or ethnic zealots, sometimes both at the same time, don't yet have the killing power of Imperial Japan or Nazi Germany or a Stalinist Russia. But they are determined to get it.

The bad news, and this really applies to our military, is that contrary to the nonsense you hear from pundits that insurgencies are never defeated, through three thousand years of history insurgencies and rebellions based on faith and ethnicity have been defeated—consistently and usually relatively quickly. The bad news is that they have been defeated only with slaughter, with significant bloodshed.

If you are unwilling to kill religious zealots or passionate ethnic zealots, you will lose. But that's not how we think—we Americans want the world to love us. Well, unfortunately, you have to deal with reality at some point. Oh, because we are so tremendously powerful, even if we walked away from Iraq tomorrow—and I don't want to see that just yet—we would still be the greatest power in history. Others would suffer, but we would move on. At some point, though, Americans, too, will have to face the harshness of this world. Our moral values had an easy ride in the last century, when so much seemed black and white. Now our humanity will be tested—and the greatest danger is that we will continue to fail to grasp that the greatest immorality isn't the over-inflated nonsense of Abu Ghraib or the infantry squad that fires on the wrong vehicle—those are issues of "little morality"—the great immorality is for the United States to allow itself to be defeated. Obsessed with ailing saplings, we're willing to let our enemies clear-cut the forest.

The reason ideological insurgencies—Marxist, Maoist, take your pick—are so much easier to deal with then the religious or ethnic insurgencies we face today is that the devotees of the recent past were not born into those beliefs, they were persuaded that it was good for them. Malaya is a good example. Why were the British able to defeat the Maoists guerillas in Malaya, apart from some good military work? The Malayan villagers were persuaded to reject Maoist ideology, which was, in any case, an unnatural fit for them. But if you look at the fights we face today, you cannot persuade an Arab to become a Kurd or a Persian to become an Arab. And you certainly will not persuade a Shi'a to become a Sunni or a Sunni to become a Christian. I really wish I could be more reassuring and charming and say, "Everything is going to be just fine—the Age of Aquarius is coming!"—but it's *not.* These are knife fights to the bone with uncompromising enemies. And we're worried about our table manners.

At present, the Islamic world of the Middle East is the crucial problem—at present. If you look at the historical mainstream, and you try to see it through the eyes of others—imagine how the Romans felt about the Jewish zealots. In the 1520s, Christianity had its Osama bin Laden, Thomas Muentzer. In a recent article I published, I cheated. I translated from a German letter that Muentzer wrote in 1525 and, instead of translating "Gott" as God, I just translated it as "Allah" and tried to make people guess where it came from. Well, the letter could have been written by Ayman al-Zawahiri or bin Laden—any of these guys—it even talked about "toppling the infidels' towers." Religious passion gone awry, this now-in-vogue apocalyptic impulse to kill every infidel, to destroy—we should have seen this coming, because it's absolutely predictable when the pattern reemerges in human events. It occurs, as in Palestine two thousand years ago, as in Germany in the 1520s, as in the Middle East today, when a social, cultural, and religious system feels utterly besieged and overwhelmed by a stronger outside force. The effect Rome had on Palestine, the effect the Holy Roman Empire, which bought into Mediterranean Catholicism, had on the German states . . . these fateful impacts generated religious fanaticism, since religion and ethnicity are the default positions of traditional human societies under threat. We don't realize how late Christianity came to the northern fringes of Europe. It was only on the Baltic fringes for a few centuries—in some spots less—by the time the Reformation arrived. Traditional ways of life were threatened, and you had this perfect storm of an outside force assaulting the old order from the other side of the Alps and threatening these highly traditional societies and their cultural practices, their values, and their religion. The result was thirteen decades of the most ferocious wars Europe experienced prior to the twentieth century.

The first thing that usually happens in such scenarios isn't actually a religious rebellion. The first thing is generally a political attempt at resolution, at parleying for the restitution of traditional privileges—which also happened in Palestine, and in the German states for over a century before the outbreak of the Peasants' War and all that followed, and it's what's been happening in the Middle East for the past half century. There is an initial attempt to settle things through political means, to work out a political solution. And when the political solutions are frustrated, whether in the Roman-occupied Middle East or the Germany of the sixteenth century or in the Middle East of the late twentieth century—when the political systems fail, when the despots rule, when Nasser disappoints, when America backs the Shah—as you know, during the Cold War we made mistakes, we backed dictators, we betrayed America's principles and it served us badly and it ultimately served Israel badly . . . well, when people fail to find a political answer, a political way out of the perceived crisis, then they default to religion. It happens every time. Those of you with extensive experience with Israel over the years have seen it. There's just a consistent pattern, where you first have the PLO with all its awful corruption—but the terror of the PLO was political terrorism. And you could bargain with them to a certain degree.

Now, I certainly wouldn't recommend bargaining with terrorists, but I think you'll see the distinction in trying to bargain with an Arafat and trying to deal with Iran's Ahmadinejad or Hezbollah's Hassan Nasrallah. We are now beyond bargaining. And Americans default to the practices of the now-dead Age of

Ideology, when men could be persuaded to change their beliefs. One of the great myths I hear right now on the American side is "Iraq can only be solved through negotiations." Well, good luck. I would bet my life that Iraq will not be solved through negotiations alone. This superstitious belief in the power of negotiations bewilders me.

Where have negotiations produced enduring results in the Middle East where the parties were not already exhausted and sick of war? War-weariness and disgust with al Qa'eda will do more for Iraq than negotiations. Israel's peace with Egypt worked reasonably well—although there are still peacekeepers in the Sinai—because Egypt was just played out. But you certainly couldn't convince Hezbollah to quit after their perceived victory last summer. Look at the evidence before your eyes. We are trying to apply Age of Ideology solutions—which didn't even work very well then—to the new Age of Debased Religion, of religion reduced to superstition, ethnicity, and blood. Which leads me to Thomas Friedman—who I think is brilliant and a nice guy and I'm jealous of his book sales. I think he's got globalization exactly wrong.

When Tom Friedman talks about globalization, he's talking about the golden crust of the human loaf. At his most acute, he's talking about the platinum specks on that golden crust. But when you get beneath that crust, when you get out of the luxury hotel and go out in the bush in Africa or the Middle East or India or Indonesia, as I have done and will continue to do, God willing—when you're down at the tribal level—the world looks very different than it does from the Four Seasons. The privileged of the world are coming together. In the 1990s, everybody was putting his or her yacht in Marbella Harbor. A few years later it was Cabo San Lucas. Those are the people to whom Tom Friedman's worldview applies. But the masses hate the changes upending their cherished verities.

We in the West turned away from the disturbing phenomenon of mass behavior after the horrors of WWII and the Holocaust. But you must embrace the obvious truth, that human beings in mass are different. The mob is a different organism, not just a gathering of individuals. Just go to a Penn State football game. Or a riot. I've seen people I knew and they just change like creatures from a horror film; they become non-autonomous parts of a greater organism—a biologically and psychologically different beast with its own malevolent dynamics. We are just so naive about mass behavior! How could Germany, the most sophisticated, educated, civilized country in Europe, do what it did in the Holocaust? You don't get the answer by looking at individuals—not even Hitler, catalyst though he was. It was a mass phenomenon.

What we are seeing in the Middle East and elsewhere, but especially in the Middle East today, is a mass phenomenon. The American approach is to try to interact with individuals and win individual hearts and minds—but we're dealing with a different organism. And far from seeing the world coming together, I believe we have entered a period of tragic breakdown. I call it "the return of the tribes." In the world of academia, you couldn't use the word "tribes" thirty years ago because it was politically incorrect, but when you go to Africa to talk to people, the first thing they tell you is what tribe they are from. Tribes are back—and not just in Africa. And by the way, not just in Tikrit, Anbar, and so on, in Iraq. Look at the 2005 French and Dutch votes against the European Constitution—those were tribal votes! Fewer Spaniards describe themselves as Spaniards—they're Catalans or Basques. Italians are Lombards or Sicilians. Obviously, the process is further ahead in some areas than others. Look at Scotland. It wants to become its own nation. It has its own parliament now. Even my own Welsh relatives imagine an historical grandeur for themselves for which there is no historical evidence whatsoever—good poets and choirs, but that's about it.

If you look around the world you see the old, European-imposed order breaking down, the mass secession from the grand collective established during the epoch of nationalism, during the age of European imperialism. People are reasserting primal identities. And not just Sunni Arabs or Shi'a Arabs, but

even subgroups within those communities—smaller tribal identities and family identities, cult identities. And then you look at
the challenges we Americans face. Israel, too, because if America
faces a problem, Israel faces it in spades. And by the way, look at
the change in Israel. The founders of Israel were overwhelmingly secular, socialist Zionists. Can you say that about Israeli
society today? Even within Israeli society, the passionate religious
believers have a disproportionate impact on the political system.

Religion is back. You remember the 1965 cover of *Time* mag-
azine—"Is GOD Dead?" God is unkillable; we are hard-wired for
faith. But I'm afraid we have entered another one of humanity's
periods when faith goes awry. We hear all about the Islamist
threat in Africa. Ethiopia has just set it back—probably briefly—
with a little quiet help from us. But that said, you go to Africa, to
Kenya, for instance—Mombassa used to be a Muslim city. What
strikes you now is that, on Sundays, Mombassa is literally jump-
ing with charismatic Christians, Pentecostal Christians, filling
parks with thousands of people. It's Christianity that's on the
march, with Islam fighting a desperate rearguard action. There
are, indeed, fault lines between civilizations—Samuel Hunting-
ton was dead right about that, although he overlooked the gory
fault lines within civilizations as well. I am not optimistic about
the chance for long-term peace where Christianity and Islam
meet in Africa—and the fault line jags right across the continent. Muslims and Christians in Africa are going to keep on
killing each other, largely unconcerned about the rest of us and
our opinions. Because a rule of humanity is "we may hate distant
enemies in theory, but prefer to kill our neighbors."

Related to the return of extreme fundamentalism we see
polarization within societies and the resurrection of atavistic religious impulses—a brute form of religion that is apocalyptic and
mesmerizes the collective. It elevates behavior over faith—it's
really the antithesis of Luther's revolutionary credo of "salvation
through faith alone." Luther, by the way, unintentionally opened
the door to modernity in the West in a number of senses. For

example, we accept that monopolies are bad in the business world and we know they are bad in government—but they are also bad for religion. It's a challenge for Israel, because of the government's granting of a de facto veto, a peculiar monopoly of power, to the least-tolerant Jews—to those who have done the least for Israel, while doing extreme damage to it. Ultimately, religious monopolies fall prey to corruption. I know of no exceptions in human history—and that's certainly the case in the Muslim Middle East today. God willing, Israel will transcend that rule. But of course Israel is, with a few exceptions, a pluralistic society, and an admirable one. But beware extremists of any stripe—the rest of us always end up paying their butcher's bill.

Now, not only do we face these challenges from extreme apocalyptic religion, from ethnicity interwoven with religion, but we in the West have educated ourselves to a fundamental misunderstanding of what warfare takes. This brings me very directly to Israel. I was privileged to be able to go to Israel midway through the war in the summer of 2006. It was heartbreaking to go up to the front lines. The IDF were very helpful; they were very open. It's probably the most open and democratic place on earth in wartime. It just broke my heart to see what was happening. To see it firsthand was painful, because Israel lost. There is no other way to put it. Israel lost. Hezbollah won. Look at the streets of Lebanon yesterday and today. Hassan Nasrallah is the first Arab since 1948 who was able to turn tens of thousands of Jews into refugees. Nasrallah was able to drive tens of thousands more Jews into underground bunkers. In the Islamic world of the Middle East, he's a hero. The only slight positive note is that a lot of Arab rulers, including the Saudis, are getting very worried—and the only good Saudi is a terrified Saudi! Paradoxically, Arab despots have always quietly counted on Israel to maintain the existing order in the region.

I worry about the price Israel is going to pay. As a lifelong supporter of Israel—although I don't think Israel always acts wisely—I'm one who, at the end of the day, comes down on

Israel's side. And there's more to it than generational romanticism. Israel represents my civilization—and, I would argue, the only humane civilization in the entire Middle East today. For all of its faults—and only God is perfect—Israel represents human decency amid the wretched moral squalor and cruelty of the forlorn landscape stunted by perverted forms of Islam and a culture of irresponsibility.

I'm going to be very blunt with you: The Israel Defense Forces absolutely need profound reform. I think Israelis realize that, but some of those reforms are going to be tougher than others. Corruption crept in; leadership was absolutely abysmal. Tactically, the IDF ground forces I saw were pathetic. There are some good units. But the reserve system doesn't work anymore. Israel's pride—the citizen soldier—doesn't work in the twenty-first century. It worked in the past, but people fight for different things today. Arabs don't fight for states; it's a foreign concept to them. They might jump up and down and declare, "We will die for you Saddam!" but they don't. People fight for different things. And Arabs and Persians and Afghans will fight for their faith, for their clan, and for their turf. Hezbollah hit the trifecta in southern Lebanon.

One American general, who watched much of this, put it to me like this: "The IDF has been living off the fumes of 1967 for too long." Bravery isn't the problem. The Israeli troops are brave. But a system that relies so heavily upon reservists simply can't attain the requisite level of professionalism. Israel is a small country; it has budgetary problems, as well, not just population problems. I know the IDF cannot go fully professional, but it's got to become more professional. The West Bank is different from Lebanon, of course. You've got rock-throwers. They're deadly sometimes, but they're slovenly and disorganized. But now they're going to study Hezbollah, and they'll learn. Regarding Lebanon, too many IDF leaders assumed, "This is going to be like the West Bank, maybe a little tougher." Even with all that prior experience in Lebanon, they called it wrong. Hezbollah had done a brilliant job of what the U.S. Army calls the "intelligence preparation of the battlefield." They studied their enemy. Hezbollah knew where they would fight and whom they would fight and what the Israeli tactics would be. Instead of making the Egyptian or Syrian mistake of trying to build a Western-model army, which Arab states, and the Arabs and Ottomans and Persians, had been trying to do unsuccessfully for three centuries, they tailored their armed forces specifically to the Israeli threat in Lebanon. They invested in antitank guided missiles, Katyusha rockets of various calibers, and a lot of small arms. Instead of having a backbone of command and control that can be broken, Hezbollah was a cellular organization that could fight autonomously from mission-type orders. I'm not glorifying Hezbollah, because in the one-on-one fighting, Israel did far better. But the casualty ratios aren't reassuring. Some five hundred Hezbollah fighters were killed, while Israel lost 117 soldiers. Hezbollah is willing to make that tradeoff anytime.

The IDF was badly led at its top. It was heartbreaking to watch Chief of Staff Dan Halutz. You know, the Tel Aviv technocrats made exactly the same mistakes, such as assuming that airpower could do everything, that the Rumsfeld Pentagon initially made in Iraq—but the United States had the residual power and command flexibility to recover. Israel has a much thinner margin of error. We live in an age when our security problems are overwhelmingly human problems. Technology doesn't solve problems of the human heart and soul. It may help you kill your enemies, but it's not the ultimate answer to people who dig bunkers in villages, use civilians as human shields, and don't care as much as we do about friendly casualties.

The Israeli air and naval forces, by the way, performed very well with civilian reservists. The air force did exactly what it was asked to do. The first night of the war—BANG!—they knocked out Hezbollah's heavy missiles left and right. I believe they got all but one of the big ones in the first day or so. And what difference did it make? Well, it did protect Tel Aviv. But Hezbollah's strategy was very robust and resilient, and it was targeted at the Israeli civilian population. What Hezbollah did was basically to embarrass the IDF by attacking Israeli civilians with means the IDF couldn't counteract.

Yes, the Katyusha attacks brought Israeli society together. But what mattered was the perception in the Arab world. And of course we saw the global media decide early on that the real story was Lebanese suffering, and so they glossed over Israeli suffering. And, by the way, the key to understanding journalists—and I have one foot in that bordello, to put it politely—is that, once *The New York Times* and a few other key outlets establish a narrative of a particular event, everybody else follows their lead. Journalists, with rare exceptions, are herd animals. That's what happened in the fighting with Hezbollah. The media pack joined forces with Hezbollah—although they certainly wouldn't put it that way.

But back to contemporary combat of the sort Israel faced and will face: Ground force commanders are the only people who can run this, not the air force—sorry. "Shock and awe" didn't work for us, and it's never going to work for the IDF. The intelligence system needs dramatic reforms. The fact is that Israel called Hezbollah so utterly wrong, and Lebanese psychology so wrong, that it stunned me. Hammering Lebanon's infrastructure just made Israel look like a bully. It alienated Israel's potential allies in Lebanon.

Israel's ground forces must become more professional. It's going to be a tough problem, and I don't have the answer as to how to solve it. The other thing the IDF needs is a noncommissioned officer corps—a professional NCO corps. The IDF has to have it. I raised this at the Ministry of Defense, and one Israeli general said, "We never had a professional NCO corps. No Jewish wife wants her husband to be a sergeant when her neighbor's husband is a captain." Well, I'm sorry, but you need nurses as well as surgeons.

The days of doing wars on the lam and hanging out at a field headquarters where most of the people are just standing around and there are pizza boxes all over the floor—those days are gone. Israel is fighting a "new model army," to borrow Cromwell's term. Increasingly, Israel's enemies are no longer emulating the European military model. This is the era of cellular networks, an era of forces tailored specifically to fight Israeli or U.S. forces. Many of these powers in the Middle East are not eager to step up and repeat yesteryear's tank-for-tank and aircraft-for-aircraft battle with Israel. They've found a better way to do battle. The hard thing for Israel, as we see with the global media, is that Israel can't win the public relations war anymore. Global media's soft-core anti-Semitism is very, very powerful. No question about it. It's the last revenge of the discredited leftist intellectuals, vanquished everywhere but in our universities and in the media. And I think the sad thing is that a lot of media people don't even realize how perversely bigoted they are, how morally sheepish.

The reason why I always support Israel is that, in the end, it's a rule-of-law state that's willing to live with its neighbors in peace. Israel's neighbors, or at least a substantial portion of them, would like to exterminate every Israeli citizen—including the Muslim and Christian citizens. When you sweep away the surface clutter, the moral lines beneath are as stark as they could be.

Which brings us back to this new age of extremist religion. Take Iranian president Ahmadinejad seriously. You know, it's funny because—just as with China, you have to worry more about failure in China, with all of China's domestic problems, than you do about a successful China—I'm more concerned about an Iran that plunges into internal turmoil, which would make it even more dangerous, should it acquire nuclear weapons.

And preventing Iran from having nuclear weapons is going to be very tough politically and even tougher militarily, if that's what we decide has to be done. Militarily, we can set the program back, but to destroy the program at this point is something else.

Imagine a scenario where Ahmadinejad or his chosen successor is in power, but there's an upsurge of anti-regime demonstrations and violence, and the regime has nuclear weapons. A time-proven technique, obviously, is to create a foreign war to unify people. Where Washington really falls short is in understanding that at least some of the Iranian leaders truly are apocalyptic in their visions. It's so hard for most people inside the Beltway to really grasp this, because Washington is not a religious town. Even among people who go to church or synagogue every week, our educations are so profoundly secular, so twentieth-century secular, that it cripples our ability to comprehend fanaticism. Our belief in "the goodness of humankind" is so discredited by abundant facts that, in holding on to it, we have trouble dealing with the world as it truly is. When I deal with the intelligence community—I still deal with it sometimes—I can't even get across to the analysts and arbiters that suicide bombers have religious motivations. They go through all sorts of contortions to prove that our enemies don't really believe what they claim to believe—it's forever argued that suicide bombers have a relative who was insulted or a sister who was spit on or that the problem is economics or demographic or that it's all of the above. What I want to know is, "Where are all the atheist suicide bombers?" Certainly, a suicide bomber may have an assortment of motivations, some stronger than others . . . but, without the assurance of his faith, he would not make his self-immolating choice.

The religious impulse is not just a question of the individual's personal history. In the Christian tradition, you see this very, very powerfully. Someone can be irreligious for years, then "see the light." The conversion can be gradual or quick as lightning. If the religious context of his society holds that suicide bombing is an admirable act, well, that's just hard to get through to Western audiences, with our tendency to mirror-image values. In such a society, the suicide bomber's mother will think it is a glorious thing that her son blew himself up in a marketplace, killing women and children. We're bewildered: How can he be a hero? Well, there are different values in different societies. We cripple our ability to understand when we pretend that all human beings have identical values, psychological needs, and desires.

Of course, the tradition of elective martyrdom isn't strictly a Muslim phenomenon. It's just that the Islamic world is in crisis today, and crises bring the martyrs out of the floorboards. In the Middle East, an entire civilization has failed—comprehensively, on every single count. It's an amazing historical phenomenon.

In medieval Granada, which was a proto-renaissance city during the Western world's Middle Ages, the Muslim rulers had a crucial and terrible problem again and again with Christian missionaries coming into the marketplace and publicly vilifying Islam and the Prophet. Again and again, the Muslim authorities would arrest these guys and implore them to plead ignorance of their insult to Islam so that they could be quietly released. But these Christians wouldn't do it. They were fanatics and they wanted to die for their cause. Which religion felt threatened at that time? Christianity. The early Christian era is full of martyrs who, admired in the church calendars, would strike us as dangerous fanatics were we to meet them in their often-tormented flesh. So it all depends on which side you are on, on the historical epoch into which you are born. The martyr impulse comes out when it is your religion and your profound beliefs that are threatened. And, by the way, there is a self-destructive personality attracted to martyrdom of one form or another in every culture.

Another invariable trait of fundamentalist religion is that it needs someone to blame. Most humans don't want explanations for their failures, for their plights—they want excuses. And supplying excuses is the job of the religious demagogue: "Its not your fault, it's the Jews," or "It's those Christian dogs," or "the Hindu pagans and idol worshipers did it." When something goes seriously wrong in our lives, our first impulse is to ask who we can blame. Well, in our culture, our civilization, we master the impulse, roll up our sleeves, and fix things. We are amazingly good at accepting responsibility. But that is not a well-developed human trait beyond Judeo-Christian civilization.

I want to stress that I'm more worried about Israel's future than I ever have been before. If the ghost of Jimmy the Greek came down and said, "Lay down your bet," I would bet that the world would not prevent Iran from getting nuclear weapons. Now, the closest thing to good news is that the Iranians are going to be arguing, "Sunni Arabs first, or the Jews first?" The Sunni-Shi'a hatred goes really, really deep. And I hope that many years after we are all gone to our just or unjust reward, there will still be an Israel. But the cautionary tale comes from the European past.

In 1099, Christian crusaders came to Jerusalem and killed everybody they could collar, regardless of faith. They held Jerusalem for almost a hundred years, and, even when they were expelled from Jerusalem, they still managed to cling to the coast for about another century. But the Middle East outlasted the foreign intruders in the end. Western Christianity was already foreign to the region—it wasn't a Middle Eastern faith any longer, it didn't fit. The religions that came out of the Middle East changed in exile. Consider how much Judaism has changed in exile, despite the power of its traditions. How close, psychologically, would any Jew of today be to a first or second century rabbi or congregation? In exile we evolve. I believe that, for Christians and Jews, the diaspora of our faiths, the lucky exile from the inhibiting influence of the Middle East, liberated us to attain levels of spiritual achievement impossible in the backward, obscurantist sands of Arabia or Egypt. Did the fall of the cradle cities of Christianity to Islam save my faith? Did the Destruction of the Temple save Judaism from atrophying into yet another Middle Eastern cult?

Now, the good news is that some Muslims are exiled, too—maybe Islam is going to evolve and maybe it will do that in Europe. But the long overdue reformation of Islam is probably coming in Dearborn, Michigan, or maybe in Toronto. America humanizes religions. It's a tough process, but it works. But I just have to ask you, is the Middle East any longer fertile soil for civilization? I don't know, I don't know the answer.

Dream Warriors

Armed Forces Journal, online edition

May/June 2007

> "Dreams have a vise-like grip on the people of Islam. We never grasped that it was more useful to let our Muslims dream than to build them schools, hospitals and factories."
>
> "You're confusing dreams with hope, aren't you?" asked Donadieu.
>
> "Possibly. But I sense that the dream is vaster and more mysterious than hope."
>
> —Jean Larteguy, *Les Praetorians*, 1961

In his best-selling novel about the French botch-up in Algeria, the former soldier and daring journalist Jean Larteguy prefigured many of the problems that English-speaking nations face today in the Middle East. While there are profound differences between Algeria and Iraq, not least the fact that Iraq has not been settled by over a million American colonists and that today's Muslim warriors are waging reactionary, not revolutionary, warfare, many of the ruminations of the officers facing Arab militants in *The Praetorians* are uncannily familiar to those of U.S. Army and Marine officers today.

The most telling insight in the novel lies in the exchange above (amended from the clunky translation published forty-five years ago): The French have been focusing on statistics and infrastructure—and losing. A veteran officer who's gotten to know the indigenous Algerians recognizes the futility of applying European analytical models to Arabs, but the vast bureaucratic machines of the army and the state plod on, obsessed with their own internal issues and rivalries.

With our armor-plated prejudice in favor of empiricism ("Just the facts, ma'am!"), we're blind to our own irrationality and susceptibility to delusions. Faced with combatively non-empirical cultures, such as those of the Middle East and North Africa, we're baffled: How can our opponents continue to deny proven facts? Our stock response is to insist, yet again, that Arabs, Persians, Afghans, and Pakistanis really want the same things we want, but haven't realized it yet and need to be convinced.

Yet it's our approach to life, although stunningly successful in other spheres, that's out of step with history and humankind when it comes to sorting out the causes for which men (and women) will fight and die—even pursuing death with fanatic enthusiasm. The glimpses we can't avoid of the mentality of other cultures are so disconcerting to us that, just as Arabs default to blaming the West for all of their ills, we default to our dogmatic insistence that the historical evidence that men fight hardest for God, bloodlines, and collective dreams is wrong and that extremist insurgents, terrorists, and suicide bombers are really fighting because they don't have high-speed internet access.

Until we are willing to confront the mentality—the soul—of our enemies honestly, we can't and won't defeat them.

We seek a logical understanding of mass violence, but war and civil strife rarely explode because of rational grievances. Complaints about oppression, poverty, or injustice may serve as superficial catalysts, but few wars can be traced to objective decision-making by the dispassionate leaders of cool-headed populations. War is an act of passion, not of policy—Clausewitz wrote of a specific period in European history, but largely misread even his own era: Napoleon was a protean, intuitive figure, not a product of the Age of Reason. For the Little Emperor, war was far more than a tool of policy—it was a glorious endeavor in and of itself, a human apotheosis, intensified by that murderous Corsican's surreal visions of universal empire (a caliphate with quiche).

In this new age of atavism and wars spawned by the most elementary human impulses—religious fervor and ethnic supremacy—we need to come to grips with the true roots of mass violence, that ecstatic phenomenon that serves the human aggregate as the equivalent of the individual's sexual passion and release. Whether we speak of the intoxicated crowds that poured into Europe's streets in August 1914, of the orgiastic joy felt by the perpetrators of pogroms, or the coital rhythms of chanting mobs, the mass consumes the individual. And that mass operates according to a biological imperative we refuse to understand, since an honest evaluation of the murderous transfiguration of human beings absorbed into an aggregate would destroy so many of our cherished myths about humankind.

The human being is a killer, and the human collective is a killing machine. The purpose of civilization is to civilize the hunter and maximize his latent abilities to contribute in other spheres—ultimately strengthening the power of the collective in other ways and making it as robust behind the phalanx as at the tip of the spear. Now we face an age in which entire civilizations are in advanced states of decay and breakdown—shutting down alternative human courses and releasing the killer again. It's far easier than we wish to believe to turn a potential neurosurgeon into a mass murderer—or to excite the dullard mass into a mob. Mundane successes placate the killer within us, but never extinguish him.

Civilization bribes us to be good; if we are not good, civilization reveals its steely side. But once a civilization has gone into collapse, a foreign power's imposition of bits of infrastructure will not arrest the process. The civilization may have to die before it can be reborn—at the very least, it requires a deeper transfiguration than any external power can impose (Cyrus didn't release the Jews from their Babylonian captivity because he was generous, but because he recognized that he couldn't change or integrate them, just as the European colonial powers ultimately abandoned their empires from an unstated sense of hopelessness). American exceptionalism aside, human identity is intractable.

By regulating, organizing, and channeling violence, successful civilizations allow the majority of their members to contribute to the general welfare while a minority provides security. Except in times of dire emergency, the superior organizational capabilities of civilized societies allow them to devote a much smaller percentage of their human capital to defense than primitive societies can do. Thus, the most successful civilization in history, that specific to the United States, has less than one percent of its population under arms, yet spans the globe with its military and corollary forms of power. Certainly, size matters—the civilization's size, as well as that of the military—but you will not find a warrior tribe anywhere in history that triumphed with under one percent of its members dedicated to warfare.

We just don't want to know what human beings, their societies, and their civilizations are really like.

WARS OF FANTASY AND NOSTALGIA

People fight for different things. Americans pledge to protect and defend the Constitution of the United States. We fight for national security and a sometimes nebulous, but ever powerful, vision of freedom. Arabs fight for faith, family, and turf—but not for constitutions. And not only do people fight for different things in different civilizations, even within their cultures they fight for different things at different times: Arab nationalism fifty years ago, fundamentalist Islam today. This second point is vital to our misunderstanding of the conflicts engaging us around the world.

From international statecraft to military counterinsurgency operations, the United States and our core allies still interpret insurrections, rebellions, and terrorism in terms of revolutionary struggle—the organizing principle, at least superficially, of so many twentieth-century insurgencies. But we've undergone a profound global shift (most advanced in the Middle East) from wars of ideology and revolutionary liberation, to reactionary violence either demanding a return to a reimagined golden age, or determined to enforce the implementation of a millenarian kingdom of heaven on earth, or both. As in the quote from Larteguy above, our enemies are fighting for dreams, and not the mundane more-bread dreams of Che Guevara, Leon Trotsky, or even Gamal Abdel Nasser, but for faith-driven fantasies and nostalgia for lost greatness.

Certainly, all warfare has a more-power-for-us component, but it's remarkable how frustrated religious visions and nostalgia for a distant past reimagined as a golden age can inspire suicidal struggles on the part of entire populations. This longing for a resurrected utopia that never really existed is so powerful that it even infiltrated avowedly secular mass movements—the Nazi philosophy, such as it was, collapsed into neo-Nordic mumbo-jumbo and third-liter-of-beer notions of a glorious German yesteryear somewhere between Valhalla and *Die Meistersinger von Nuernberg*. In societies regulated by religion, the propensity to believe in Eden betrayed and waiting for redemption is incomparably more powerful. If suicide bombers plague us today, suicidal struggles by rebellious groups empowered by metaphysical visions have plagued civilizations since the murky dawn of history.

Today's insurgents and terrorists aren't fighting for freedom, but for voluntary subjugation to a stern, even punitive regime. Freedom is terrifying. Most human beings welcome just a little more freedom in their daily lives, but are ill-equipped to bear the responsibilities that American-style freedom thrusts upon them. Adults secretly crave rules as surely as do misbehaving children (and every mob quickly produces a leader with a commanding voice). Anarchy in the streets isn't a rebellion against rules, but a protest at their absence: Give an anarchist the right demagogue to follow, and you'll turn him into a storm trooper marching in lockstep.

This phenomenon varies in intensity from society to society and from civilization to civilization, but it manifests itself particularly strongly in today's Middle East. Iraqis may not want Saddam Hussein and the Mukhabarat, but they do require structure to a degree that Americans would find intolerable. Left without rules we would find insufferably strict, Arabs become lost and angry outside their womblike families. Conditioned by their religious culture to life-by-the-checklist, they require a distinctly non-Western degree of regimentation to function as a society.

Instead of simply decrying the fact that our fiercest enemies "want to return to the seventh century," we should attempt to understand why that's their fervent, professed desire—and why the rallying cry appeals to such an astonishing range of people. Not least, they imagine Islam's "golden age" as a time of good order similar to medieval Europe's "great chain of being," when everyone supposedly knew his place and found contentment in it.

Of course, even members of al Qa'eda or the Taliban would find it unpleasant to return entirely to the turbulent aftermath that followed the Prophet's death, or, for that matter, to the mythologized era of the Caliph Harun al Rashid a few centuries later: The cell phone and the dentist would soon be missed.

Yet, even such an assessment is too literal, too Western. The bin Ladens and al Zawahiris aren't interested in the perfect replication of the distant past, but in the galvanizing vision of a better, godlier world for which a fairy-story past serves as an inspiration and affirmation. The airbrushed past is just a catalyst for the dream—and, as Larteguy's Frenchman suggests, a mighty dream will mobilize far more potential martyrs than a new sewage system.

In Iraq, we tried to share our own dream, one that's worked remarkably well for us. But our efforts may be as hopeless as an attempt to convince a friend obsessed with a destructive lover to decide, on a rational basis, to choose a less-menacing partner: Reason is an ineffective weapon against passion, whether in love or war. Many in the Middle East, perhaps even a majority, have fallen madly in love with fantasies that can only be sustained through a culture of blaming others for all that goes wrong, by embracing self-contradictory conspiracy theories, and by rejecting—in a rage—the contours of more successful civilizations. Like that lovesick friend of ours, humans don't want sober advice, but affirmation that their folly is wisdom.

We're left with a war not of ideas, but of competing visions: On one hand, the congenial disorder, bounded by humane laws, that has allowed us to rise to such heights of power and influence, and, on the other, the reality-shunning fantasies of grandeur resurrected and militant sanctity that blinds the people of the Middle East to their own practical self-interest.

After their basic physical needs are satisfied, what invisible needs drive human actions? Certainly it's not the Western admonition to be reasonable. Whether the fantasy is of eternal salvation or of a vanquished national glory revived, human beings will rush to their deaths to sustain their irrational, but satisfying, beliefs.

THE GREAT REACTION

Over the last few centuries, men and women gave their lives for man-wrought utopian visions. But all the invented ideologies not only failed to work, they ultimately failed to satisfy. Now the great reaction has set in, the retrograde shift to defensive intolerance. Even in our own incomparably successful society, both extremes of the political spectrum are no longer occupied by progressives, revolutionaries, or reformers, but by ferocious reactionaries who dream either of a return to a godlier age that never existed as they imagine it, or who fantasize about a neo-agrarian society that has no more chance of coming to pass than al Qa'eda has of reestablishing the caliphate.

From the Taliban to the People for the Ethical Treatment of Animals (PETA), and from the foreign extremists haunting Iraq to the opponents of women's rights in North America, our age is characterized by self-righteous fanatics who—terrified of freedom—believe it their duty to impose their rigid social norms on the rest of humanity. Their rigid visions are unanimously about turning back the clock to a "simpler" age that supposedly didn't suffer from the ills afflicting our own, Eden without the serpents. (It's piquant to note that Hitler, a strict vegetarian and animal-lover, would have backed PETA to the hilt.)

Yet humans are humans. There never was a perfect golden age, and Atlantis remains a dated pop song, not an archaeological site awaiting lucky scuba divers. Nonetheless, the longing for the "lost" golden age or the perfect future is endemic to the human condition—like the poor, fantasies will always be with us for those who cannot accept the challenges of the here and now. The difference today is that both the tumultuous pace and the universal awareness of change is more threatening than it ever has been in the past: Our enemies are fighting either to stop the clock, to turn back the hands, or to make the clock irrelevant by achieving timeless perfection. The one thing they all dislike is American-style progress.

Human beings have always been frightened by change. Today, most of humanity is terrified. And tens of millions, if not more, will fight for dreams that promise them an escape from the reality plaguing them with a sense of inadequacy and failure.

We seek to improve the reality of the Middle East, but the people of the Middle East just want to escape reality.

UNDERSTANDING THIS ENEMY

If we are to avoid the fate of that fictional French officer who, faced with comprehensive failure, belatedly recognized that a people's dreams are more inspiring than the arrival of traffic lights, we have to challenge our own illusions about both our enemies in particular and humanity in general. In some respects, our own behavior patterns have been disturbingly similar to those of the Middle East—just as our opposite numbers reject empirical data in favor of comforting fantasies, we, too, flee from reality when it makes us uncomfortable: The liberal fantasies that "all men want peace," that "war doesn't solve anything," and that's it's in the natural order for societies and civilizations to get along just fine all defy the historical and contemporary evidence.

Just because we don't like the truth, doesn't mean that we can declare it false.

We may heartily desire it otherwise, but far too many human beings enjoy killing and abusing others; perhaps a majority of humanity is convinced that its path should be imposed upon all others; and the impulse to wage collective violence, whether in spontaneous massacres or in wars, is irrefutably embedded in the mass psyche—to which the individual is tethered in ways that we refuse to acknowledge or investigate.

When faced with the facts of the human experience, the "enlightened" citizen closes his mind and starts calling the messenger nasty names. But if war is not part of our makeup, why have there been so many wars? Can we really blame a tiny numbers of individuals who suffered unhappy childhoods? Isn't it time that we seriously investigated the ugly phenomena of mass behavior and the collective organism that devours the individual's conscience in times of stress and disorder? A mob is not a collection of individuals, but an organism with its own biological and psychological dynamics. If we continue to see humanity only as a collection of individuals, we will never understand war or insurgencies or terror—or even the popularity of *American Idol*.

As reality forced our military—or at least the Army and Marines—to confront the changed security environment since 1991, the services entered a painful learning process. In the beginning, there was well-intentioned "cultural understanding," the essential purpose of which was to avoid offending a terrorist's value system. Since then, we've moved on to seeking a more tactically useful grasp of our enemy's culture, the sort of insight that allows us to operate more effectively. But tactical successes, although vital, lead nowhere if our strategic analysis is wrong: We study the individual and extrapolate to the mass, when the correct approach is to seek to understand the mass, then use that knowledge to control individuals. We've got it exactly backward.

Veterans of Iraq and Afghanistan, as well as special-operations forces in general, viscerally grasp that the asymmetries we face today go deeper than mismatches in organizations and weaponry. The problem is that thinking officers have yet to discipline their knowledge into words, into articulate insights and appropriate doctrine. Paradoxically, one of the greatest obstacles we have to understanding our enemies is that our officer corps is too well educated in the formal sense. Officers with master's degrees in international relations and Ph.D.s in government have become prisoners of the outdated theories they encountered in graduate school (alchemy in the age of particle physics).

Perhaps the best piece of advice you can give to an officer with advanced degrees is, "When the reality confronting you contradicts the theory you learned at Harvard or Stanford, believe the reality." This sounds like common sense, but it's routine to encounter dutiful officers struggling to fit a confounding and deadly reality into the cookie-cutter formulas their professors insisted would turn human lead into strategic gold. Post-graduate education, if its teachings are in error, can cripple a talented officer and leave him a menace to his subordinates—or to the entire force, if he rises high enough.

The military can't look to the academic world for answers— the campus is as out of touch with reality as an al Qa'eda cabal in a cave fantasizing about the revival of the caliphate. Academics will defend their obsolete theses to the last infantryman in the streets of Baghdad. Our military leaders, at all levels, must scrutinize their own experiences in the field and do their best to see the facts clearly, to discard the Vaseline-coated lenses their educations convinced them to wear. You can't understand today's conflicts from Cambridge or Ann Arbor. Military men and women have the experience to achieve a fresh, more accurate under-standing of human motivation and the roots of conflict. It's their duty to reject the intellectual alchemy of liberal-arts faculties and the circular logic of think tanks.

The professors will tell you that it's all about deprivation and demographics, mistaken American policies and, yes, the need to build those schools, hospitals, and factories. Nothing wrong with a clinic here and a co-ed classroom there, but the real problem is that our opponents refuse to accept the empirical reality we insist is the global standard. If we continue to misunderstand the psychological and spiritual environments in which we operate, the clinics will continue to be bombed and the classrooms will remain empty, their teachers assassinated.

We need to spend at least as much time asking ourselves what our enemies want as we do telling them what we think they should want. Unless we accept the power of the enemy's dreams and deal with those dreams as a motive-shaping reality, we'll get it every bit as wrong as the French did in Algeria.

Faith's Civil Wars

USA Today

June 25, 2007

Though history's religious battles often pit one faith against another, today's struggle is a very different, and universal, one. Virtually every major world religion (not just Islam) faces an internal tug of war. Indeed, religion today is caught between the saint on one side and the suicide bomber on the other.

The rebellion of Islamist extremists against the West obscures the greater religious conflict looming over the twenty-first century: The decisive struggle will occur not between religions, but within them.

The great religious civil war of this century afflicts not only Islam but also Christianity, Judaism, Hinduism, and Buddhism. It's the conflict between those in every faith who promote a punitive, disciplinary deity and those who worship a merciful, loving god. Not all confrontations will be violent, but many will be venomous.

Alarmed by the atrocities that a relative handful of radicalized Muslims have committed against us, we overlook the fact that, overwhelmingly, the victims of Islamist terror have been other Muslims. Compared with the intrafaith savagery at work, the events of September 11, 2001, were a sideshow.

Viral elements within Islam have graduated from fundamentalism to fanaticism. That shift might be a harbinger, not an echo. A global transition is underway from the believer to the enforcer, from the fundamentalist who warns us of consequences after death, to the fanatic who threatens consequences here and now.

Because of the comprehensive failure of the Middle East to compete in the modern era, this devolution from a transcendent god to an ill-tempered warlord, from the luminous to the ominous, is immediately evident in Islam's old homelands. But apart from the Muslim-on-Muslim atrocities staining the region, this battle also rages, if in less violent forms, in the USA—as well as in Africa, Latin America, India, and wherever faith is extant. In an age when Buddhist monks indulge in violent protests and Hindus level mosques on mythic pretexts, when extremists haunt both sides of the Israel-Palestine question and American Christians seek to legislate the behavior of fellow citizens, there are three related struggles underway:

- The contest between those who obsess about external forms and behaviors and believers whose faith is spiritual first and last. The surest indicator of a religion in crisis is an expanding list of things forbidden.
- The demotion of the divine to worldly dimensions—God as a real-estate magnate obsessed with owning blood-soaked dirt. (One of the many blessings Americans enjoy is that God hasn't staked any property claims here.)
- The global war to deny equal rights to women or to revoke the rights they have gained. The insistence by religious elders that they know how their god wants women to comport themselves is a blot on every faith: When old men make the rules, young women suffer.

THE GLOBALIZATION OF INSECURITY
Why do we face this universal rift in faiths today?

In the past, each major religion has suffered its share of crises. But now elements in all religions perceive themselves as living under siege and demand a barracks-room rigor in response.

Blame globalization. Contrary to the claims of pop best-sellers, globalization and its attack dog, the internet, do not portend a harmonic convergence of human cultures. While globalization is a boon to the educated, the capable, and the confident, to the practically and emotionally ill-equipped it's a destabilizing, terrifying force.

Yet the premise upon which we have to act is that globalization is a fact, and neither Islamist extremists nor trade unions will be able to force the process into reverse. In a globalizing world, many are helped, some are damaged, and the masses are just confused.

Those masses are the prize at which religious demagogues aim. Overwhelmed by a torrent of information (often wildly inaccurate) delivered by ever more numerous communications means, the average global citizen literally does not know what to think. And humans crave certainty, especially during periods of upheaval. They need little encouragement to default to debased forms of religion that provide condensed answers and reassure them of their eternal superiority—even if the infidels are richer and more powerful at the moment.

THE TRENCHES

This global response to a crisis of confidence reflects the old maxim that "there are no atheists in foxholes." Entire civilizations perceive themselves as trapped in embattled trenches, with powerful shells of change bursting all around them. The more traditional the society, the harder it is for its members to rally and respond constructively.

We are witnessing an inspiring reinvigoration of faith on one hand and, on the other, a redaction of faith's complexities to exploit the fear and jealousy abounding—promising vengeance on this side of the grave. Twenty-first century religion will be caught between the saint and the suicide bomber. The nemeses of every faith will be those who can't tell the difference.

This doesn't mean that interfaith struggles will disappear: I've seen firsthand how Christianity threatens to become a "church militant" in response to Muslim imperialism in Africa, and have been similarly appalled by exchanges with Arabs who hope to exterminate Jews and with Jews who argue for ethnically cleansing Arabs. Terror in the name of faith is a growth industry.

But even as we confront that terrorism, we need to look beyond it to the sword-of-Damocles question hanging over our new century: Not "Is God Dead?" (that bit of nonsense from a frivolous yesteryear), but "Will the god of love and mercy triumph over the god of battles?"

Better Than Genocide

Ethnic Cleansing in Human Affairs

National Review

August 13, 2007

Ethnic cleansing is evil. It can never be condoned. Yet our repugnance at the act leaves us with a dilemma: What are we supposed to do in cases where ethnic cleansing may be impossible to prevent—cases in which well-intentioned efforts to interrupt ethnic cleansing actually make a conflict deadlier?

One problem we face is a muddle in terminology, employing "ethnic cleansing" and "genocide" interchangeably; in fact, there is a profound difference between these two human habits. Genocide is the attempt to *exterminate* a minority. Ethnic cleansing seeks to *expel* a minority. At its less serious end, ethnic cleansing may aim only at the separation of populations deemed incompatible by at least one side, with psychological, legalistic, or financial machinations brought to bear to achieve the desired end. At the other extreme, ethnic cleansing can involve deadly violence and widespread abuse. In the worst cases, ethnic cleansing efforts may harden into genocide.

It must never become the policy of the United States to abet ethnic cleansing. Yet our all-or-nothing reaction when confronted with this common human phenomenon has proven to be consistently ineffective, from the Balkans to Iraq. Until we make an honest attempt to understand the age-old human impulse to rid a troubled society of those who are different in ethnicity or religion, we will continue to fail in our efforts to pacify and repair war-ravaged territories. If our conflicts over the past decade and a half offer any lesson, it's that the rest of the world refuses to conform to our idealized notions of how human beings are designed to behave. We never stop insisting that the peoples of the former Yugoslavia, the tribes of Somalia, the ethnic groups of Afghanistan, and, most painfully, the religious and ethnic factions of Iraq learn to live in harmony. Those we hope to convince ignore us.

If ethnic cleansing can be prevented and the society rejuvenated, that's an admirable accomplishment. But not all enraged passions can be calmed, no matter how vociferously we insist otherwise. Once ignited, some human infernos must burn themselves out; and you had best position any firebreaks correctly. To date, our reactions to situations in which ethnic cleansing cannot be arrested have been inept; in Iraq, for example, well-intentioned attempts to stymie neighborhood ethnic cleansing efforts may have led to the targets' being murdered as opposed to merely forcibly removed. We struggle to keep families in their homes; in response, the families are massacred in those homes. We pretend that embedded hatreds are transient misunderstandings, but we're not the victims who pay the price for our fantasies.

As uncomfortable as it may be to face the facts, ethnic cleansing has been a deeply ingrained response of human collectives since the dawn of history, and it's preferable to uncompromising genocide.

A LONG HISTORY
Why do human collectives feel compelled to expel neighbors with whom they may have lived in relative peace for generations or even centuries? It's a difficult question. The Western model of studying the individual and then extrapolating our findings to the society prevents us from understanding mass behavior, which is far more complex (and murky) than the sum of individual

actions. In much of the world—not least, in the Middle East—a more incisive approach is to examine the mass first, then extrapolate to the individual. We're astonished when foreign actors we know as affable individuals are swept up in mob behavior, but the mob may be their natural element and the reasonable character we encountered on a personal level a fragile aberration: Even in our own society, the mass remains more powerful than the man.

A related obstacle to understanding the insidious appeal of ethnic cleansing is that our leaders and opinion-makers interact disproportionately with foreign urban residents who have a higher education level, a greater English-language ability, and a more cosmopolitan outlook than the rest of their society. As a result, we're instructed that a given society doesn't support ethnic cleansing, since there are mixed marriages in Sarajevo or Baghdad or Weimar Germany. But the impulse to expel those who are visibly or behaviorally different—or who are merely accused of being different—is deeply rooted in the human soil. The man in the mansion may tell you one thing, but the unemployed citizen out on the street may bring to bear a very different psychology—along with an inchoate desire for vengeance inseparable from the human condition.

In the Old Testament, you can search fruitlessly through book after book for an example of disparate populations living happily side by side as equals. Ethnic cleansing and genocide appear early and continuously; and it is the differences between the various nationalities and tribes, not the commonalities, that are stressed in the foundational text of our civilization. We read not of a multicultural, tolerant society, but of a chosen people charged to conquer. Tribal genocides erupted throughout history when competition for scarce resources intensified; genocide is fundamentally Darwinian, as one group seeks to annihilate another for its own safety or other perceived benefits. Above the tribal level, though, full-scale genocides have been relatively rare; the more common practice, even in the case of the ever-cited Mongols, was selective mass-murder to instill fear—the slaughter of a city's population to persuade other cities not to resist.

The Romans knew how to punish convincingly but had little taste for outright genocide. Their preference was for forms of ethnic cleansing that resettled troublesome tribes or dispersed rebellious populations—such as the Jews, following the rebellions of the first century A.D. (The Greeks, whose "civilized" behavior was a myth, had been more apt to slaughter rivals, whether in the poetry of Homer or the reportage of Thucydides.) From the Babylonian captivity down to Stalin's practice of uprooting restive groups (such as the Chechens), ethnic cleansing as a tool of state-craft has a long, if hardly proud, tradition, with genocide reserved as the fail-safe answer.

Further confounding our preconceptions, state-organized programs of ethnic cleansing, for all their heartlessness, look relatively humane compared with the countless outbreaks of ethnic or religious cleansing inspired by roving demagogues, *agents provocateurs*, or simply rumors. While state genocide is the most potent form, state-backed ethnic cleansing tends to be less lethal than popular pogroms, since the state seeks to solve a perceived problem, while the mob wants blood (the horrific genocide perpetrated against the Armenians fatally combined state policy and popular bigotry in a muddle of genocide and ethnic cleansing). Once the people of a troubled society get it into their heads that their neighbors who look or sound or worship differently are enemies bent on subversion, outbursts of extraordinary savagery are the norm.

In this context, ethnic cleansing might be the least horrific of the alternatives. Which atrocity was worse, the French massacre of Protestant Huguenots in the sixteenth century, or Louis XIV's expulsion of them in the seventeenth (a process that harmed the French economy, while benefiting German-speaking states)? The Spanish expulsions of the Jews and then the Moors were a vast human tragedy that ravaged Iberian civilization—but weren't those forced exiles preferable to Hitler's attempt to exterminate

European Jewry? Even at the extremes of man-wrought evil, there
are gradations of cruelty.

The historical evidence is troubling, since it suggests that
ethnic cleansing can lead to peace. For example, the German
presence amid Slavic populations in northeastern Europe lasted
for eight oppressive centuries before all ethnic Germans were
expelled in the wake of the Nazi collapse; after almost a millennium of torment, the region now enjoys an unprecedented level
of peace and social justice. Certainly, other factors influenced
this new calm—but the subtraction of Baltic, Ukrainian,
Pomeranian, Silesian, and Sudeten Germans from the social and
political equations appears to have been decisive.

In the wake of World War I, Greece and the Turkish rump of
the Ottoman Empire exchanged millions of ethnic Turks and
Greeks, under miserable conditions. The ethnic cleansing was
harsh on both sides and the suffering of these hereditary enemies was immense. Yet despite their history of violent antago-
nism, Greeks and Turks have remained at peace for more than
eight decades since those mass expulsions, with the conflict over
Cyprus confined to that unhappy island.

Meanwhile, trouble spots in which populations remain inter-
mingled continue to erupt in violence, from West Africa through
the Middle East to the subcontinent and Southeast Asia (where
anti-Chinese pogroms are almost as predictable as the monsoon
season).

Nor can we Americans claim perfect innocence when it
comes to ethnic cleansing. Our treatment of Native Americans
remains, along with slavery and its consequences, one of the two
great stains upon our history. And our present situation goes
unexamined: On one hand, the unprecedented degree of ethnic and religious integration we have achieved (largely in the
last half-century) blinds us to the depth and operative power of
hatreds elsewhere in the world; on the other, our own society
has devised innovative, relatively benign forms of achieving ethnic separation. The "gentrification" of neighborhoods in cities

such as Washington, D.C., is a soft form of ethnic cleansing by checkbook and mortgage.

There is also an enduring self-segregation of various groups within our society. Many individuals prefer the familiarity and sense of security delivered by a collective identity, by the codes and symbols of belonging, whether displayed in a barrio or in the economic segregation of a suburban gated community. Even in our remarkable multi-ethnic, multi-confessional society, there are still race riots—in the course of which interlopers whose skin is the wrong color end up beaten beyond recognition or dead.

Human collectives are still, essentially, warrior bands protective of their turf (even in those gated communities—just attend a homeowners' association meeting). Group competition is powerfully embedded in our psyches. Successful societies channel such impulses constructively, but struggling societies and those that have already succumbed to anarchy revert to narrow (and safe) identities—race, tribe, faith, cult—and respond to perceived threats with assertive group behavior: The individual is lost once the group is awakened. We can deny it as often as we like, but the historical pattern is timeless and enduring: When the majority feels threatened, it lashes out at minorities in its midst. When a minority's ethnicity and religion *both* differ from the mainstream of a traditional society, that minority is living on borrowed time. The span of imagined safety may last for centuries, but then, one day, the zealots appear on the street corner, whether in brown shirts or wearing Islamist robes.

THE PRACTICAL IMPLICATIONS

It cannot be stressed too often or too forcefully that ethnic cleansing is a crime against humanity that cannot be excused. The purpose of this essay is to try to understand it—not to condone it—and to consider the implications for our military and diplomatic missions abroad.

Given that we would prefer to prevent any ethnic cleansing, what do we do when it cannot be prevented, when the hatred is too intense and the process already has gone too far? While there will never be a universal answer, given the complexity of each specific case, it can be argued as a case study that ethnic separation at an earlier stage might have prevented the massacre at Srebrenica (of course, no such separations will ever be fully just). Indeed, U.S. diplomats gave tacit approval to the Croatian cleansing of Serbs during the endgame in Croatia and Bosnia. Later, in Kosovo, we sought to persuade Serbs not to drive ethnic Albanians from their homes, but, as soon as victory was delivered to the Kosovars, they set about ethnically cleansing Serbs with high-testosterone vigor. The dynamic in play was such that none of our pleas, lectures, or scoldings were going to alter the hardened attitudes prevailing in either camp. What if the *only* hope for peace in the territory some still pretend is a unified Kosovo is ethnic separation and partition?

Meanwhile, in Iraq, ethnic-cleansing efforts have been savage. They still fall short of genocide: Confessional murders to date have aimed at intimidation and expulsion, at punishment and advantage, not at annihilation. What if the best hope for social peace is the establishment of exclusive Shi'a or Sunni (or Kurdish) neighborhoods—or towns and cities and provinces? We aren't alarmed by the existence of various ethnic quarters in Singapore or, for that matter, Brooklyn, and we accept that Saudi Arabia would not welcome an influx of Christian settlers to Riyadh. What if the last chance for Iraq to survive as a unified state is for its citizens to live in religiously or ethnically separate communities? What if efforts to prevent ethnic cleansing in Baghdad, for example, not only are doomed to fail, but exacerbate the ultimate intensity of the violence? Would we really prefer that a family die in its home, rather than be driven from it? Our principles are noble, but it's shabby to expect Iraqis to die for them.

There are no easy answers to these questions. But it should be absolutely clear by now that ethnic cleansing is an issue we will face again and again in the decades ahead, and it may not always be possible or even helpful to stop its march. We must face the unsettling question as to whether it's always desirable to force a halt to such purges, instead of acting to ameliorate the suffering of those displaced.

Idealists will continue to insist that Arabs and Jews, Sunnis and Shi'as, Kurds and Turks, Tajiks and Pashtuns, Sudanese blacks and Arabs, or Nigerian Muslims and Christians can all get along. Would that it were so. But to decline to study the possibility that they might refuse to get along, that the individuals we think we know may be consumed by mass passions that reasonable arguments won't tame, is folly. The old military maxim applies: You may hope for the best, but you prepare for the worst.

There is nothing welcome about ethnic or religious cleansing. But if we do not recognize its insistent reemergence in human affairs, and the fact that—in contrast to full-scale genocide—it remains the lesser evil, we will continue to act ineffectually as the innocent suffer.

America's Two Terror Wars

Armchair General

January 2008

Mention "two terror wars" and the automatic assumption is that you're talking about Iraq and Afghanistan. But *geography* isn't the smartest way to demarcate the threats Americans face. We're currently under attack from Sunni terrorists and Shi'a extremists. Both are deadly; but they have conflicting agendas and pose profoundly different strategic threats.

Our instinct today is to focus on al Qa'eda and the Sunni side of the problem, but our troubles with Shi'a radicals predate the wildfire spread of Sunni militancy (with our shortsighted support) during the Soviet engagement in Afghanistan (1979–89). Iranian Shi'as seized our embassy in Tehran after the Shah fell (1979), and Shi'a Hezbollah bombed the Marine barracks in Beirut (1983) during President Reagan's first term. Sunni terrorists only shifted their attentions to us after the Red Army retreated across the Amu Darya.

Does that mean that Shi'a fanatics are the greatest threat to our security? Should we make it our priority to counter the extremist regime in Iran, Muqtada al Sadr's army of thugs in Iraq, and Hezbollah in Lebanon?

Makes sense—if all you're worried about is the Middle East. On the other hand, it wasn't Shi'a terrorists, but Sunnis, who reached out from their homelands to attack the Twin Towers (twice), the Pentagon, our embassies in Kenya and Tanzania, the train system in Madrid, the London Underground, nightclubs in Bali, and all the other targets struck around the globe.

Both terrorist denominations have killed Americans. The key difference is *where* they killed them.

Shi'as have a *regional* agenda, whether speaking of Iran's madcap President Ahmadinejad, Muqtada al Sadr and his Iraqi Jaish al Mahdi, or Hezbollah's cold-blooded leader, Hassan Nasrallah. They want us out of the Middle East. They want Israel erased from the map. And they want hegemony over the Persian Gulf's oil supplies. Yet they've remained sober enough to realize it would be counterproductive to attack us on American soil.

Sunni fanatics, on the other hand, are fired by an insane vision of reestablishing the medieval caliphate at its geographical extremes—stretching from Spain to Mozambique and from Hungary to the subcontinent. They also believe that their severe brand of Islam is destined to master the entire globe over time.

So should we concentrate on the fanatics currently hijacking Sunni Islam? Not if we want a bearable outcome in Iraq, a peaceful future for Lebanon, and Israel's survival. Strategy isn't easy.

Americans have to deal with *both* denominations of terror. But we must tailor our approaches and prioritize among our enemies. In Iraq, al Qa'eda remains our number one enemy—as it is to others around the world. At present, ever more Sunni tribes have become disillusioned with their erstwhile allies from al Qa'eda and have switched to our side to fight against them. Between death squads and government shenanigans, Iraq's problem looks increasingly like a Shi'a one.

Meanwhile, Shi'a Iran is pursuing nuclear weapons while arming Hezbollah for another round with Israel. Paradoxically, progress in the Persian Gulf demands that we control the Shi'a extremists, while the Global War on Terror (whatever we're calling it this month) requires a concentration on Sunni Islam's internal civil war.

Watch: Will we muster the will to take down the Shi'a militias in Iraq before drawing down so many troops that we can't? Can Iran's nuclear program be stopped? Will we finally call the Saudis—who still foster Sunni extremism abroad—to account? And how will Western political leaders react when terrorists strike with the next wave of attacks?

Crisis Watch Bottom Line: Our Iraq policy remains adrift and our will continues to decay—despite the tactical progress our troops made in Iraq last summer, ever more politicians from both parties want to retreat to salvage their electoral hopes. We need to contain the Shi'a threat *and* keep the Sunni terrorists on the strategic defensive.

The Global Nuclear Underground

Armchair General

May 2008

Last September, Israeli aircraft raided a nuclear weapons facility under construction deep in the Syrian Desert. Tel Aviv tipped its possession of breakthrough anti-air defense technologies to make it clear to Damascus that Israel will never tolerate Syria's pursuit of nukes. The generals of the Israeli Defense Forces (IDF) believed that laying down an ace was worth it.

Rogue states that spent big money on Russian-built air defense networks panicked over the IDF's ability to penetrate Syrian airspace undetected. Moscow's generals had a great deal of explaining to do—both to the Kremlin and to foreign customers. But Israel and the West have greater worries.

Syria's determination to develop nuclear weapons apes Iran's and North Korea's nuke programs, as well as Pakistan's successful bid to join the club of nuclear powers. Even Libya flirted with a similar effort before U.S. carrots and sticks stopped it.

Analysts agree that rogue states seek nuclear weapons because they realize they can't withstand the military power of Israel or the United States. But there's more to it—and more alarms should be sounding.

This rash of nuclear programs signals that regimes such as those in Tehran and Damascus have realized that terrorism ultimately isn't an equalizer, as terror can't produce decisive results. Nukes now seem to be their only hope—not only of leveling the playing field but also of taking apocalyptic revenge.

This doesn't mean that the Iranians or Syrians or others of their ilk have abandoned terrorism. Far from it. Even if terror isn't a war winner, it remains a useful tool for lesser ends: It diverts Western attention and resources; it channels local radicalism against external targets; and it is emotionally satisfying—a small revenge in lieu of comprehensive vengeance.

Nor are nukes the only weapons of mass destruction that interest rogue states. Syria and other actors run germ warfare programs and keep a hand in the poison gas game, too. But leaders of rogue states realize that the massive use of chemical weapons on Israel, for example, would draw a nuclear reply. Moreover, designer diseases are notoriously difficult to control.

Increasingly, nuclear weapons look like the only serious game in town.

Given the tenacity—and duplicity—of rogue states around the world, the terrorist underground that should worry Americans even more than al Qa'eda is the network of nuclear engineers and scientists whose services are for hire individually or who are farmed out as "nuclear sharecroppers" by their governments: Pakistanis, North Koreans, Russians, and global freelancers.

Of course, this network of nuclear mercenaries supports regimes whose interests often converge with those of al Qa'eda and other terrorist organizations. But loyalties are not always clear—some scientists may have additional affiliations that the regimes employing them do not detect.

Then there are the proxies, the wealthy states who secretly bankroll those sharecroppers. Saudi Arabia financed Pakistan's nuclear program while Iran may have funded Syria's effort. Regimes that pretend to be America's allies—such as the Saudi government—yearn for a nuclear veto over Israel but want plausible deniability in the meantime.

Given a choice between taking out Osama bin Laden and his entire leadership network and eliminating renegade nuclear engineers, the latter option might do far more for our long-term security.

Watch: Syria has tried to obliterate traces of its nuclear facility. Will it try again elsewhere? Will Iran keep the West talking as Tehran's secret facilities expand? Will Washington continue to insist, against the evidence, that North Korea is serious about eliminating its nuclear capabilities and discarding the relevant skills? How safe is Pakistan's growing nuclear arsenal?

Crisis Watch Bottom Line: As long as the West dithers, a nuclear conflict in Eurasia grows ever more likely. The only question is who will be the first target.

Tribes vs. Democracy

Armchair General

July 2008

From Afghanistan and Iraq, through Kenya and Nigeria, to the *altiplano* of the Andean Ridge, tribal and ethnic identities frustrate attempts at democracy, impede modernization, and trigger violence that threatens to rupture nations.

Students of military history get it. The problem is that the ruling class in Washington refuses to face the facts—confronting reality is just too daunting—while the intelligentsia continues to pretend that tribal aggression is caused by everything *except* tribal identity.

We've made some progress: Thirty years ago, we weren't allowed to use the word "tribe" on a campus. Tribes, whether African, Middle Eastern, Southeast Asian, or American Indian, were supposedly a "European construct" invented to divide and oppress innocent indigenous peoples. The problem with the politically correct academic model was that the tribes refused to play along. Speaking different languages, with different DNA in many cases, and with powerful group identities grounded in history, myth, and religion, the tribes insisted that they really did exist (the yoo-hoo! factor).

Certainly, not all tribal identities are pure. Whether in Ghana, South Africa, North America, or post-Roman Gaul, victorious tribes often integrated defeated populations. Some tribal identities remain highly exclusive while others are elastic. But they *all* matter—for our military engagements, our strategic interests, and ultimately for the security of our country.

The 9/11 hijackers from Saudi Arabia were bound not only by religion but also by tribal ties. In the Arab portions of Iraq, tribal identity proved indestructible—until we decided to deal with tribal sheikhs, we simply weren't making progress. Afghanistan has such strong tribal and ethnic identities that (like Pakistan) it just may not endure with its present artificial boundaries intact. And tribes were certainly a deadly problem in Somalia.

Then there are countries where tribal rivalries are overlaid with religious differences—for instance, Nigeria, the vast stretch of Africa where the desert meets the Savannah, or outer-island Indonesia. Watch those spaces.

Basic "default" identities—ethnicity and religion—continue to reassert themselves throughout the world's trouble spots, from Chechnya to Myanmar/Burma, and from Kosovo to Central America. Our political leaders must stop pretending that such identities don't matter. The rest of the world *isn't* just like us.

Nor are tribal identities entirely negative. While any state with an alpha tribe that dominates elections will have trouble making Western-style democracy work, tribes exist because, since the days of prehistory, they've functioned as protective associations based on blood ties or, initially, just proximity. Today, tribal networks ensure that their members have food, receive hiring preference, start married life with a boost, and have a backstop in times of crisis.

But tribal members vote for the chief, or his designated representative. They hire the second cousin and do business within the tribe, and if they get the least scrap of power in the government, they favor the tribe any way they can—exacerbating the plague of corruption and stifling the development of mature market economies (forget meritocracy).

In Kenya, Ghana, Zimbabwe, Iraq, Burma, Pakistan, and dozens of other countries (even Belgium, to stretch a point), tribal identities remain resilient while national identities are as fragile as a top-heavy wineglass.

And tribes *don't* love one another. They cooperate when forced to do so by circumstances, not out of affection. And they don't need much of an excuse to start killing—even after decades of drowsy peace.

The operational point? When we're confronted by tribal-based societies, profoundly different rules apply than when we deal with Western-style governments. Our statecraft just doesn't work: We want to negotiate with cabinet members when the real power often lies with a tribal chief or even a shaman.

Watch: How often we insist on one-man-one-vote balloting where elections simply mean that the largest tribe wins and loots the country. Whether those who remained behind in Washington will be willing to learn the lessons our troops are learning in war.

Crisis Watch Bottom Line: With the Age of Ideology dead and gone, we're back to violent unrest and wars over ethnic and religious differences. And it's not going to be pretty.

Man on the Move

New York Post

May 27, 2008

We Americans see our illegal-immigration crisis in isolation, as if we alone face failing borders. But we're in good shape compared with migrant-flooded countries around the world.

It's a global phenomenon—a new age of mass population transfers that bedevils rich, stable countries and overwhelms the infrastructure of weaker states. And there's no end in sight.

For us, it means focusing seriously (at long last) on securing our borders and facing up to our economy's needs. For struggling states, the scale and speed of population movements mean scarcity, explosive crime, terrorism, and anti-immigrant riots that climax in murder.

Just this month: In South Africa, pogroms butchered refugees from Zimbabwe and economic migrants from Mozambique. In India, Muslim fanatics among a mass of Bangladeshi immigrants (to whom even India appears wealthy) set off a string of bombs in Jaipur.

Central Asians fear a demographic takeover by Chinese moving westward; European states struggle to absorb unskilled African illegals and Muslim immigrants out to exploit welfare benefits (while avoiding social integration). The United States confronts the prickly question of what it means to be a nation of immigrants in the twenty-first century.

Within states, the rural poor swell monster-cities such as Lagos, Karachi, and Mumbai. Fleeing such cities, desperate people overload wooden boats, walk across deserts, or stow away in aircraft cargo—headed for other continents that offer a glimmer of hope.

On the plus side, the new mobility means a brilliant Indian software engineer in Silicon Valley or a drop-dead-gorgeous Polish barista in a London Starbucks. But all too often it means Salvadoran gangbangers in Virginia, no-prospect Muslim kids simmering in Paris, or deadly economic competition in Johannesburg.

Why is this happening now? First, it isn't really new. This is only the latest great global migration—the last one occurred as the Roman Empire faded. Back then, entire tribes moved, driven from their grazing grounds on the steppes or searching for richer worlds to conquer.

Today's migration is more chaotic and individualized, but swifter. Instead of moving on horseback and fighting hostile tribes, today's migrants fly or ride overcrowded buses, and do battle only with immigration officials or border police. But the world is on the move again.

The immediate reason for these explosive population transfers is simply that we've been stunningly successful at improving nutrition and reducing disease in poverty-stricken countries. Nature no longer takes its natural toll—but few developing states can absorb the results of reduced mortality.

With our hard-learned humane values, Western states have been slow to recognize global migrations as an accelerating challenge—and not a temporary phenomenon bound to wither away. Demographic pressures are only going to increase.

The bottom line? Europe is already on a disastrous course with its won't-assimilate Muslim immigrants—not toward "Eurabia," but toward another period of population expulsions.

Developing states inundated by migrations will behave brutally (and Western leftists will make excuses for every atrocity, as long as it's committed by dictators hostile to Washington).

But what about us? What about this country composed of immigrant stock (save for our Native American population)? Who are we? What sort of country do we want to be? Which of our fears are grounded, and which are folly?

The problem with our immigration "debate" is that it isn't a debate, but a shouting match among the deaf. A realistic, humane immigration policy that acknowledges our economic needs would make neither the militant left nor the extreme right happy.

Let's start with the admission that we need to control our borders—and are entitled to do so. We're not required to accept everyone who wants to come here. We're not required to admit criminals or the diseased or those who reject our fundamental values.

If it takes a fence to control our borders, just tell me how high. But we also have to accept reality. Our feckless leaders—Republican and Democrat—have allowed 12 million illegals to enter our country. And the U.S. Army is not going to line them up four abreast and march them back across the Rio Grande.

My solution would be to create a new form of residency, short of full citizenship: No one who broke the law to enter our country should ever be able to vote in our elections.

But we also must be honest about our needs. Immigrant labor is essential at both the bottom and the top ends of our economy. If talented individuals educated at foreign expense want to come here to help us create wealth, we should be tripping over ourselves to grant them visas.

Contrary to left-wing myths, a Ukrainian physicist won't put an American auto worker out of a job. And that auto worker isn't going to accept a job harvesting garlic in Gilroy, California.

If we want to maintain our global lead (which we have not lost), we're going to have to accept that our economy will always need new blood.

On the other hand, we must be much tougher on criminal immigrants. One felony? Serial misdemeanors? You're gone, dude. No appeals.

What's the worst thing we could do about the new global migration? Ignore it. Postpone solutions. Pretend—as we did twenty years ago—that illegal immigration is a temporary phenomenon curable with a "one-time" amnesty.

What's the best we could do? Control our borders, but be honest about our needs and treat legitimate immigrants with dignity and decency.

The status quo is not only unworthy of our values, it's a disaster.

Al Qa'eda's Market Crash

New York Post

July 19, 2008

If you think the US markets have problems, look at the value of al Qa'eda shares throughout the Muslim world: A high-flying political equity just a few years ago, its stock has tanked. It made the wrong strategic investments and squandered its moral capital.

In the immediate aftermath of 9/11, Osama bin Laden was the darling of the Arab street, seen as the most successful Muslim in centuries. The Saudi royal family paid him protection money, while individual princes handed over cash willingly: Al Qa'eda seemed like the greatest thing since the right to abuse multiple wives.

Osama appeared on T-shirts and his taped utterances were awaited with fervent excitement. Recruits flocked to al Qa'eda not because of "American aggression," but because, after countless failures, it looked like the Arabs had finally produced a winner.

What a difference a war makes.

Yes, al Qa'eda had little or no connection to Saddam Hussein's Iraq—but the terrorists chose to declare that country the main front in their struggle with the Great Satan. Bad investment: Their behavior there was so breathtakingly brutal that they alienated their fellow Muslims in record time.

Fighting enthusiastically beside the once-hated Americans, Iraq's Sunni Muslims turned on the terrorists with a vengeance. Al Qa'eda's response? It kept on butchering innocent Muslims, Sunni and Shi'a alike. Iraq exposed al Qa'eda as a fraud. Where do Osama & Co. stand today? They're not welcome in a single Arab country. The Saudi royals not only cut off their funding, but cracked down hard within the kingdom. A few countries, such as Yemen, tolerate radicals out in the boonies—but they won't let al Qa'eda in. Osama's reps couldn't even get extended-stay rooms in Somalia, beyond the borders of the Arab world.

And the Arab in the (dirty) street is chastened. Instead of delivering a triumph, al Qa'eda brought disaster, killing far more Arabs through violence and strife than Israel has killed in all its wars. Nobody in the Arab world's buying al Qa'eda shares at yesterday's premium—and only a last few suckers are buying at all.

Guess what? We won.

The partisan hacks who insisted that Iraq was a distraction from fighting al Qa'eda have missed the situation's irony: Things are getting worse in Afghanistan and Pakistan not because our attention was elsewhere, but because al Qa'eda has been driven from the Arab world, with nowhere else to go.

Al Qa'eda isn't fighting to revive the caliphate these days. It's fighting for its life.

Unwelcome even in Sudan or Syria, the Islamist fanatics have retreated to remote mountain villages and compounds on the Pakistani side of the Afghan border. That means Afghanistan's going to remain a difficult challenge for years to come—not a mission impossible, but an aggravating one.

But we all need to stand back and consider how much we've achieved: A terrorist organization that less than a decade ago had global appeal and reach has been discredited in the eyes of most of the world's billion-plus Muslims.

No one of consequence in the Arab world sees al Qa'eda as a winner anymore. Even fundamentalist clerics denounce it. For all of our missteps, Iraq's been worth it.

How is it that the media missed this stunning victory? Will they start to admit it after November 4?

Yes, al Qa'eda remains dangerous. It's a wounded hog still grunting down in the canebrake: More innocent people will be gored—and it's going to take a lot of pig-sticking to finish it off.

But I'm proud of one call I made last year: The prediction that the "Sunni flip" in Iraq's Anbar Province announced the high-water mark for al Qa'eda. Increasingly, that call looks correct.

Democrats make a great fuss over the Bush administration's failure to capture Osama (although they themselves have no idea how to do so). But it now looks like the judgment of history—after the political rancor has settled into the graves of today's demagogues—will be that the administration of George W. Bush defeated al Qa'eda.

There's plenty of work still to be done. Al Qa'eda will behave viciously in its death throes. Other terrorist groups await their turn to appall the world.

But the second-greatest irony of our time is that, fumbling all the way, the Bush administration did what it set out to do after 9/11: It exacted vengeance on those who attacked us and top-pled *their* towers—al Qa'eda's fantastic dreams of global jihad.

So what's the greatest irony? The president's oft-mocked declaration of "Mission Accomplished" wasn't wrong, after all—just premature.

Why Putin Should Scare Us

USA Today

September 17, 2008

Possessing a clear vision of where he wants to go and the ruthlessness to get there, Russian Prime Minister Vladimir Putin is the world's most effective national leader. He also might be the most misunderstood.

Grasping what Putin is about means recognizing what he isn't about: Despite his KGB past and his remark that the Soviet Union's dissolution was "the greatest geopolitical catastrophe" of the twentieth century, Putin isn't nostalgic for communism. By the time he joined the KGB in the mid-1970s, the organization was purely about preserving the power structure—not upholding abstract philosophies.

Far from being a Marxist, Putin belongs to a long tradition of aggressive Russian nationalists. A complex man, he's cold-bloodedly pragmatic when planning—as both his rise to power and his preparations for the recent invasion of Georgia demonstrated—yet he's imbued with a mystical sense of Russia's destiny. The ambitious son of a doctrinaire communist father and a devout Orthodox mother, Putin is straight from the novels of Fyodor Dostoevsky (another son of St. Petersburg).

Putin's combination of merciless calculation and sense of mission echoes an otherwise different figure, Osama bin Laden.

116

In both cases, Western analysts struggle to simplify confounding personalities and end up underestimating them. These are brilliant, driven leaders who flout our rules.

Nonetheless, Putin did carry over specific skills from his KGB career: As a former intelligence officer myself, I'm awed by his ability to analyze opponents and anticipate their reactions to his gambits (Russia is, of course, a nation of chess masters). Preparing for the dismemberment of Georgia, the prime minister accurately calculated the behavior of that country's president, Mikheil Saakashvili, of President Bush, of the European Union, and of the Russian people. He knew he could get away with it.

Putin has a quality found in elite intelligence personnel: the ability to discard all preconceptions when scrutinizing a target. And when he decides to strike, he doesn't look back. This is not good news for his opponents, foreign or domestic.

Among the many reasons we misjudge Putin is our insistence on seeing him as "like us." He's not. His stage-management of the Georgia invasion was a perfect example: Western intelligence agencies had been monitoring Russian activities in the Caucasus for years and fully expected a confrontation. But our analysts assumed that Russia wouldn't act during this summer's Olympics, traditionally an interval of peace.

Putin had been conditioned to read the strategic cards differently: The world's attention would be focused on the Games, and key world leaders would be in Beijing, far from their crisis-management staffs. Europe's bureaucrats and senior NATO officials would be on their August vacations. The circumstances were ideal.

It has also become a truism that Putin is foolish for relying on oil, gas, and mineral revenue while failing to diversify his economy. But Russia's strongman knows what he's doing: He prefers a wealthy government to a wealthy society. Putin can control a handful of oligarchs whose fortunes flow from a narrow range of sources (Mikhail Khodorkovsky, once Russia's richest man, sits in prison for crossing the Kremlin), but a diversified economy would decentralize power.

Putin's obsession with control—another national tradition—serves an overarching purpose: restoring Russia's greatness. He realizes he can't restore a Soviet Union that sprawled deep into Europe. What he hopes is to reconstruct the empire of the czars, from eastern Poland through Ukraine and the Caucasus to Central Asia. Putin's expansionist model comes from Peter the Great, but his methods resemble those of Ivan the Terrible, not least when it comes to silencing dissent. The main thing the prime minister has salvaged from the Soviet era is the cult of personality. He knows what Russians want—a strong czar—and his approval ratings have exceeded 80 percent.

Does this ruthless, focused leader have a weakness? Yes: his temper. Despite his icy demeanor, Putin's combustible. He takes rebuffs personally and can act impulsively—and destructively. Instead of lulling Europeans into an ever-greater dependence on Russian gas, he angrily ordered winter shutoffs to Ukraine and Georgia, alarming Western customers. Rather than concealing the Kremlin's cyber-attack capabilities, he unleashed them on tiny Estonia during a tiff over relocating a Soviet-era memorial—alerting NATO.

Putin's invasion of Georgia was also personal. In addition to exposing the West's impotence in the region, he meant to punish Georgia's defiant president. The lengths to which Putin was prepared to go in a personal vendetta should worry us all.

Such outbursts of temper suggest that Putin's campaign to restore Russia's greatness could end very badly. We needn't take his dispatch of a naval squadron to Venezuela or bomber flights over U.S. Navy carriers seriously. They're staged for his domestic audience and militarily absurd. But Putin's willingness to use naked force against regional democracies suggests that, like so many strongmen before him, he'll ultimately overreach.

Meanwhile, our next president will have to cope with this brilliant, dangerous man. That's going to require the experience and skills to exploit every element of our national power, to convince Europe that appeasement will only enlarge Putin's appetite, and to draw clear lines while avoiding drawn guns. Above all, our president will have to take Putin's measure accurately and not indulge in wishful thinking. Managing Putin's Russia could emerge as our No. 1 security challenge.

The Halfway War

Armchair General Online

January 22, 2009

The Israeli government's decision to break off its punitive expedition into Gaza prematurely—despite the superb performance of the Israel Defense Forces—calls into question not only the utility, but the ultimate morality, of this "pocket war."

When a rule-of-law democracy embarks upon a military campaign its leaders are not committed to pressing to a decisive conclusion, it upsets the ethical calculus. In war, worthy ends can justify ruthless means. But a feckless, inconclusive application of military force that does not produce an improved postwar environment is difficult to justify.

After enduring years of terrorist rocket attacks from Gaza, followed by Hamas's one-sided abrogation of an extended-truce proposal, Israel acted in self defense. The initial cause of this three-week war was just.

The subsequent application of heavy, but discriminate, firepower by Israel in dense urban warrens in which Hamas employed noncombatants not only as human shields, but as propaganda sacrifices, was also justified—but only if Israel meant business and intended to continue operations until Hamas was shattered and its senior leadership cadres had been killed or captured.

Stopping short of the campaign's logical goals abruptly calls into question the level of destruction and civilian deaths. Collateral damage can only be excused when the end attained is greater than the cost.

For example, the relentless bombing campaign against the cities of Nazi Germany was justified as part of a total effort to eliminate Hitler and his regime. But the massive loss of civilian life would not have been acceptable had the Allies agreed to a peace that left the Nazis in power. In war, you may do evil to achieve a greater good, but not without a transcendent moral purpose.

Likewise, the employment of fire-bombing and, ultimately, of atomic bombs against Japanese cities was morally acceptable because of the stakes involved, previous Japanese behavior, and the potential for a far greater loss of life (on all sides) were we forced to invade Japan's home islands. But a premature peace that accepted a continuation of the militarist regime in Tokyo would have reduced our behavior to wantonness.

The end not only can justify the means, but must.

In the conduct of war, the innocent will always suffer, no matter how scrupulous targeting cells and decision-makers may be. But the misery should not be disproportionate to the value of the results.

The paradox isn't that Israel caused too many casualties, but that it failed to continue killing Hamas terrorists until the civilian casualties could be justified by the war's results.

With 1,300 Palestinians dead (most of them Hamas terrorists, but not all) and zones of severe damage within the Gaza Strip, Israel has betrayed its own morality by letting Hamas survive. When the IDF unilaterally ceased fighting on the weekend before the U.S. presidential inauguration, the terrorist leaders, who had hidden in deep Iranian-engineered bunkers under hospitals and schools, had only to emerge into the light of day as survivors to declare themselves the victors.

Life isn't fair, and neither is war—especially the challenge of fighting faith-fueled terrorists. To win, we have to kill enough of them to destroy their organization and break the will of any survivors. The terrorists only need to survive in sufficient numbers to pop back up and thumb their noses. Yet the necessity of killing terrorist leadership cadres in large numbers is a lesson Western states, including Israel, have difficulty absorbing and remembering.

From a diplomatic standpoint, Israel did have multiple justifications for stopping short. Hamas had received a significant drubbing and a local humiliation. The Olmert government had timed the operation to exploit the remaining weeks of the Bush administration and, with the inauguration of President Obama looming, the Israeli "triumvirate" of Prime Minister Ehud Olmert, Foreign Minister Tzipi Livni, and Defense Minister Ehud Barak (the latter a decorated war hero) decided it could not afford to appear as the prime mover in the first foreign-policy crisis facing the new U.S. administration. With President Obama a worrisome unknown to Tel Aviv and Jerusalem, the Israelis decided not to risk a public repudiation from Washington.

Furthermore, Israeli elections loom in a few weeks, and the ruling coalition fears an opposition victory under the leadership of the charismatic Binyamin Netanyahu, whose firm approach to the Palestinian problem resonates with Israelis sick of rocket attacks and still mortified by the mess of the 2006 conflict with Hezbollah (in a peculiar sense, the Gaza incursion was Netanyahu's war, although he had no direct involvement: the Olmert government felt compelled to act to show it could be as tough as "Bibi").

Israel also faced the inevitability of significant greater casualties—friendly, enemy, and civilian—if the IDF were ordered to penetrate to the heart of Gaza's cities. And, contrary to anti-Israeli myths, Israel is ever cognizant of the human cost of war.

Additionally, the global media and anti-Israel regimes around the world were screaming, exaggerating the carnage in Gaza and ignoring the fact that all Hamas had to do on any given day to stop the fighting was to stop firing blind terror-rockets into Israel and agree to live in peace. While Israeli leaders should have learned by now that their only hope of achieving a durable success in the course of a conflict is to ignore the media, the UN, and other terrorist fellow travelers until the job is done, the Olmert government lost its nerve again.

What will emerge as the smoke of battle clears? Perhaps the hammering Hamas received will have chastened the terrorist organization and, despite the current crowing, might have weakened it sufficiently to loosen its death-grip on the Gaza Strip. But the odds are better that Hamas will be able to maintain its local monopoly on violence against its own people and, with the assistance of a multitude of international aid organizations, return to employing aid as an internal political weapon while renewing the smuggling of Iranian-supplied weapons.

While we can't yet know which trend will emerge the stronger, the odds are that nothing will have been decided by this halfway mini-war. While Israel has set back Hamas's development of a full-blown second front to complement Hezbollah's primary front in southern Lebanon, it left Iran's proxies alive to proclaim themselves resistance heroes.

Israel's unwillingness to do all that was required to crush Hamas also may have encouraged Iran to intensify its nuclear-weapons program, assured that Israel lacks the guts and wherewithal to stop it.

A half-fought war—that bizarre vice of democracies—doesn't save lives in the long run, but guarantees a future round of violence—probably with higher stakes and definitely with greater ferocity. In stopping short of its essential goals, Israel broke a fundamental rule of all warfare. He who is unwilling to pay the butcher's bill promptly will pay it with compound interest in the end.

Taliban from Outer Space

New York Post

February 3, 2009

A fundamental reason why our intelligence agencies, military leaders, and (above all) Washington pols can't understand Afghanistan is that they don't recognize that we're dealing with alien life forms.

Oh, the strange-minded aliens in question resemble us physically. We share a few common needs: We and the aliens are oxygen breathers who require food and water at frequent intervals. Our body casings feel heat or cold. We're divided into two sexes (more or less). And we're mortal.

But that's about where the similarities end, analytically speaking.

In my years as an intelligence officer, I saw colleagues make the same blunder over and over: They rushed to stress the ways in which the Russians, the Chinese, or the Iranians were "just like us." It's the differences that kill you, though.

I was an effective intelligence officer. Why? In junior high, I matured past the French Existentialists and started reading science fiction. The prose was often ragged, but the speculative frameworks offered a useful approach to analysis.

Begin with the view that all opponents are aliens from another cultural planet. Build your assessment from a blank slate. What do the alien collectives desire or fear? How do they perceive the galaxy? What are their unique weaknesses?

Regarding Planet Afghanistan, we still hear the deadly cliché that "all human beings want the same basic things, such as better lives and greater opportunities for their children." How does that apply to Afghan aliens who prefer their crude way of life and its merciless cults?

When girls and women are denied education or even health care and are executed by their own kin for minor infractions against the cult, how does that square with our insistence that all men want greater opportunities for the kids?

What about those Afghan parents who approve of or even encourage suicidal attacks by their sons? This not only confounds our value system, but defies biological reason.

So: These humanoid forms with which we must deal don't all want or value the same things we do. They form different social aggregates and exchange goods and services within wildly different parameters (and exhibit hypocritical sexual tastes that diverge from procreative mandates—ask our troops about that).

These alien tribes seek to destroy physical objects and systems valued on Planet America. They perceive time differently. They treat other life forms more harshly than we do. Their own lives are shorter, with different arcs. They quite like our weapons, though. . . .

The point isn't to argue that Afghans are inferior beings. It's just that they're irreconcilably different beings—more divergent from our behavioral norms than the weirdest crew member of the starship Enterprise.

As an analytical exercise, try to understand Afghanistan as a hostile planet to which we have been forced, in self-defense, to deploy military colonies. How do the bizarre creatures on that other planet view us? What do they want? What will they accept? Is killing us business, pleasure—or both?

Are there tribes among these aliens with which we can cooperate? Which actions of ours inflame the alien psyche? What will the alien willingly die for? What does the alien find inexplicable about us? Must we preserve a useful climate of fear?

Do we intend to maintain our military colonies out there in deep space? For how long? Can the angry planet ever be sanitized of threats?

Of course, there's more in play than images of our "starship troopers" combating those alien life forms that call themselves "Taliban." This exercise is just meant to break our mental gridlock, to challenge our crippling assumption that we're all merry brothers and sisters who just have to work through a few small understandings.

This is a "war of the worlds" in the cultural sense, a head-on collision between civilizations from different galaxies.

And the aliens don't come in peace.

Ghost States

"Inconvenient" Reality

New York Post

February 27, 2009

Pakistan's bloodied Northwest Frontier Province is getting a new name: Pakhtunkhwa, or "Land of the Pashtun" tribesmen. A key demand of Taliban radicals, the new title isn't an end, but a beginning.

Obsessed with the "integrity" of dysfunctional, artificial borders, U.S. policymakers struggle to come to grips with the Taliban, an overwhelmingly Pashtun organization. For its part, the Taliban functions as the shadow government of a ghost state sprawling across huge stretches of Afghanistan and Pakistan.

Pakhtunkhwa already exists in fact, if not in the UN General Assembly. The writs of the governments in Islamabad and Kabul run up to the international border on our maps, but not in reality. We play along with the fantasy.

Census numbers are flimsy, but up to 42 million Pashtuns (or Pakhtuns or Pathans) live in the region, with perhaps 13 million in Afghanistan and double that number in Pakistan. That would make Greater Pakhtunkhwa a middle-weight nation, population-wise.

United by old blood and various dialects of Pashto, the Pashtuns are a collection of five dozen major tribes that long have functioned as a primitive state, governed by tribal councils amid

127

hundreds of sub-tribes. Although briefly united at a few junctures in history, their primary goal has been the defense of local territory against outsiders, not central administration.

Now the Pashtuns, as manifested by the Taliban, seek an authentic state governed by Sharia law. It isn't good news for us, for women, or for the feeble states of Afghanistan and Pakistan. But how much of our blood and treasure is it worth to keep those wretched states on life support, while denying the vigor of a ghost state fighting to become flesh?

A Pakhtunkhwa that includes all of the Pashtuns would be culturally abhorrent. But it may be inevitable. Are we fighting forces our measures can't defeat?

Nor is the ghost-state problem limited to our confused efforts in Afghanistan. The 6 million Kurds in northern Iraq are ethnically, linguistically, and culturally different from the oppressive Arab majority to the south. Iraq's Kurds are also the most-advanced Middle Eastern population outside of Israel (and the most pro-American).

Well, the ghost nation of Kurdistan isn't just three Iraqi provinces, but a broader Kurdish state struggling to be born. Iraq, Iran, Turkey, Syria, and the southern Caucasus hold 30 million Kurds between them, nearly all subject to Jim Crow laws and worse.

The Kurds are struggling for freedom. We find them an inconvenience.

But "inconveniences" don't go away just because we ignore them. Consider yet another ghost state where U.S. troops have engaged: Greater Albania.

Again, census numbers are sticky, but Albania itself has a population of 3 million to 4 million, with another 1½ million ethnic Albanians in Kosovo and a half-million more in Macedonia and Montenegro.

How much effort should we expend to prevent the natural emergence of Greater Albania? Doesn't self-determination count in the clinch? (As for a "Muslim menace," a third of Albania's inhabitants are Christians. In the Balkans, organized crime's a far greater threat than Islam.)

Of course, a ghost state of a different sort exists on our Southwest border and in northern Mexico. But, apart from a few rabid activists in La Raza, that's one ghost state that doesn't seek a real state. The difference? Individual rights and fair opportunities, guaranteed by the rule of law (on our side of the border).

Contrary to racist myths, few Latinos want to return our Southwest to the Mexico they fled. Nobody's going to vote for death squads, corruption, poverty, and a narco-state. While we need to fully control our border and boot out convicted criminals immediately, self-interest and economics will handle the rest.

Yet we do need to recognize that the age of European Imperialism, to which we were an adjunct, left a legacy of international borders that range from the awkward to the impossible—and no state wants to give up an inch of territory, even when its efforts to control separatists appear suicidal.

We don't need to play along, though, except when it's clearly in our national interest. The question before us is blunt: Should our soldiers die to preserve the disastrous borders Europeans left behind?

Should Free Kurdistan, or Greater Albania, or even a full-fledged Pakhtunkhwa be opposed simply because their emergence would mean shifting desks in the State Department? Can our policymakers even tell the difference between the expedient and the inevitable?

The borders Europe left behind are prisons. How long will we be the guards up on the walls?

Border Bloodbath

New York Post

March 27, 2009

While Washington focused on terrorists halfway around the world, a narco-terror crisis exploded—with 8,000 dead in two years—along our border with Mexico.

Were we blindsided? Only because we closed our eyes on purpose. One administration passed the problem on to the next. And the next.

Are we taking this crisis seriously at last? Let's hope.

After her disastrous pilgrimage to Beijing, Secretary of State Hillary Clinton appears to have gotten a big diplomatic move right: On Wednesday, she acknowledged both the seriousness of Mexico's narco-insurgency and our complicity as a huge drug consumer and the major source of drug-cartel weaponry.

Our top domestic problem is that this issue's been politicized by extremists on both the political left and right. So let's cut through the hot air and look at what's happened—and what we need to do.

How did it come to this bloodbath? The warning signs were there fifteen years ago. In 1994, I did an on-the-ground drug-war analysis for the U.S. Southern Command. Among the key conclusions: Mexico was headed for a crisis.

The logic was simple. For five centuries, Latin America has suffered boom-bust commodity cycles—in gold, silver, tin, beef, rubber, oil, and, last but not least, cocaine.

All booms lead the countries of origin to overproduce. The end market becomes saturated. Where does the surplus go? It's sold at discount rates in the transit countries—which lack the infrastructure to deal with the sudden economic distortions and soaring corruption.

It was obvious that Mexico would become a market-share battleground. It was also clear that cocaine's appeal would peak and other drugs would be introduced. (Welcome to the toxic world of meth.)

The Clinton administration simply didn't care. Latin America was a backwater, and Mexico (a massive country vital to our security) was an afterthought. George W. Bush did come to office with a Latin-America agenda—only to be consumed by 9/11.

And here we are. Mexico's border cities are killing fields, the Mexican army's in the streets (and not always winning)—and violence is spilling north of the border.

Our bad? Thanks to political biliousness on the hard left and extreme right, weapons we sell kill Mexican cops and soldiers, while our own citizens go unprotected from ferocious criminals who enter our country illegally.

What should we do? The medicine's bitter:

- Decriminalize marijuana. I hate the idea. But marijuana doesn't kill and it's not an "inevitable gateway drug." We need to concentrate our resources on the killer drugs and the murderers who push them. Make hard-drug smuggling and vending crimes with mandatory life sentences. (I wish we could make them capital crimes.)
- Create a serious paramilitary force to control our border: Expand, up-arm, and legally empower our Border Patrol. Thanks to vile activists, Border Patrol agents have gone to

prison for wounding drug criminals. We need to authorize deadly force and stop second-guessing those who defend us.

The political left needs to stop protecting criminal aliens. Unfortunately, the Obama administration's ballyhooed shift of several hundred Immigration and Customs Enforcement agents to the border is a phony trick to appease pro-illegal-immigrant activists: It means far less domestic enforcement of immigration law.

The political right needs to accept that, while firmly protecting the gun-owning rights of law-abiding citizens, we must crack down fiercely on the supply chain that puts automatic weapons in the claws of drug cartels. The Founding Fathers wanted to protect our rights of self-defense. They didn't intend to equip foreign thugs.

• Enforce the laws we have. And tighten those laws as necessary. Immigration is a great strength for our country, but we have every legal and moral right to decide whom we welcome as future Americans. Illegal immigration and narco-terror are inextricably intertwined.

What won't work? A wall—at least along the eastern half of our border, from El Paso to Brownsville. As border expert Dave Danelo points out, we really have two borders. First, there's the grisly, out-of-control stretch from El Paso west to the Pacific. That's where walls do help.

But a wall on the southern border of Texas would hand the Rio Grande River to Mexico. And law-abiding Hispanic families have lived on both sides of the river for centuries, visiting back and forth. They're not the problem. (Been there, seen how it works.) The problem is interloping narcos.

We shouldn't penalize honest citizens just because Los Angeles or San Francisco protects gang-bangers from deportation.

Bottom line? If we want to worsen the problem, keep politicizing it. To solve it, ignore the extremists: Empower our officials, punish criminals, and concentrate on the drugs that kill—not on busting aging hippie potheads.

And help Mexico every way we can. If President Felipe Calderon's brave efforts fail, the next president south of the border will be a tool of the narco-terrorists.

PART III

Fit to Fight

Wanted: Occupation Doctrine

Armed Forces Journal

April 2007

Together, the Army and Marines shoulder the combat duties in Iraq, supported by the other services. But the primary burden of occupation has been borne by the Army—as it always will be. Given the difficulty of overcoming the breathtaking range of errors committed by political ideologues during this occupation's early phases—when it wasn't even permissible to term it an "occupation"—and the uphill struggle to salvage the situation now, one of the last things the Army wants to contemplate is another occupation in the future.

But that future occupation is going to come. Followed by others. If the Army does not demonstrate the foresight and character to write and print honest, comprehensive, and adaptable occupation doctrine now, it will have itself to blame when next it's tasked to repair a broken country with inadequate support and confused lines of authority—while a politically charged environment bedevils the home front.

Army leaders have yet to grasp two vital points: First, the refusal to prepare for a given mission is not an effective means of avoiding the mission. Second, doctrine isn't just for the military's internal use—manuals can function as both a contract with and warning to inexperienced civilian leaders whose geopolitical ambitions are not always tethered to reality.

In this ruptured world, with artificial borders collapsing, debased religions raging, ethnic identities resurgent, and entire civilizations in crisis, the pretense that, since we don't want to conduct occupations, we shall therefore be able to avoid them, is absurd. If, miraculously, we do not need to occupy any other state, large or small, in our lifetimes, so much the better. But we had better have sound, no-nonsense doctrine in case miracles prove to be in short supply.

The immediate need for doctrine that addresses the various forms and durations of occupations under differing mandates and in different cultural environments is, obviously, to allow our military to plan wisely, act effectively, and leave the occupied territory under conditions favorable to our own security requirements. But that second aspect of doctrine—the cautionary education of policymakers—may prove even more important to mission success.

Imagine how different the situation in Iraq might be today had the Army possessed an up-to-date manual, "Occupation," that laid out the complexity and challenges involved prior to our move against Saddam Hussein's regime. Oral arguments and position papers are weak tools compared to an approved doctrinal manual, in black and white, that our uniformed leaders could lay in front of the president, his advisers, and Congress to detail the probable cost to achieve our goals.

The absence of such doctrine grants madcap civilian theorists a license to fantasize about bloodless war followed by easy, self-financing occupations (or worse, the assumption that occupation won't be necessary). If the Army doesn't draw its lessons learned from Iraq (and previous occupations it conducted successfully) and forge those lessons into useful doctrine, the institution will have only itself to blame the next time we blunder headlong into a reality that doesn't match the merry expectations of policymakers for whom our military is merely a global janitorial service.

Army leaders have to be hardheaded about this: Formulate realistic doctrine—neither blithely optimistic nor so pessimistic it obviously was framed to discourage occupations. While our doc-

trine can help politicians make wise decisions by instructing them
what their visions truly involve, it's also essential that the Army
doesn't fall into the "can't do" trap in which it caught itself in the
mid-1990s. This isn't a matter of the Army getting to choose its
missions, but of giving decisionmakers a sense of reality when
unavoidable missions arise.

Occupation doctrine must be forged with absolute integrity.
Taken along with further evolutions of our counterinsurgency
doctrine (the title of the next version of the manual should be
plural: "Counterinsurgencies"), it must provide our forces with a
dependable framework for occupation efforts, while imparting a
sense of sobriety to elected and appointed officials. The formulation of such doctrine, as onerous as the Army may find it, isn't
an optional activity. It's a duty.

IMPROVISED EXPLOSIVE MYTHS (IEMS)

The first step in formulating usable doctrine is to sweep aside
the politically correct myths that have appeared about occupations. Occupations are military activities. Period. An Army general must be in charge, at least until the security environment
can be declared benign with full confidence. Historically, the
occupations that worked—often brilliantly, as in the Philippines,
Germany, and Japan—were run by generals, not diplomats. This
is another mission the Army doesn't want, but no other organization has the wherewithal to do it.

As Iraq illustrated so painfully, security must come first. That
requires military decisiveness, not diplomatic quibbling. All else
is secondary to the provision of security to the occupied population, and all longer-term goals depend upon quiet in the streets
and peace in the countryside. A governor-general means a general as governor—we can choose more palatable terminology,
but civilians cannot be put in charge in a theater of war before
the shooting stops. The place for civilian decisionmakers is in
Washington, not in a future travesty imitating Ambassador Paul
Bremer's personal Disneyland in the Baghdad Green Zone.

Consider just a few essential rules for successful occupations—all of which we violated in Iraq:

* Plan for the worst case. Pleasant surprises are better than
  ugly ones.
* All else flows from security. Martial law, even if imposed
  under a less-provocative name, must be declared immediately—it's far easier to loosen restrictions later on than to
  tighten them in the wake of anarchy. This is one aspect of
  a general principle: Take the pain up front.
* Unity of command is essential.
* The occupier's troop strength should be perceived as
  overwhelming and his forces ever-present.
* Key military leaders, staff officers, intelligence personnel,
  and vital civilian advisers must be committed to initial
  tours of duty of not less than two years for the sake of con-
  tinuity.
* Control external borders immediately.
* Don't isolate troops and their leaders from the local population.
* Whenever possible, existing host-country institutions
  should be retained and co-opted. After formal warfare
  ends, don't disband organizations you can use to your
  advantage.
* Give local opinionmakers a stake in your success, avoid
  penalizing mid-level and low-level officials (except war
  criminals), and get young men off the streets and into jobs.
* Don't make development promises you can't keep, and
  war-game reconstruction efforts to test their necessity, via-
  bility, and indirect costs (an occupation must not turn
  into a looting orgy for U.S. or allied contractors).
* Devolve responsibility onto local leaders as quickly as possible—while retaining ultimate authority.
* Do not empower returned expatriates until you are certain they have robust local support.

- The purpose of cultural understanding is to facilitate the mission, not to paralyze our operations. Establish immediately that violent actors and seditious demagogues will not be permitted to hide behind cultural or religious symbols.
- Establish flexible guidelines for the expenditure of funds by tactical commanders and for issuing local reconstruction contracts. Peacetime accountability requirements do not work under occupation conditions and attempts to satisfy them only play into the hands of the domestic political opposition in the United States while crippling our efforts in the zone of occupation.
- Rigorously control private security forces, domestic or foreign. In lieu of a functioning state, we must have a monopoly on violence.

Such a list captures only a fraction of the complexity of an occupation. But these elementary truths must be driven home to counteract the myths that have appeared about how occupations—and our government—should function. Consider the prevailing claim that an occupation is a team effort involving all relevant branches of government: The problem is that the rest of the team doesn't show up. The State Department, as ambitious for power as it is incompetent to wield it, insists that it should have the lead in any occupation, yet has neither the leadership and management expertise, the institutional resources, nor the personnel required (among the many State-induced debacles in Iraq, look at its appetite for developing Iraqi police forces and its total failure to deliver).

The military is the default occupier, since its personnel can be ordered into hostile environments for unlimited periods; State and other agencies rely on volunteers and, in Iraq, the volunteers have not been forthcoming—even when the tours for junior diplomats were limited to a useless 90 days and dire warnings were issued about the importance of Iraq duty to careers.

Under prevailing political circumstances, it will probably be necessary to offer a dual-model approach to occupations in the manual—one for situations in which the lead time allows the government to build interagency organizations staffed full time, resourced and trained in advance, and another, military only, for circumstances when immediate action is required or when the other government agencies cannot or will not make firm, long-term personnel commitments. Even now, the situation in Iraq remains disgraceful—with unfulfilled promises by other government departments and agencies leaving the occupation's burdens on the military's shoulders. To prevent another such shambles, the Army must assume that it will have to conduct every on-the-ground aspect of the mission by itself from the occupation's zero hour. If the rest of the government comes through, great. But the Army must be prepared to execute the occupation mission with only the support of the other uniformed services.

Although military personnel are ever in short supply, it would be worth the overhead for the Army and the other uniformed services to establish a permanent occupation-planning headquarters staffed by experienced officers (and offering joint-duty credit). It would not need to be heavily manned and, yes, there would be a danger of such an organization turning into Sleepy Hollow—but the likelihood that we will face future occupation requirements makes it worth the investment to gather, preserve, and further develop how-to expertise for occupations. We should never again face a debacle such as the chaos that prevailed in the buildup to Operation Iraqi Freedom and immediately after the fall of Baghdad—situations exacerbated by the moral cowardice of senior military officers unwilling to take a stand on much of anything.

EDUCATING THE GENIUSES
In Washington, everybody who works across the river from the Pentagon "knows" that he has a better grasp of military strategy than the generals. Whether new congressmen or novice foreign

service officers, their lack of military service (or even of interest in things military) doesn't stop D.C.'s best and brightest from scheming how to employ our armed forces.

This situation isn't going to change. The draft has receded so far into the past that we can be certain that each successful round of elections will further diminish the firsthand knowledge of military affairs on Capitol Hill. Those in uniform who imagine that the manner in which civilian ideologues steamrollered the Army in the buildup to our invasion of Iraq was an exceptional case that will not be repeated are indulging in fantasies as dangerous as those that got us where we are today. Ignorance doesn't simply disappear; arrogance is and always will be endemic to Washington, and ideological extremism of the sort that short-circuited the planning process for OIF and its aftermath is a bipartisan plague.

If military leaders do not lay out a realistic scenario for future interventions and occupations, decisions of life, death and national security will once again be made on the basis of political dogma.

The fundamental reason why the Cheney-Rumsfeld-Wolfowitz-Feith-Cambone cabal forbade the military from planning for a full-scale occupation was straightforward: They feared that any such plan would project high troop numbers, serious financial costs, and a lengthy presence—and that the plan would inevitably leak to an already-jumpy Congress. Their attitude was, "Just get the war and everything else will sort itself out."

They got their war. But everything hasn't sorted itself out.

In the absence of current printed doctrine, even former Army Chief of Staff Gen. Eric Shinseki's judgment that an occupation of Iraq would require hundreds of thousands of troops could be dismissed as simply one opinion among many. Now consider how differently such a scenario might play out if a future chief of staff—or chairman of the Joint Chiefs—testifying before Congress could slap down a manual in front of the C-Span cameras and state, "Senator, this doctrine lays out the requirements for an occupation. It's the U.S. Army's institutional position, based upon the professional judgment of veteran officers. Its tenets have been tested against a full range of historical examples."

Or, as Martin Luther put it, "Here I stand. I cannot do otherwise."

Even if the ideologues of the future, on the political right or the left, again moved to prevent the Pentagon from occupation planning, the manual would still exist, impossible to censor and available to Congress and the media. Civilian "experts" anxious to insist that everything could be done on the cheap would be thrust onto the defensive—simply by existing, the doctrine would seize the high ground for the military. And a printed manual blessed by the Army's leadership (or joint doctrine, for that matter) is a far more powerful tool of persuasion than a frantically compiled position paper or an oral answer to a senator's query during a hearing.

Of course, the point of producing a manual for occupations isn't to avoid legitimate responsibilities by raising the bar impossibly high. Such doctrine must be developed with absolute integrity—describing fairly what can be done and what it takes to do it. The internal purpose is to guide our military efforts wisely. The external purpose is to force civilian decisionmakers to face the probable costs and consequences of their actions up front, but not to frighten them into paralysis. Such doctrine would not be intended to deter the National Command Authority from doing what must be done—only to ensure that deployed military forces are given both the authority and the full array of resources to accomplish their assigned mission.

Every occupation will have its unique qualities and special requirements. Even the best doctrine will only provide us with an initial framework, not a complete set of infallible answers. While recognizing that all occupations share some common and irreducible requirements (such as those highlighted above), we must avoid down-in-the-weeds prescriptions that may be case-specific: The goal of doctrine is to provide a strong skeleton; specific circumstances flesh it out. There will always be surprises, in war and in the occupations that follow. But this much is certain: It would be nothing short of dereliction of duty for the Army leadership ever to allow our military and our country to be blindsided on this issue again by unelected charlatans who felt entitled to use the military to advance their ideological theories.

If the Army has not formulated a frank, practical doctrine for military occupations before the next such requirement draws in our soldiers, the generals will have only themselves to blame when our troops are misused and our national purposes frustrated.

The Army doesn't want to face another occupation, so it doesn't want to write occupation doctrine. But the Army has to shoulder this burden for the nation. No one else will.

Learning to Lose

The American Interest

July/August 2007

Hamlet thinks too much. Chewing every side of the argument to mush, he lacks the courage to swallow hard and kill an assassin at prayer—a philosophical "war crime." The archetypal academic, theory-poisoned and indecisive, Hamlet should have stayed at the university in Wittenberg, where his ability to prattle without resolution surely would have gained him early tenure. Mistaking himself for a man of action, he remains self-obsessed throughout the play, taking less interest in the rest of the world than the most narcissistic blogger. To put it mildly, his perception of others is faint, as Ophelia, Polonius, and a platoon of others might testify. Hamlet loves players, because real human beings perplex him (not least his mama, who seems too meaty a woman to have given birth to such a scrap). The unmanly prince dithers, stalking himself, until his belated action—inevitably, too complex in its conception—leaves the stage covered with bodies, including his own.

Henry V, by contrast, was a real king who won battles because he wasn't afraid to get close to the enemy and kill him. Both Shakespeare's titan and the historical figure triumphed militarily over bowel-draining odds, yet neither propounded a high-flown theory of warfare. Both Henrys believed in the doctrine of kingship, but doctrine guides action, while theory inhibits decisiveness. Henry led from the front and checked up on his troops in the dead of night, unlike the slothful chain of command responsible for the Abu Ghraib debacle. In contrast to Hamlet, Henry's violence was prompt and always had a point. King Harry could make a decision. His leadership inspired and he never lost sight of his essential requirement: to win, at any cost. First he won militarily, *then* he negotiated from a position of strength.

How easy it is to imagine Hamlet scheming for a higher chair within an Ivy League faculty. If Henry V showed up in the quad, the first graduate assistant to spot him would speed-dial the campus police.

What do Shakespeare's polar-opposite characters have to do with the education of the officer corps of the U.S. Armed Forces—apart from the fact that Shakespeare has to do with nearly everything? Only this: Our military needs Henrys, yet for half a century it's been hellbent and determined to turn out Hamlets with stars on their shoulders.

Setting aside practical training, a task at which the U.S. military is incomparable, an officer's formal education after commissioning comes in two varieties (one is tempted to write "comedy and tragedy"): In-house courses conducted by the services, for the services; and advanced civilian education for officers selected for specialized roles, for those identified as likeliest to rise in rank, and, not least, for those who don't really want to be soldiers and scheme to cajole a free education out of the bureaucracy. (A fourth category is composed of officers who gain a master's degree or the equivalent on their own, in their scarce free time and at far more expense to their personal lives than to the taxpayer, but no officer who saves the government tens of thousands of dollars can be taken seriously.)

The in-house courses, of which there are many, do a competent job of preparing officers for their previous rank. The most effective of the courses through which all officers must pass is the

Basic Course (for simplicity's sake, we'll use the nomenclature common to the Army and Marines, since service terminology can vary). The students are lieutenants fresh from a service academy, from the Reserve Officers' Training Program on a civilian campus, or from Officer Candidate School, which commissions soldiers harvested from the enlisted ranks. The Basic Course, followed by a block of specialized training, welcomes the young officer into the service and provides a grounding in his or her branch (Infantry, Military Intelligence, Ordnance, and so forth). It functions as a transition stage before the young officer is thrust into the never-enough-time atmosphere of a battalion.

Along with the follow-on specialized course, the Basic Course gives the second lieutenant a professional vocabulary and a sufficient sense of what he or she will have to do "in the field" to allow the officer to get started in a first assignment—where the real education of any officer begins.

At the conclusion of their apprenticeships, captains attend the Advanced Course, where the system begins to fray. With at least two assignments behind them, student officers arrive with a disruptive knowledge of how things actually work. They are then instructed by a faculty not always selected from the military's strongest performers on how their branch's doctrine insists they should have done what they did successfully but incorrectly. Some Advanced Course programs are better than others, but few officers learn much of use from them. Their greatest value comes from giving the officer a bit of time with his or her family in a not-quite-serious environment, and in bringing peers together so they can sniff each other—an important matter for those who inevitably will need to rely on one another in future assignments.

The next educational gate is Command and General Staff College (C&GSC) for majors and captains on the promotion list. Once selective, the Army program is now inclusive—and healthier for it. C&GSC's purpose is, as the name suggests, to prepare officers for higher command and staff positions. Once again, the student is asked to forget what he or she has learned in practice in order to master obsolete or obsolescent doctrine approved by a hierarchy of committees, few of whose members have the recent wartime experience common to the students. While elective courses can have real value, major end-of-term exercises in the past have been so far divorced from military reality that only the most careerist students pretended to respect them. As with the Advanced Course, the real value of C&GSC is the gathering in of the tribes, the opportunity for peers—this time from all of their service's branches, as well as from sister services and foreign militaries—to get a sense of each other, to learn from each other, and to build relationships that can have profound effects in future years.

The last formal phase of in-house officer education is the War College, where largely civilian faculties instruct colonels and lieutenant colonels on the countless theories academics have devised for avoiding war. Failed theories of international relations form the core curriculum, augmented by courses on how to lose wars politely, and lectures from government functionaries who never rose quite high enough to discount such ego-boosting appearances.

The value of the officer's year at the War College depends overwhelmingly on whether he or she is interested in learning. This is a year for those who recently relinquished command—an all-consuming endeavor—to read. The best thing that has happened to the various service war colleges in recent years has been the assignment of new war veterans and more creative officers as seminar leaders, but the tenured academics will surely wait them out.

At all levels above the Basic Course, veterans are challenging faculties composed of academics, aging military retirees, and administrators who would rather lose a war than attract uncomfortable attention by exploring controversial subjects (one war college journal has been forbidden from mentioning religion when discussing our current conflicts, which means interpreting Islamist terror as a virgin birth). A few innovators have infiltrated the system and hopeful signs have increased, but one suspects that the force of tradition and the bureaucratic might of the institutions will continue to prevent the military education system from being all that it could be.

As any officer above the rank of second lieutenant knows, our military's real education occurs in units and on their staffs, where doctrinal manuals are only consulted to ensure that a piece of paper has been paragraphed properly before being transmitted to higher headquarters.

Although the reality can be opaque to outsiders, the U.S. military is remarkably supple once it escapes the classroom—considering the institution's behemoth size and complexity. Frankly, we can continue to prosper under the current mediocre system of in-house military education as long as practical *training*, from infantry patrolling to flying combat aircraft, is superbly conducted. Talent, commitment, and field experience carry us through. Yet we could do far better. The problem is that, to construct an incisively useful military education system for the twenty-first century, we would need to discard most of the current system and start afresh. That would mean taking on hallowed traditions (the Army's C&GSC has its roots in the nineteenth century) and gutting deeply rooted bureaucracies. Iraq is easier.

What might a more effective in-service education look like? That depends on what we really need it to do.

At present, captains and above are taught dubious schoolhouse solutions to problems they have already faced and resolved under fire. The war colleges offer the potential to raise an officer's perspective to the strategic level, but faculties are trapped in dysfunctional twentieth-century theories of international relations and conflict (often in jealous emulation of their civilian campus peers). Unless he draws a strong, uniformed seminar leader, the officer may, indeed, learn a great deal at the war college: most of it wrong.

If you queried commanders in Iraq, Afghanistan, or else-where as to what additional skills would be of the greatest bene-fit to the officers under their command, you initially might get muddled answers. Their subordinate officers are already very good at the applied combat and support skills at which the U.S. military excels. You would have to calm them down a bit and press them, perhaps even leading the witness. Given time to think it over, thoughtful line-unit commanders probably would agree that nothing would give their officers a greater additional advantage than better language skills.

Anyone who has witnessed a lieutenant, captain, or lieu-tenant colonel interacting with Iraqis through an interpreter immediately grasps the problem: Even with the best hired help, information is filtered and nuances disappear. The officer may be as good as any combat leader in the world when it comes to combat, but he's crippled in his ability to read the signals that may be leading to a fight. As signals intelligence operators used to put it, he's condemned to "reading externals," making judg-ments based upon outward manifestations, as opposed to deci-phering the immediate human message.

While not every infantry officer can be trained as a fluent Ara-bic, Pashto, or Farsi speaker, nor should he be, the inability to com-municate and understand, to activate the magic that comes to those who master the opponent's language, leaves us in the role of eternal outsiders. The widespread dismissal of the importance of language skills for officers in command positions is simply aston-ishing given the nature of the conflicts we have faced in recent years and will likely face for decades to come. You will find hun-dreds of senior officers who have been immersed in theories of civil-military relations or (obsolete) deterrence models for each one who can construct a sentence in Arabic or Farsi (or Chinese, for that matter). But nothing could be more irrelevant to today's and tomorrow's enemies than Western theories of statecraft, while the language skills and cultural grasp that foster adroit (and swift) evaluations of the multidimensional conflict environment comprise, in military jargon, a major "combat multiplier."

Wars are won by officers who know the smell of the streets, not by those who swoon over the odor of political science texts. Under the press of tradition and inertia, we continue to train officers according to dreary patterns established decades or even centuries ago. Yet we have been selective (and often penny-wise, pound-foolish) about the educational traditions we chose to preserve: U.S. Army officers on the eve of the Civil War were far more likely to be able to read professional texts in at least one foreign language than their counterparts today. Our military education system for senior officers, especially, concentrates more energies on teaching them about Washington than on exposing them to the world beyond our shores; thus they rise through the system better prepared to fight for additional funding on Capitol Hill than to fight our enemies abroad.

If we could reform the in-house military education system to make it relevant to the requirements of the twenty-first century, it would first require a great sweeping away of the current system's deadwood. Military *leaders* need to set aside emotion and the force of habit to ask themselves honestly which current courses and institutions are a waste of time. If the issues are "staffed," the bureaucracies will always justify themselves. We need military-education reformers in uniform. Unfortunately, we're likeliest to get more sheep in wolves' clothing—the best description of today's general officers I can offer.

To get a sense of the current misplaced priorities, let us return for a moment to the issue of language skills. At present, language training goes overwhelmingly to enlisted personnel on the unspoken assumption that officers don't have time for that sort of triviality. And even the enlisted personnel who receive language training are almost always from the Military Intelligence Branch. Certainly, MI needs all the linguists it can get. But so do infantry companies—and platoons. Yet the few officers who do receive serious language training of sufficient length to allow conversational fluency are Foreign Area Officers (FAOs) destined for strategic or embassy assignments. While FAOs make an enormous contribution to our military, there are never enough of them to go around—and certainly not enough to beef up ground patrols in Baghdad or the badlands on Afghanistan's border with Pakistan.

The current military leadership—children of the Cold War still—simply cannot bring itself to take foreign language skills for line officers seriously. In a recent dinner conversation, a certain Army Chief of Staff agreed that, yeah, developing language skills is important—right, got it, sure. But it isn't a "wartime priority." Well, first, this struggle we are now in is going to be a very long one, and second, war is the *only* time when you really can change a military. In peacetime, the bureaucrats always win.

There are many other twenty-first-century skills that officers require, some of which are being learned the hard way. But the reluctance to send officers for language and cultural studies programs of serious length in lieu of other timewasting military-education programs (such as the Advanced Course or C&GSC) reflects institutional prejudice at its most hidebound and destructive. Consider how many American soldiers and Marines may have died in Iraq because their leaders didn't understand what the locals said or scrawled on a wall. Imagine how much more effective our forces might be if language skills were rewarded with increased promotion-board advantages (the crucial link in making any reform stick).

Of course, military officers needn't master every last tribal language, and could not do so in any case. We live at a time when the key languages officers should study are finite in number: Arabic, Farsi, Urdu, Chinese, Swahili, Spanish, African-French, Portuguese, Turkish, Russian, and a few others. And as all those who ever mastered a single foreign language know, the ability to live in another tongue opens new mental horizons transferable to still other cultural environments. Foreign language skills, taken seriously, teach us not only how to communicate, but how to think like the other side, how to see differently, and, sometimes, even how to feel differently. But instead of studying the world and how it communicates, we continue to teach officers how they should have formatted that staff report in their assignment before last.

The current status of in-house military education is suboptimal but bearable because even if it doesn't much help officers, it doesn't ruin them either. The graver problem is our habit of sending talented officers to "top" civilian universities, where their critical-thinking faculties are destroyed and their common sense is retarded. Can it be coincidental, after all, that across the half century during which the cult of higher civilian education for officers prospered, we have gone from winning wars to losing them?

The basic question regarding university and postgraduate education for military officers is, "How much is enough?" Certainly, every officer should have a four-year degree, without which he or she would not be sufficiently attuned to the broader frequencies of American society. For many officers, a master's degree or the equivalent makes sense, as well. But a Ph.D. is deadly (if not to the officer receiving it, then to his subordinates). I know of not a single troop-leading general—not one—whom I believe is a more effective combat commander because he holds a doctorate. On the contrary, too much formal education clouds a senior officer's judgment, inhibits his instincts, and slows his decisionmaking. I have watched with dismay the process of unlearning necessary for the too-cerebral officer to become the visceral killer any battlefield demands. For the better sort, war does eventually knock the Hamlet out of them, but at what interim price? Even Schopenhauer, hardly an illiterate, warned that an excess of theoretical knowledge obscures reality.

Certainly, we need *intelligent* generals. But we should fear *intellectual* generals. America won its wars largely by avoiding the soldier-butchering theories of warfare concocted by French and

German staff officers with too much time on their hands. Pragmatism is at the heart of America's cultural and economic success, and it long remained the key to our military success. When we began to theorize, we began to lose. In the military context, theory is a killer.

Theory kills both actively and passively. The horrific massacres perpetrated in the name of political theory in the twentieth century should be revelatory to officers with intellectual pretensions, but the lure of theory is simply irresistible to certain breeds of officers. Having pursued an active profession for decades, when suddenly exposed to the theoretical world they become enchanted with its novelty—like the new girlfriend who clouds the devoted husband's judgment. Ill-equipped to navigate the murky waters of theory, they jettison their common sense and the lessons of experience to doggy-paddle behind professors who couldn't swim in real world currents without dragging down every lifeguard in sight. You should never let any full-time university professor near any form of practical responsibility, and you should never let a rising officer near a professor.

My own experiences with officers who pursued doctoral degrees have ranged from the ludicrous to the horrifying. One lieutenant colonel, upon receiving his doctorate, took to smoking a bent-stem pipe and wearing a cardigan. I would've had him shot. Another, more recent experience with an officer who let his education pervert his judgment involved a discussion about how an Army doctrinal manual had gone so terribly wrong. A lieutenant colonel responded to an observation of mine by puffing himself up and beginning, "Speaking as a social scientist—"

"You're not a social scientist," I told him. "You're a soldier."

He looked startled. "Well, I'm a social scientist *and* a soldier."

"No. You can't be both. Which is it?"

To a lay reader, this conversation may strike no chords, but soldiering is a vocation akin to a religious calling. One may have other skills, but no soldier—no *real* soldier—would ever define himself first as a social scientist or as anything else. All else is secondary to the calling, and when the calling fades, it is the soldier's last duty to shed his uniform before shaming it.

The conversation got worse. The "social scientist" had published a book based on his academic work on campus. Having addressed mid-twentieth-century counterinsurgency operations, he was determined to apply "his" solutions to radically different twenty-first-century conflicts. In the best academic tradition, he had no intention of letting the facts interfere. Unfortunately, this officer had been tasked to write Army doctrine. The draft manual he produced was utterly out of touch with reality. Its irrelevance was the topic of our meeting.

Confronted with the utter nonsense the manual propounded, the officer was challenged to defend his winning-hearts-and-minds, don't-shoot, negotiate-with-the-sheikh-and-don't-hurt-his-feelings approach to defeating insurgents (one is compelled to add that the officer and his associates also honored the academic tradition of writing very badly). Pressed, the officer admitted, in front of several of his peers, that the most effective technique employed by the unit with which he had served in Iraq wasn't handing out soccer balls, but strapping dead insurgents across the front of their tanks and driving around for the locals to get a good look—after which the relatives had to come to the military base to ask for the bodies.

"Well, why isn't that in the manual, if that's what worked?" I asked.

It was a rhetorical question. The manual in question wasn't about defeating insurgents, but about political correctness.

The officer isn't a bad man nor even the worst sort of careerist—on the contrary, he's quite talented. But he was determined to defend his thesis to the end, no matter if we lost the struggle in Iraq. He couldn't see that his airy theorizing was going to get soldiers killed for nothing. He had compartmentalized the techniques that actually worked for him and his peers in Iraq from those which he knew the military and political establishment wanted to hear. No conscious decision was involved: This is what the campus had done to him.

The military's adulation of dead theorists at the expense of current experience would be laughable were it not costing the lives of our soldiers and Marines while failing to accomplish the missions assigned to our forces. Even the most talented general with a doctorate must go through the process of unlearning to rid himself of the last century's intellectual baggage, finally enabling himself to see "*das Ding an sich*," reality itself.

In speaking with officers during their classroom courses, I warn them that, when confronted with a reality that contradicts the theories they have studied at Harvard's John F. Kennedy School of Government, they should believe the reality. Most think I'm just making a joke, but I'm not. That officer who wrote dishonest doctrine to protect his dissertation's reputation had lost all perspective on his profession and his duty. In yet another hallowed academic tradition, he was determined to cram the vast complexity of the world into a neat theoretical briefcase.

Perhaps the most perverted romance of recent decades (Lord knows, that's quite a standard) is the love affair between the military and civilian academics. I challenge any reader to cite a single example of a social science professor's work contributing to any military victory. On the contrary, we have produced generations of officers so diseased with theory that some no longer possess the mental health to grasp the reality unfolding before them. It has been heartbreaking to watch our timid military leadership tie itself into knots in Iraq as it tried to wage the sort of conflict academics assured them was necessary. And then, for ill measure, the academics they revere solemnly warned the public that the generals they had castrated were an unruly threat to the republic. We had, simultaneously, generals who lacked the guts to tell the president the truth and stay-at-home academics who insinuated that coups were just around the corner. The contrast between cowering generals and crowing professors was surreal. And our troops died from the blindness, incompetence, and cowardice of leaders who knew everything except how to make war.

Worse, they didn't even know they were in a war. Many still don't. But the academics who seduced them with fairy-tale theories will prosper from writing texts explaining the failure of the generals.

Imagine how much better it would be to train an officer in a useful language and then launch him into a foreign country for a year to perfect his fluency, instead of sending him to Yale or Princeton. Not one of the generals and admirals who won our nation's wars had doctorates, but they often had extensive experience of the world beyond our shores.

A young George Marshall spent months inspecting Russo-Japanese War battlefields on the Asian mainland, while a not-yet-vinegary Joe Stillwell literally walked across China. Douglas MacArthur had long years of service in the Philippines before the first Japanese aircraft appeared over Luzon. Would they have served our country so well if their time had been spent on a campus instead of getting Asian dust on their boots?

Again, it's a question of the right level of education. A master's degree is useful because it broadens horizons, but a doctorate usually narrows them. Moreover, one should always be suspicious of a line officer willing to spend so much time away from troops. If he wants to spend his life pondering the modern astrology we term "social science," let him take off his uniform. Officers don't need to study elaborate theories of conflict resolution (none of which work, anyway). They need to know how to fight and win wars. They need to have the guts to do what it takes. Above all, they need integrity, which is a hallmark of good military units, but certainly not of the contemporary American campus.

Should we really send our future generals to Princeton, instead of shipping them off to Pakistan for six months or a year? If we are going to use tax dollars to send officers to graduate school, we should at least refuse ever to send them for degrees in political science or sociology. With special exceptions for officers destined for technical assignments, future leaders should study history, languages, and foreign cultures (a bit of anthropology, but light on the postmodernist mumbo-jumbo). In current practice, a master's degree in marketing counts as much for promotion purposes as does a degree in Middle Eastern studies. It's about the merit badge, not the merit.

The natural charge against the arguments advanced here is "anti-intellectualism." And the accusers would be exactly right. Our military should prize intelligence and broad learning, but should abhor intellectual posturing. At present, intellectual posturing trumps practical intelligence. Personally, I value the officer who painstakingly builds a library of cherished books, but fear the officer who revels in academic credentials. The most admirable general officer I've known—a brilliant man and a ferocious battlefield leader who also writes with unfashionable clarity—mocks the master's degree the Army forced him to get as worthless. He's a member of a dying breed.

Reading to aid thinking is a habit usually acquired early on. One of my favorite memories is of sitting in a cavernous classroom as an instructor droned on at Officer Candidate School and thinking myself awfully smart as I read a German translation of Solzhenitsyn under my desk—only to be humbled when I realized that the officer to my right was reading Tacitus in Latin, while the officer to my left was reading medieval poetry in French.

The issue of the future of military education, either within the services or on civilian campuses, comes down to what we expect of our military. If we want our generals and admirals to continue to lose wars while fearing to tell the president the truth, by all means continue with the present system. If, however, we imagine that we might want senior leaders who understand the real and dangerous world beyond our shores, who realize that wars are not won with good table manners, and who believe it their duty to tell the truth to our country's elected leaders, then it's time to stop trying to turn first-rate officers into third-rate academics.

What kind of men do we want to lead our military? Do we want generals who understand the importance of "a little touch of Harry in the night," or Hamlets who spend the night contemplating what they aren't going to do in the morning? Do we want battlefield leaders who inspire their men to "imitate the action of the tiger," as Henry V does before the walls of Harfleur, or do we prefer generals who wring their hands in the face of deadly enemies and ask, "To be, or not to be?" Now *that* is the question.

The Geezer Brigade

Armed Forces Journal

July 2007

In these years of relentless stress on our understrength Army and Marine Corps, one pool of talent foolishly goes unexploited: military retirees, the "Geezer Brigade," those of us who have career-long experience and retain the patriotic will to serve.

This isn't about mobilizations from the Individual Ready Reserve or involuntary recalls of any kind, all of which constitute an unjust and selective draft from those who've already contributed their share. On the contrary, a your-country-needs-you appeal to capable retirees to return to an innovative category of uniformed service would capitalize on the willing.

It's a contemporary cliché that "sixty is the new forty" in terms of fitness, lifestyle, and longevity. Although this may be something of an exaggeration intended to make baby boomers feel good about themselves (as if we aren't sufficiently self-satisfied), there's enough truth to the sound bite to merit a reconsideration of military personnel policies. At present, the personnel system's mandatory retirement age and term-of-service limits assume that physical health still matches profiles from the 1940s, when some of the earliest casualties of World War II were over-age officers who went down with heart attacks—while others simply proved unfit to lead.

Times have changed. The chain-smoking, whiskey-drinking generations of officers have given way to fitness buffs wary of cholesterol. In purely physical terms—and physical fitness reflects mental readiness—today's officers on the edge of retirement, as well as those who've already taken off their uniforms, are put out to pasture while they still have plenty of races left in them. At a time when we expect active-duty officers to serve ever-lengthening, successive tours of duty in combat zones, we're ignoring a chance to give them at least some slight relief.

Consider a few practical examples of how we waste expertise: Foreign Area Officers, no matter how successful, are forced out just when the foreign peers beside whom they studied and served are becoming chiefs of staff or defense ministers (or presidents) in their home governments. Officers who've mastered the arcane details of acquisition and program management are given no choice but to flip over to the dark side and use their knowledge to benefit the defense industry, rather than the troops or the taxpayers. And there's many a military intelligence colonel, lieutenant colonel, or master sergeant at the mandatory retirement point who could help pull the overloaded coach in Iraq or Afghanistan. Combat-arms officers who are years beyond the current punch-out point could help us in countless wartime jobs.

Reinventing the way in which we regard retired or about-to-retire officers and senior NCOs could provide us with one means to relieve the pressures on staffs in war zones or on the training base. (I do not envision re-greened retirees in command positions, but only in supporting roles that ease the commander's burden.) At present, skilled soldiers and Marines are lost to the system once their date of birth or years of service dictate. The manner in which we shrug off retirees as professionally dead and buried makes the government's response to Hurricane Katrina look like a model of efficient management.

Easy to say. But how might a new system of voluntary military service for retirees and end-of-career officers and senior NCOs actually look?

OX OFFICERS

As stated above, we would rely on volunteers, not on the double-jeopardy mistreatment of members of the IRR who have lost their taste for uniformed service or who cannot leave their new lives without making ruinous sacrifices. The goal is to attract those who retain the will and the ability to serve—a twenty-first-century version of FDR's "dollar-a-year" men (although we'd have to pay them a bit more than that).

Step one: a new rank. Offer these officers and senior non-commissioned officers a chance to wear the uniform again. That's the crucial bargaining chip. I cannot adequately stress my conviction that many who wouldn't dream of doing defense-related work for a private corporation would welcome a chance to resume the dignity of uniformed service—at a fraction of the salary offered by "the suits." At the same time, we don't want to clog the system with aging officers who block the progress of those still on the rise: We need an innovative approach to a rank structure that hasn't really changed since the eighteenth century.

At present, we assume that any officers brought back to active duty must be reinstated in their old rank (or in a higher rank, at the discretion of the president). Who says? What we need, rather, is a new sidecar rank specifically for retirees who volunteer for a year's reactivation and for those officers and senior NCOs who elect—and deserve—to remain on duty beyond the present mandatory retirement limits. We may choose a different term, but, for now, let's just call the new rank "auxiliary officer," or (inevitably) the "ox."

Congress would have to approve both the new twenty-first-century rank and the necessary funding. It seems reasonable to assume we could easily gain Capitol Hill's backing for a $50 million pilot program (less than the cost of a single defense-conglomerate CEO's retirement package) as long as we didn't mind seeing it saddled with an earmark for a $500 million pogo-stick research facility to be located in, say, Johnstown, Pennsylvania.

The only way to make such a system work would be to create a single new rank to stand apart from the current promotion ladder. Whether the retired or about-to-retire volunteer was a master sergeant or a lieutenant colonel, a sergeant major, or a major general, his ox rank would be identical to all others. Every ox would wear the standard duty uniform and the badge of his special rank but would be available for a wide range of responsibilities and missions—at the commander's discretion and in accordance with unit needs.

Ox service should be in voluntary increments of one year, because those who have built successful civilian careers can be asked to serve no longer—although those who wish to continue to serve might remain in uniform if their performance merits it.

Ox officers would work on staffs or in specialized positions and take their orders from officers who hold the rank of lieutenant colonel or above, although their work might be managed by qualified majors or captains. They would not command, except in emergencies when no regular officers at the rank of captain or higher were present. Out of respect for their previous ranks, they would be required to salute only colonels and above, or lieutenant colonels in command positions, and would receive salutes from all other soldiers. And yes, that means that former senior NCOs would get the same treatment and returned-to-service rank as retired generals (knowing retirees of every eligible rank, I don't think it would be a problem, because most retirees get over the active-service rank differentiations quickly—and those who don't wouldn't volunteer, anyway).

Why mention so minor a point as who salutes whom so early in this proposal or make ox officers salute at all? Actually, it's critical. You have to make these volunteers feel like soldiers and Marines again, to make it clear that they're full-fledged members of the Corps or Army team. The pride and dignity of a return to military service would appeal to such men and women far more than money could, and the surest way to kill the program would be to treat those who've built (often remarkably) successful careers on the outside as Christmas help in Baghdad or Kabul.

Unlike those who sign up with private contractors, ox officers would be fully subject to the Uniform Code of Military Justice. But it's safe to assume they would create fewer disciplinary problems than any other class of service member ("OK, men–empty your pockets and dump your Viagra in the amnesty box."). They would have to meet appropriate fitness standards and would have to look like soldiers. And we would need to be certain that personal health concerns would not cost the system more than an individual's contributions merited. But forget age as the decisive indicator: Today, a sixty-five-year-old who maintains pride in his person might be healthier and more energetic than a forty-five-year-old who stacked arms the day he took off his combat boots.

Speaking of costs: Just as there should be only one rank for all volunteers, pay should be identical for all. Maximum-rate O-5 pay is probably right, although O-6 pay would still give the nation an incredible bargain. And, recognizing that retirees who entered other service professions upon retirement from the military won't have accumulated the same levels of wealth as those who went into the business world, don't touch the retired pay they receive. This would still be one of the best deals the taxpayer would ever get. Except for a few weeks of in-processing and cram-course updates on new systems at use in their branch, there would be no training overhead. After just a month in the field, ox officers would be full contributors to the units in which they served.

Nor do I think we'd see many know-it-alls ("Back in my day, we used to . . . "); on the contrary, the sort of retired soldier or Marine who would volunteer would be humble in the face of today's professionalism and, if anything, would go to excessive lengths to avoid the "And there I was . . . " syndrome. If anything, ox officers, with their long and varied experiences in and out of uniform, would be more likely to provide emotional ballast during periods of crisis (and given that they have no prospect of further promotion, they'd be inclined to tell the truth to the chain of command).

And if any ox officers fail to measure up, for any reason, out they go. A review at the six-month mark would determine whether their good intentions just weren't enough to imbue their service with practical value.

Oh, and you wouldn't have to force them into war zones. They'd volunteer—although, unlike more expensive contractors, they could be ordered to execute any required mission. There's simply no one so useful in a combat zone as a real soldier or Marine who has taken his oath.

Again, I may be naive. But I believe that if the country called such men and women, we would find that there are thousands of them and they would answer the call, at least at the rate of several hundred a year. Consider how useful even a few hundred experienced veterans might be, were they deployed to augment staffs and support units in Iraq or Afghanistan. Some active-duty officers or senior NCOs might get to spend a full twelve months at home with their families—and those who didn't might at least get a little sleep.

We have so many skilled retirees going to waste in wartime—men and women with sophisticated skills in logistics, intelligence, planning, administration, and security—that it only makes sense to ask them whether they'd be willing to give one more piece of their lives to our country's military, to spend one more year away from their families in a time of national need. Some won't answer, while others will find that, for personal reasons, they can't answer. But we are foolish not to issue the call and find out.

PRIDE IN THE MISSION

Essential to making this work would be to give ox officers meaningful work and to involve them in serious missions. We don't need retired colonels to make coffee or sergeant majors to sit around answering the phone. To borrow half of a term from our old enemies: "From each, according to his abilities." If foolish staff principals regarded such men and women simply as duty bodies, the program would fall apart. They must be given appropriate levels of responsibility (not authority—responsibility). Put bluntly, they would need to be challenged, not treated as some well-meaning old coots. You can't expect men or women to leave jobs in the private sector in which they're making six-figure incomes and going home to the good life every night to sit on their butts in Baghdad drinking Gatorade and counting the days.

How could we make sure the program proved both worthwhile and efficient? First, don't just assign these volunteers blindly or as individual replacements (with some exceptions—there are always exceptions). Form them into groups, from squad size to platoon size, destined for specific units. We all know that team spirit matters, that ineffable sense of belonging. Time their activation to coincide with scheduled unit deployments (most would serve at division level or higher, although some could be deployed down to brigade if their overall fitness and skill levels were suitable).

And don't just ship them off to Unit X. Ask the deploying units if they actually want such augmentation and how they would use their oxen. Ask the unit what it believes it needs and make certain that the commander values this no-cost support (most commanders would view such an augmentation as a godsend). Then the unit should welcome them in as full members of the family—no matter how busy he might be, a wise CG would personally hand each re-greened retiree his unit patch. (In Baghdad last year, I was impressed by the way Col. Tom Vail, then commanding the 506th Brigade Combat Team, made all attached and supporting personnel feel that they were full-fledged Currahees—the heightened morale was worth an extra battalion.)

On a practical level, these teams of now-active retirees would be dispersed throughout the gaining unit's staff and subordinate commands, and the ox officers would need a go-to guy or gal at the unit headquarters to oversee their utilization. So, acknowledging human vanity, anoint the officer who held the highest active-duty rank as the unit's "Master Auxiliary Officer" (the "Big Ox," but with no difference in pay). The highest-ranking NCO (or a volunteer from among the oxen) would serve as the team's administrator (probably the toughest job of all, given the nature of our military's bureaucracy).

I can't believe that any commander in the field would turn down the opportunity to gain an additional 40 or 60 or 100 skilled and screened retirees that he could allocate across his corps or division or training effort to reduce the burdens his Marines and soldiers bear. And the importance of deploying most of these volunteers to war zones cannot be overstated: If you wish to persuade them to volunteer, such men and women would need to know they would contribute to the war effort in a direct and meaningful way that justified their personal sacrifices; paradoxically, promising them that they would not be deployed outside of the United States would be a disincentive for the very best retired officers.

Of course, such a program wouldn't solve all of our personnel shortages or the system's many woes—but it could help our troops, who deserve all the support they can get. Shouldn't we at least try it? Even if such a program failed, the cost would be a tiny fraction of what we waste daily on hiring staff mercenaries from contractors.

Patriotism is alive and well among military retirees—although the system's done its best to kill it.

Enlisting new soldiers or Marines for a single year would be an utter waste. But one additional year of service from still-qualified retirees could make a genuine contribution to our war effort. You don't get just a year of service, but the skills and, yes, wisdom accumulated in twenty or thirty years of wearing the uniform. Imagine if a conscientious retiree, rather than an equal-opportunity hire, had been in charge of the Abu Ghraib facility in its fateful period.

For their part, the Army and Marine Corps would need to keep the program streamlined and efficient (and, for the love of Christ, Moses, and Mohammed, don't hire a contractor to manage it—which would be an insult to the entire concept). And we also would have to be willing to admit it, in four or five years, if the program turned out to be a bust. The entire effort would have to be cost-efficient and could not be allowed to become an employment option of last resort for retirees who regarded it as a glorified welfare ticket: The point would not be to serve retirees who need jobs—on the contrary, we need successful men and women, the sort who made things happen in uniform and continued to make things happen after they retired.

Far more details would need to be hammered out. But there is no practical reason why such a program could not be designed swiftly and inaugurated with sufficient speed to take at least a bit of the burden off our troops. Retirees aren't going to win these conflicts for us. But given the chance to do their parts, they could help in fields ranging from staff planning and intelligence analysis, through automation management, to serving as impartial investigating officers, gathering lessons learned, or representing the commander as a liaison with host-nation elements. The best retirees would rise to the missions assigned to them—and wouldn't complain if those missions fell short of the prestige they enjoyed in their previous service.

Many of us would welcome the opportunity to serve our country in such a capacity. But the current system tells us that we're worthless.

I would pose only one caveat: If the heraldry folks design a gray-on-gray Geezer Brigade patch with crossed crutches over a wheelchair, we ain't coming.

Bribing Troops to Quit

New York Post

October 6, 2007

The problems with military outsourcing go far beyond last month's massacre of civilians by Blackwater USA's hired guns: Wartime profiteers are bleeding our military.

Astonishingly, contractors are free to approach those in uniform, offer them generous salaries to leave their service in wartime, and then profit from the skills your tax dollars taught them.

This isn't just about Navy SEALS or other special operators. In intelligence, for example, we train young soldiers for complex missions and expensively process their security clearances—then contractors bribe them to leave the military, raking in big bucks from your investment in their new employee.

Maybe we could look the other way in peacetime. But we're fighting multiple wars. Would we have allowed contractors to hire away some of the most highly skilled men and women in uniform during World War II? (Of course, most lawmakers really were patriots then. . . .)

It's fundamentally wrong to let contractors go head-hunting among our troops in wartime. Those in government who've elevated outsourcing to a state religion pretend it helps our war effort—with the whopper that outsourcing military functions saves taxpayer dollars.

Exactly how does that one work? You get stuck with the training and security-clearance costs; the soldier lured to the private sector gets his salary doubled or tripled—then the contractor adds in a markup for his multiple layers of overhead costs and a generous profit margin, and bills the taxpayers. How is that cheaper than having soldiers do the job?

The scam artists tell us that using contractors saves money in the long run, since their employees don't get military health care and retirement benefits. But the numbers just don't add up.

Contractors are looting our military—while wrapping themselves in the flag.

Thankfully, the finest soldiers and Marines aren't in it for the money. But we're still losing personnel with vital in-demand skills.

Here's how one disgusted special-ops veteran puts it:

"I got tired of old SF buddies handing me their business cards as I exited the dining facility in Iraq [and] asking me to come over and work for them. I'll go teach high school English in the inner city first."

In a follow-up message, this veteran—who's sticking by the colors—wrote:

"The saddest thing I see in those 'flesh peddlers' is the part of the conversation when they admit that they really miss the unit and the people in it. A true warrior isn't in it for the money, but, rather, for those things that money can never buy: mutual respect, camaraderie, and the self-worth that comes with it.

"Every one of my contractor 'buddies' eventually breaks down and admits these things to me. Unfortunately, they can also pick up on a malcontent quickly, therefore acquiring the 'easy sale.'"

The disgraceful cycle works like this: Contractors hire away military talent. The military finds itself short of skilled workers, so contractors get more contracts. With more money, they hire away more uniformed talent.

Here's what we need to do to right a wrong that borders on treason:

- Congress must defy its campaign contributors and criminalize attempts to hire those in uniform away from their service during periods of war and conflict.
- If a service member put in a full twenty years or more and retired, he or she should be free to take a job with any law-abiding firm. But any soldier short of twenty who accepts specialized training and a security clearance at government expense should have to wait two years after his or her discharge before moving to a related private-sector position.
- Defense contractors who hire young veterans with advanced skills or security clearances should have to reimburse the government 50 percent of their training and background investigation costs.

The current system is intolerable. The problem, of course, is Congress. Although the Hill is halfway to approving stateside prosecutions for criminal conduct by government contractors abroad, your representatives only did so because they were caught out by the Blackwater scandal.

The truth is that most members of Congress, Republican or Democrat, will favor a contractor who pays in campaign contributions over soldiers who pay with their lives.

We saw classic congressional behavior last week, when Blackwater founder Erik Prince testified on the Hill and set a new standard for smugness. A solid Republican phalanx defended a major contributor. The Dems, who failed to do their homework on the issues, looked stupidly partisan themselves—just harassing a GOP donor.

And Prince got away with his shameless claims that he and his trigger-happy thugs are true-blue patriots. If so, why hire talent away from our military in wartime? Why give heavy weapons to under-supervised "malcontents," endangering our battlefield progress?

And if the independently wealthy Prince is so patriotic, why not provide Blackwater's services to the government on a no-profit basis?

Well, Blackwater ain't no red-white-and-blue charity, and Prince isn't one of FDR's dollar-a-year men. The company lacked serious credentials when it landed its first security contract—and one suspects it would never have been hired if not for Prince's campaign contributions and political connections.

People like Erik Prince aren't patriots. They're vampires sucking the blood of our troops—war profiteers growing rich while soldiers die.

We didn't just outsource services in Iraq. We outsourced our nation's honor.

Dishonest Doctrine

Armed Forces Journal

December 2007

A year after its publication, the Army and Marine Corps counterinsurgency manual remains deeply disturbing, both for the practical dangers it creates and for the dishonest approach employed to craft it.

The most immediate indication of the manual's limitations has been Army Gen. David Petraeus's approach to counterinsurgency in Iraq. The manual envisions COIN operations by that Age of Aquarius troubadour, Donovan, wearing his love like heaven as he proceeds to lead terrorists, insurgents, and militiamen to a jamboree at Atlantis. Although the finalized document did, ultimately, allow that deadly force might sometimes be required, it preached—beware doctrine that preaches—understanding, engagement, and chat. It was a politically correct document for a politically correct age.

Entrusted with the mission of turning Iraq around, Petraeus turned out to be a marvelously focused and methodical killer, able to set aside the dysfunctional aspects of the doctrine he had signed off on. Given the responsibility of command, he recognized that, when all the frills are stripped away, counterinsurgency warfare is about killing those who need killing, helping those who need help—and knowing the difference between the two (we spent our first four years in Iraq striking out on all three counts). Although Petraeus has, indeed, concentrated many assets on helping those who need help, he grasped that, without providing durable security—which requires killing those who need killing—none of the reconstruction or reconciliation was going to stick. On the ground, Petraeus has supplied the missing kinetic half of the manual.

The troubling aspect of all this for the Army's intellectual integrity comes from the neo-Stalinist approach to history a number of the manual's authors internalized during their pursuit of doctorates on "the best" American campuses. Instead of seeking to analyze the requirements of counterinsurgency warfare rigorously before proceeding to draw impartial conclusions based on a broad array of historical evidence, they took the academic's path of first setting up their thesis, then citing only examples that supported it.

To wit, the most over-cited bit of nonsense from the manual is the claim that counterinsurgency warfare is only 20 percent military and 80 percent political. No analysis of this indefensible proposition occurred. It was quoted because it suited the preformulated argument. Well, the source of that line was Gen. Chang Ting-chen, one of Mao's less-distinguished subordinates. Had the authors bothered to look at Mao's writings, they would have read that "political power grows out of the barrel of a gun," that "whoever wants to seize and retain state power must have a strong army," and that "only with guns can the whole world be transformed."

Sorry, but Mao didn't believe that round-table discussions were a substitute for killing his enemies, party purges, mass executions, and the Cultural Revolution. Mao believed in force. In our COIN manual, he's presented as a flower child.

Anyone looking objectively at the situation in Iraq could hardly claim that it's only 20 percent military and 80 percent diplomatic. Even the State Department doesn't really believe that one—or they would've kept a tighter leash on their private security contractors.

Wishful thinking doesn't defeat insurgencies. Without the will to establish and maintain security for the population, nothing else works.

The manual's worth revisiting a bit longer to underscore the dishonesty of the selective use of history. Citing a narrow range of past insurgencies—all ideological, all comparatively recent—the authors carefully ignored parallel or earlier examples that would've undercut their position. For example, the British experience in Malaya is cited ad nauseam (although it's portrayed as far less bloody than it was in fact), but the same decade saw a very different and even more successful British campaign against the Mau Mau insurgency in Kenya. After realizing (a bit ploddingly) that the Mau Mau could not be controlled by colonial police forces, the British took a tough-minded three-track approach: concentration camps for more than one hundred thousand Kenyans; hanging courts that sent more than one thousand Mau Mau activists and sympathizers to the gallows; and relentless military pursuits that tracked down the hardcore insurgents and killed them. It worked. A few years later, British rule ended in Kenya—but only because Britain had decided to give up its empire. And the thousands of British citizens who remained behind in Kenya weren't massacred.

However, citing the British experience in Kenya wouldn't have been politically correct—no matter that it worked after gentler methods had failed. The COIN manual's authors weren't concerned with winning but with defending their dissertations.

DOES IT MATTER?

An apocryphal anecdote from World War II has a German staff officer expressing his frustration that American commanders don't know their own doctrine. Recently, a retired officer and friend argued that doctrine really only matters for us in terms of the atmospherics, the outlook, that it shapes. Well, if that's so, the dishonest atmosphere propagated by that COIN manual is profoundly troubling as a warning of problems to come.

The Army and Marine Corps in Iraq have already moved beyond the manual's grossest limitations, and the document will be rewritten in a few years, so we may be able to shrug off its core contention that the best reply to a terrorist is a big, wet kiss. We had better be concerned, though, about the implications for the next round of doctrine-writing on other military subjects. Can we afford to have future drafting teams employ the same dishonest techniques, allowing the use only of historical examples that support predetermined theses? Must our manuals be politically correct? Don't we care about the truth, about winning, about giving our soldiers and Marines doctrinal tools that keep them alive while helping them kill their enemies?

The formulation of doctrine isn't about persuasion. It's about evidence. If a doctrinal proposition cannot withstand the force of countervailing examples, it's a bad idea. Historical examples and vignettes have a valid, useful place in doctrine: They can serve to illustrate why a commander made a decision or how a particular technique worked in the field. Inevitably, some selectivity comes into play, because no manual can contain all of humankind's military history. But the examples employed must serve honest ends, and they must be counterbalanced, when appropriate. In short, it's fine to cite Malaya as an example of one variety of COIN operation, but it's unacceptable to imply that all counterinsurgency situations will mimic Malaya. You've got to cite Mau Mau, too.

And what about the Moros, the Islamist fanatics in the Philippines who only succumbed to U.S. Army Gatling guns? The bloodiness of that campaign didn't suit the authors of the manual, so the details of one of our own most challenging and ultimately most successful counterinsurgency efforts were glossed over—the facts would've undercut the manual's argument.

Education, clearly, is not synonymous with intellectual integrity. Doctrine should be written by successful battlefield commanders, not by doctors of philosophy playing soldier.

MYTHMAKING AND MONKEY BUSINESS

From ancient Greece through the contemporary Middle East, leaders and peoples have rewritten history to suit them. Historians all too often contributed to the disinformation, whether it was Edward Gibbon, whose lack of firsthand experience with Islam left him intoxicated with Muhammad and his ghazis, or the ludicrous Paul Kennedy, who, on the eve of the Soviet Union's collapse, published a ballyhooed book arguing that it was the United States that was about to go under. We in the West have molested the historical facts to create national myths from Belgrade to Moscow and on to Edinburgh. We've twisted the facts to advance political agendas, claiming either that colonialism was an unalloyed evil or that the future belonged to militant socialism or that Iraq is worse than Vietnam (a proposition that fifty thousand dead Americans would challenge, if they could).

Robust societies can afford a good bit of such monkey business, but selective mythmaking can lead fragile societies to disaster. And no military can afford to indulge in the selective use of history. Soldiers must seek the truth.

Intellectual integrity is ultimately more important to the doctrine writer than intellect itself. The formulation of doctrine has to be an act of selfless service, not the construction of a personal monument. If our military is unwilling to face the most troubling evidence history offers, it would be better served by swearing off the use of history entirely.

Of course, not all doctrine writers are intellectually corrupt. But a final difficulty we have with the use of historical examples to illustrate or underscore doctrine is that most of us have so few of them in our mental catalog. The study of history isn't a matter of a year or two on a campus to get a piece of paper and a personnel-file notation. For an officer, the immersion in history in the broadest sense must be a lifelong pursuit. Beware the officer who reads just a little and falls in love with a single book (say, *Seven Pillars of Wisdom*). He'll cite that book as if quoting from the Gospels, and he'll insist on its relevance even when the problem facing him is of a profoundly different nature.

We'd be better off having our military doctrine written by officers with no historical knowledge than by those with just a few narrow areas of interest: A little knowledge truly is a dangerous thing.

Of course, the best situation would be to have doctrine drafted by veterans who possess a broad sense of history—and who have no personal theories to validate at the expense of our men and women in uniform. But there ain't enough of that commodity to go around.

It's hard to have much hope, given the deplorable state of history studies at every educational level. Wars have been banished from the K-12 curriculum, while universities, determined to discard the West's intellectual advantages, insist on taking as selective an approach to history as any band of Islamist terrorists (to say nothing of their similar interpretations of the past).

But our military can't afford to make excuses. We have to get our doctrine right—both because it helps us fight effectively and because it explains to civilian decisionmakers what it is that soldiers do. If doctrine creates false expectations, those decisionmakers will make flawed choices—and those in uniform will pay the price.

Better no doctrine than bad doctrine. Better no history than bad history. The saving grace of our military—historically—has been pragmatism. Unlike European generals, we never sent our soldiers to die for a theory (at least, not until Operation Iraqi Freedom). If our own history has a lesson for those responsible for military doctrine, it's that the only admissible criterion is that the doctrine has to work.

Dethroning the King

Armchair General

November 2008

The U.S. Army appears determined to cripple itself. Cuts in field artillery strength promise to weaken the "king of battle" to the point where the Army will have sacrificed its greatest historical advantage: the ability to put a storm of steel precisely on target faster than the enemy can react.

Midlevel officers with combat experience have taken aim at this crisis in the Army, but so far, their salvos have had no apparent effect on the leadership. Meanwhile, gunners are pressed into infantry roles in Iraq, thanks to the "peace dividend" shortage of grunts. Artillery skills are plummeting, while doctrine veers ever deeper into fantasies of precision strikes by airpower as the universal answer.

Why would the Army throw away its killing power? Because nearsighted senior officers and inexperienced civilians don't believe we need killing power anymore. They're convinced that from now on our conflicts will be all counterinsurgency, all the time. Yup, they're already fighting the last war again, and the last war isn't even over yet.

The Army can't prepare only for asymmetrical warfare against terrorists and insurgents. It has to be able to walk and chew gum at the same time—to fight irregulars today and be prepared for the big, hyper-conventional war that might come tomorrow.

Having spent much of the 1990s arguing that the Army's focus solely on conventional operations left us vulnerable to threats from an asymmetrical "new warrior class" ranging from Islamist terrorists to narco-militias, I now find myself obliged to holler, "OK, enough's enough! We have to maintain a balance. There's more to our national defense than hunting roadside bombs!"

The U.S. Army simply doesn't have, and never will have, the luxury of preparing for just one form of conflict. However remote a conventional war might appear today, we must be ready for that "impossible" war.

The stock answer these days is that the Air Force will be the Army's "flying artillery," hitting targets precisely with low-yield warheads and reducing collateral damage. That's not merely foolish, it's nuts. In a conflict between major powers, it may be the collateral damage that ultimately forces the enemy to surrender (remember Japan?).

In a *real* war—a long slugging match—the new generation of Air Force fighter-bombers would be confined to bunkers for heavy maintenance within weeks. There won't be enough of these planes, either. In a serious conflict with a power such as China, precision strikes would accomplish even less than "shock and awe" did in Baghdad.

You can't just impress an enemy into surrendering. You have to *defeat* him.

In a major fight, U.S. forces would exhaust their reserves of precision munitions within a few months—and Americans couldn't build replacements fast enough. As for aircraft, we're going to lose plenty, and we now face the reverse dilemma of World War II, when we could build fighters or bombers faster than we could train crews. Despite the greater complexity of flying in the twenty-first century, we can now train pilots much faster than we can build aircraft.

We can't send our troops into battle without deep reserves of robust killing power, and artillery long has been America's strong suit. From the brilliant use of "flying" batteries in the war with Mexico through World War II, when our gunners were the finest in the world, to Vietnam, where artillery saved countless American lives, our troops could go into battle confident that all our nation's strength was behind them as the redlegs yanked their lanyards.

We won't always be chasing snipers down Baghdad's alleys. When the next "big one" comes, our soldiers on the front lines had better be able to call for responsive, overwhelming fires—in all weather, in all terrain. If we're unwilling to pay the price in steel, we'll pay it in blood.

Watch: Any further cuts to artillery assets.

Crisis Watch Bottom Line: Slashing field artillery units may be the dumbest organizational decision ever made by the U.S. Army. Killing power matters.

Fighting Words

Armed Forces Journal

October 2008

If our troops shot as wildly as our politicians and bureaucrats fire off words, we'd never win a single firefight. The inaccurate terminology tossed about by presidents and pundits alike obscures the nature of the threats we face, the character of our enemies, and the inadequacies of our response. If we cannot, or will not, label our opponents, their cause, and their motivations correctly, how can we forge an efficient and effective national strategy?

Let's begin with the most-abused word in Washington, "ideology." Flocks of Potomac parrots in Brooks Brothers suits tell us, again and again, that we're in a "war of ideologies," or a "contest of ideologies" with the terrorists we face. The speakers—not one of whom seems to have thought the issue through—appear to believe that ideology can be used as a pleasant euphemism for religious fervor, that ideology has been with us since the days of cave paintings and really bad hair days, and, oddest of all, that we ourselves are fighting for an ideology.

In fact, political ideologies are a relatively new phenomenon in the bloody pageant of history. If you open Samuel Johnson's dictionary, published in London in 1755 (and still my favorite dictionary), you will not find the word "ideology." The term first appears as "ideologie" in 1796, in Paris, in the noisy aftermath of

the French revolution. The word and what it represents are products of the madly misnamed Age of Reason, when human beings
discovered vast new horizons of causes about which they could
behave unreasonably.

How does the current *Oxford English Dictionary* define "ideology"? The pertinent entry runs as follows: "A system of ideas or
way of thinking pertaining to a class or individual, esp. as a basis
of some economic or political theory or system, regarded as justi-
fying actions and esp. to be maintained irrespective of events."
That's a fine definition of communism, Maoism, Nazism, fascism,
anarcho-syndicalism, Trotskyism, Fourierism, and on through the
-ism of the individual malcontent's choice. However, it does not
describe Islamist fanatics determined to sacrifice their lives to
honor their god.

Religion is a deeper, far more enduring factor than ideology.
Ideologies come and go, often making quite a mess along the
way, but the remarkable thing about successful religions—those
that survive over millennia—is their galvanizing resilience. They
may evolve or devolve, adapt or mutate grotesquely, but they last
and continue to inspire. In historical terms, ideologies are closer
to fads, to deadly hula hoops. Religion, on its mundane side,
may develop subordinate ideologies—such as liberation theol-
ogy or other passing militancies—but no ideology has ever produced a religion.

Religion and ideology are essentially antithetical. Religion is
not "a system of ideas," but a matter of faith subduing and transcending reason. Religion may give birth to ideas, but ideas
never give birth to a religion. So our devout enemies—and they
are, indeed, devout—are not engaged in a battle of ideas or ideologies with us. They are driven by unreasoning faith, by passion, by furies, by a perverted vision of eternity.

And what about us? Are we fighting for an ideology? Absolutely not. Democracy isn't an -ism. Democracy is a technique of
human governance that uses the tool of elections. In the United

States, ideologies in their true sense only exist on the extreme margins of the political spectrum (where they belong, to the extent they belong anywhere). We are not fighting for an American ideology. There's no American equivalent of Marxism or fascism, and we should be very glad of it. We're fighting to defend our values.

Now, the relevant definition of "values" from the *Oxford English Dictionary* is: "The principles or moral standards of a person or social group; the generally accepted or personally held judgment of what is valuable and important in life."

The "American way of life" and the values that have made it a success are a matter of national consensus that transcends our individual differences; an ideology is the opposite of a consensus approach to society—it's dictated, one way or the other. Our consensus has developed organically, by trial and error. Ideology is artificial, constructed by an individual or small group and foisted on a society. There is no American ideology with its *Das Kapital*, Mao's *Little Red Book*, or *Mein Kampf*. The nature of this confrontation—between the all-or-nothing religious fanaticism driving our enemies and the cherished values motivating us, between a merciless interpretation of a god's will and an ongoing experiment in human freedom—is yet another asymmetrical aspect of postmodern conflict.

If we were simply in a duel of ideologies, our task would be a lot easier.

THE TIMELESS FANATIC

We desperately want our enemies to be reasonable, to operate from motives we can nail down neatly and explain without too much discomfort. But religious extremists are, by definition, not reasonable. The fanatic is driven by faith in a greater reality than that which our senses identify in our waking hours. And what is faith? I know of no better definition for our purposes than that proposed three centuries ago by Jonathan Swift and cited in Johnson's magisterial dictionary:

"Faith is an entire dependence upon the truth, the power, the justice, and the mercy of God; which dependence will certainly incline us to obey him in all things."

In other words, there is no truth but your god's truth, no power comparable to his and his is the only justice, while mercy is also his alone. Above all, faith is not to reason, but to obey "in all things."

Unlike political ideologues, religious fanatics have been with us since the infancy of history. For Johnson, a "fanatick" was "a man mad with wild notions of religion," while the *Oxford English Dictionary* defines a "fanatic" as "a mad person; a religious maniac." Those seem rather more appropriate descriptions of men who saw the heads off living prisoners to please their god or who walk into a marketplace crowded with fellow believers and detonate a suicide bomb.

Nonetheless, various U.S. government outlets and agencies, from military publications through intelligence organizations, have been discouraged or forbidden outright from bringing religion into their analysis of our enemies, or from using terms such as "Islamist terrorist," because we would rather avoid giving the least offense than accurately describe the ambitious murderers we face. It's a bit like banning the word "Nazi" when describing Hitler.

Political correctness has no place in the intelligence world and no place in (what should be) hard-headed government documents. If your enemy declares himself an Islamist and your enemy is a terrorist self-avowedly motivated by his religion, then it hardly seems unjust to describe him as an "Islamist terrorist."

Nor does political correctness infect only the left. The conservative version simply obsesses on different terms. For example, some well-meaning (and some downright nutty) Internet activists on the right have argued that we should never use the terms "jihad" or "jihadi" when referring to al Qa'eda, the Taliban, and their ilk. In a bizarre confluence, those on the hard right find themselves sharing common ground with the extreme left, both agreeing that "jihad" isn't really about war at all, but about an unarmed personal struggle (somewhere between morning-after guilt and a bowel obstruction).

This is nonsense. A personal struggle is an anomalous and far lesser form of jihad. Since the first conquering Arab armies exploded out of the desert thirteen centuries ago, "jihad" has consistently described warfare waged on behalf of the faith. Were the hand-wringers to inspect the historical record, they would find "jihad" used from the start to describe campaigns against unbelievers, against schismatic Muslims, against Crusaders, against Byzantines, against Slavs, Austrians, Hindus, the British, the French, Americans in the Philippines, the Israelis, the Soviets, and, now, the West in general. An armed struggle waged on behalf of the faith of the Prophet is a jihad. Period.

Nor is there a supreme terrestrial authority who can give a jihad the thumbs up or thumbs down: jihad is practically "every mullah for himself." While only the Pope could declare a Crusade in the pre-Reformation West, Islam is not only divided between Sunni and Shi'a, but is a semi-anarchic collection of diffuse institutions that seldom agree on much. When it suits their whims, the Saudi royal family may be able to influence domestic clerics to declare a given jihad invalid, but that won't stop Islamist extremists who view the entire Saudi establishment as corrupt and illegitimate. If a cleric of middling standing can persuade a sufficient number of people to launch a jihad, it's a jihad. And those who wage it are jihadis.

The notion that non-Muslims have sufficient authority to declare that jihadis aren't real jihadis reaches heights of absurdity rarely encountered outside of the House of Representatives. Do we really think that the Muslims of the Middle East hang on the words of our domestic pundits? If an American scholar of Anglo-Saxon heritage writes a carefully footnoted article "proving" that al Qa'eda isn't engaged in a jihad and that its members don't conform to classical Koranic values, can we really believe that al Qa'eda gives a damn? If a Saudi, Egyptian, or Iranian authority declared that our soldiers and Marines fighting in Iraq and Afghanistan were not true Christians, just how seriously would we take it? We're babbling for our own consumption—our enemies are not impressed. The terrorist enemies we face view themselves as jihadis and they are viewed as jihadis by many millions of Muslims (even by many who don't approve of their actions—just as our domestic left accepts that a Marine is a Marine, like him or not).

The inability or unwillingness to speak clearly generally arises from the inability or unwillingness to think clearly. Our slovenly use of terminology—whether from intellectual sloth, political correctness, or both—is a serious obstacle to understanding our enemies and fighting them effectively. We continually describe the enemies we want to face, rather than those who are determined to kill as many of us as possible.

If we lack the judgment and courage to speak plainly, where shall we find the strength to defeat men of such passion and will as those jihadis? No enemy has ever been defeated by a heavy barrage of euphemisms.

Good Dr. Johnson, who understood the value of specificity as well as any English-speaking man, gives us this definition of "folly": "Act of negligence or passion unbecoming gravity or deep wisdom."

Our official blasts of inaccurate terminology are folly, indeed. But that negligence only masks Washington's deeper foolishness—the refusal to think honestly.

Learning from Georgia

Armchair General

March 2009

Last August, a resurgent Russia won a swift victory over tiny, democratic Georgia. Sticking with tradition, Moscow relied on mass. The "new" Russian military couldn't use its precision weapons effectively; its combined arms coordination was poor; pilots flying the latest aircraft couldn't hit their targets with smart bombs; and the Black Sea Fleet could only deploy a five-ship squadron. On the ground, lawless Chechen mercenaries did Prime Minister Putin's dirtiest dirty work.

The United States was powerless to stop any of it.

Setting aside the question of whether a military response would have been appropriate, the core issue facing our military had already arisen, in another variant, in Afghanistan.

Had we wanted to counter Russia's move militarily, we literally "couldn't get there from here." A few angry voices called for bombing. But we just couldn't have done it.

Responding with aircraft would have required flyover permission from, at the very least, Turkey. And Turkey has no intention of provoking Russia, despite Ankara's NATO membership. The only other conceivable route would have crossed the Black Sea from Bulgaria or Romania. However, we would've needed not only permission to use their airspace but also a green light from several countries to their west, as well. Another no-go.

We also would've needed permission from states such as Turkey, Germany, and Italy to fly missions from our bases on their soil. Not one of those states would've granted it.

As for a naval response, the Black Sea is a Russian shooting gallery. Even so, getting there requires sailing up the Dardanelles, past Istanbul, and through the narrow Bosporus Straits. By international treaty, the Turks are required to grant passage to noncombatant ships from states at peace. But Ankara can close those waters to combatant ships during a crisis. It took serious diplomatic pressure just to get Turkey to allow a few U.S. Navy and Coast Guard ships to pass to deliver nonmilitary aid.

Send in ground troops? Even if we could've deployed them, we couldn't have supported them or provided air cover. We—and the Georgians—were stuck.

To the east, Afghanistan poses a related dilemma. Supporting our forces and those of NATO requires not only an air bridge (and overflight rights from Pakistan and other states) but also the use of Pakistani port facilities, rail lines, and roads. When naive U.S. politicians suggested sending our ground forces into Pakistan's troubled border regions to root out al Qa'eda and the Taliban, they didn't understand that, were Pakistan provoked by what local politicians would brand as an American invasion, Islamabad could simply deny us the use of its lines of communication. That would mean "game over" in Afghanistan.

The challenge of reaching landlocked and other distant regions with meaningful military power in a hurry isn't going away (imagine trying to protect an independent Kurdistan). We've just had back-to-back wakeup calls: Not one of the combat systems projected for any of our military services would've been a game changer. Not one of the hyperexpensive weapons currently envisioned could've gotten to Georgia.

The answer is obvious: We need weapons that don't require permission from third-party governments for their use. That means weapons that can intervene from space.

While the primary focus of "Star Wars" type systems has been on defeating nuclear-tipped missiles, the more practical (and easier) approach would be to pursue space-based weapons that can make aggression tactically expensive and operationally embarrassing for tomorrow's enemies.

Note that I didn't write "defeat our enemies." Victory in warfare will still require conventional combat systems and, above all, boots on the ground throughout our lifetimes. Space-based tank, ship, and aircraft killers wouldn't replace anything in our present arsenal; rather, they'd expand that arsenal to fit the evolving demands of the twenty-first century. These would be punitive, not decisive, weapons. But they'd have their uses.

Watch: If the big-bucks programs currently pushed by the defense industry cartel proceed with business as usual, not only are we not pursuing weapons that would help in "dirty little wars," we seem out of touch with the needs of tomorrow's major wars, as well.

Crisis Watch Bottom Line: While the West is desperate to deny it, great power confrontations are back. We're going to need intervention means that don't rely on other players who refuse to play.

The Damage Done

Armed Forces Journal

March 2009

The quickest way to discredit a good idea is to execute it incompetently. Human nature will blame the idea along with those who botched it. The presidential administration of George W. Bush came to power with a number of sound, even crucial, military and strategic concepts in mind, such as regime change, preemptive attacks, punitive expeditions, and decapitation strikes. Unfortunately, the implementation of such strategic endeavors was entrusted to a cadre of inexperienced, stunningly arrogant pseudo-academics who were, at best, close-minded and naive. The result was a succession of disappointments, setbacks, and outright failures that triggered the emotional rejection of sound ideas that had been misapplied.

Much has been written about the concrete errors of the Bush administration in the military and strategic spheres, but the focus is ever upon the immediate costs, with little regard to the crippling of future policy formulation and the diminution of our range of options in the crises of tomorrow. Even allowing for the faddish nature of Bush hatred among the intelligentsia, the damage done to our conception of what can or cannot be done by our military and what is or isn't permissible in war may hamper our effectiveness for decades.

Perhaps the greatest paradox of the Bush administration's military legacy is that the intelligentsia finally got what it wanted—academically credentialed officials in virtually every top position and the shunning of the advice of military professionals. That this occurred under a Republican president should not obscure the lesson about what happens when theoreticians without practical experience are put in charge of life-and-death decisions. For all its cowboy iconography, the Bush administration was not composed of Rough Riders, but of senior appointees insulated from break-your-nose reality since childhood. They could not grasp the ferocious aspects of human nature that war reveals and empowers. Only the quality of our military rescued the administration's foreign endeavors—to the extent they have been rescued—and now we face a future in which our military is going to be underfunded, operationally restricted, and strategically misapplied.

The Bush administration's mismanagement of its wars did not set defense thinking back a mere three decades to the post-Vietnam era, but a full century: The greatest power in history is determined to become a strategic Lilliput.

REGIME CHANGE: AN IDEA SUBVERTED

The Bush administration's strategic illiteracy regarding Iraq robbed not only the United States, but humankind, of a critical tool to facilitate peace, human rights, development, and improved governance. During the Cold War, the age-old tradition that legitimate states enjoy the right to do as they wish within their own borders metastasized into a defense of monstrous dictators hiding behind artificial frontiers. A figure such as Saddam Hussein could seize power through a coup and maintain it in a sea of blood, then claim "sovereignty" when faced with foreign dismay. As I write, "President" Robert Mugabe, who has ravaged a once-rich country to the point where hunger prevails and cholera kills thousands, is considered untouchable. Murderous thugs rule Myanmar; Sudan butchers its own citizens; and Iran, the government of which has stated its intent to destroy Israel, pursues nuclear weapons with essential impunity. Meanwhile, the true basis of all legitimate sovereignty—the will of the population—goes ignored.

No moral human being can maintain that a dictator has the right to slaughter his own people—yet, the international community defends that right. In 2003, with the dismantling of Saddam's regime, there was a brief, wonderful glimmer of hope that things might change. Around the world, frightened dictators hastened to make nice, while states that had tolerated or even abetted terrorists suddenly found it necessary to shake the offending crumbs from their aprons. The Bush administration's noble decision to remove the Baathist regime had the potential to move human governance forward. Instead, the incompetence with which it was done set back freedom and decency elsewhere: The strongmen gained a new lease on life.

The immediate failing of the administration was its reluctance to send enough troops and show the right mettle for an effective occupation—or even to anticipate the need for an occupation. The administration's notion of how developments would unfold was formed not from the sober assessments of generals, diplomats, or senior intelligence officials, but through a bizarre combination of mirror-imaging and wishful thinking that led a supposedly tough-minded vice president to rely for his situational awareness on an Iraqi fortuneteller. (Dick Cheney and his national security adviser spoke with then-indicted fraudster Ahmed Chalabi daily during the invasion and its aftermath, while angrily dismissing unwelcome reports from Americans on the ground.)

The problem wasn't what we did, but how we did it—and, above all, unrealistic expectations. The hermetic circle around the president, vice president, and Defense Secretary Donald Rumsfeld talked itself into a congenial fantasy: Not only would a country that had been raped for two generations prove instantly problem-free and capable of democratic self-government, but its rehabilitation would pay for itself (even netting a tidy profit for well-positioned American firms).

The most worthless words in the English language may be "if only," but consider how differently things might have turned out that first year in Iraq had we held sensible expectations and made the traditional preparations to assume an occupation's responsibilities. The administration's ideological theorists assumed that removing Saddam would inevitably lead to optimal results. Instead of exploring rational options based upon worst-case scenarios—the standard military planning procedure—the administration simply crossed its fingers. The realist's basic choices would have been to break the regime's hold on power and then leave and let the Iraqis sort themselves out, or to accept that staying on to nurture a new government demanded a full-blown, no-nonsense, shoot-the-looters occupation. Instead, the cabal inside the administration chose a third option: Remove Saddam as cheaply as possible, at great risk, and then loiter in Baghdad, hoping for the best. The well-intentioned but startlingly arrogant neoconservatives were certain they understood the use of military force better than any generals.

In the wake of the Bush administration's transfer of power to its successor, Iraq does have a chance at maintaining a customized pseudo-democracy, but the agony and tangible costs along the way discredited the inherently sensible idea of regime change. Chastened, the Bush administration abandoned its ideals and reembraced the Middle Eastern authoritarian regimes it initially had sought to liberalize. In 2003, our actions terrified Iran, Libya, and even America's No. 1 enemy, Saudi Arabia. By 2009, they barely took us seriously—and we had defaulted to betting, once again, on the regime of Egypt's aging president, Hosni Mubarak, with a pile-on-the-chips enthusiasm reminiscent of the hand we played with the last shah of Iran.

Clichés become clichés because they convey tested truths, and we can pile them on when analyzing the Bush administration's failures: "The devil is in the details," "Anything worth doing is worth doing well," "There's no free lunch," "If something can go wrong, it will," "Always plan for the worst case," "Always have a Plan B," and, not least, "Speak softly, and carry a big stick." But no amount of criticism is going to redeem the administration's genius for doing the right thing appallingly badly. Had it gotten regime change right, we would live in a different, better world today. But its execution was so inept that millions more human beings will suffer and die because incompetence discredited an idea whose time had come.

PREEMPTIVE ATTACKS

Another valuable tool has been banished, for now, from our arsenal of concepts: preemptive attacks. By focusing exclusively on spurious claims that Iraq was readying weapons of mass destruction in a secret program, the Bush administration made doing the right thing look like bullying justified by lies. Unaccountably, the administration failed to play the human-rights card—which would have been sounder policy, putting "Old Europe" and its profiteers on the defensive. The catastrophic perversion of intelligence has been amply discussed elsewhere, but what remains bewildering is the way the administration crammed all of its justification eggs into one basket—then waited for the WMD bunny to appear.

In an age of the proliferation of WMD—notably, nuclear weapons—preemptive strikes must remain an option. Unfortunately, the standards of proof of hostile capabilities and intentions have soared to the point where decisive U.S. action in a timely manner seems unlikely for years, if not decades, to come.

The dangerous age in which we live cannot afford to indulge in moral equivalency. Even as we insist that our enemies really don't mean the threats they hurl in our direction, they move along with their preparations to fulfill their murderous promises. As the cardinal example of the moment, Iran's nuclear program menaces Israel, the Sunni Arab states to the west and southwest, and our own interests and freedom of action in a vital region.

Thanks to the botch-up in Iraq, though, it's unlikely that we will take effective preemptive action, no matter the evidence compiled about Iran's purposes. While this is not intended as an argument for attacking Iran today, we need to recognize the possibility that our reluctance to act boldly in the future may have terrible consequences—far worse than the most comprehensive preemptive strike would generate. This isn't about cure-all prescriptions, but preserving options. Again, the Bush-era incompetence at war making rendered the astute and timely employment of military force far more difficult for future administrations.

In this new, second age of WMD, when great-power rivalries subject to rational calculation have been replaced by knife fights between gods, we appear apt to wait until we have witnessed a regional apocalypse before acting. Without behaving as warmongers, there are times when we have to shoot first for the good not only of ourselves, but of civilization. Thanks to the Iraq debacle, we won't.

While the term "punitive expeditions" is far too honest to be used by any administration or the Pentagon (where the very model of a modern major general would rather be politically correct than effective), the concept is of tremendous practical value. Suppose we had sent enough forces to Afghanistan to do it right—to corral and kill al Qa'eda's remnants while convincing the Taliban that the United States and its citizens meant business—instead of trying to do things on the cheap (only to find ourselves bogged down in a deepening tar pit). Suppose that, after slaughtering al Qa'eda's cadres and leaders, while bloodying the Taliban, we had simply withdrawn—with the promise to return, if provoked again. Would we be safer? We certainly would have more strategic options, and more young Americans would be alive. And the world's only superpower would not be at the mercy of corrupt Pakistan.

What if, after reaching Baghdad, pummeling the Baathist regime, and then capturing Saddam (after killing his sons), we had come home—after making it clear that we would not tolerate open

interference by Iraq's neighbors? Would the subsequent civil strife
have been deadlier than the bloody mess we fostered by flopping
indecisively on the Iraqi couch and chowing down on ideological
junk food for almost four years before growing serious about
restoring public order? While we cannot know precisely what
course Iraq would have taken, we can be certain that al Qa'eda
would not have thrived, that (again) more young Americans would
still be alive, that we would be less indebted (although various private gunslinger organizations would be poorer), and that the Iraq
that emerged, whatever its other qualities, would not have been
defiant toward the United States.

Perhaps the greatest practical failing of the administration's
idealists was their unquestioned assumption that, when the
United States sends in our troops, we must remain to fix every
local plumbing leak. We can't afford that and it doesn't work.
God and occupations help those who help themselves. Frequently, an occupation isn't the answer, but a new problem.
Defending our citizens and our interests does not mean we have
to adopt our former enemies. While full-scale occupations may
be necessary or wise in specific cases, more often we just need to
convince violent enemies that it's dumb to take on those bad-
hombre Americans. Why is this so difficult for our leaders to
comprehend? How could President Bill Clinton expect to foster
good governance in Somalia? How could President George W.
Bush expect Iraqis to turn into flower children overnight? How
can President Barack Obama expect Afghanistan to become a
modern, unified state?

The most-promising concept in play is, in fact, a postmodern version of the punitive expedition: our Predator attacks,
occasional airstrikes and black operations in Pakistan and elsewhere. Having seen the utility and effectiveness of such actions
on a small scale, can't we envision taking punitive actions on a
greater scale, when appropriate? Call them by whatever innocu-
ous name or acronym you wish, but punitive expeditions are
effective, relatively economical and—critical to the American

psyche—relatively quick. We should no more assume that our troops must remain wherever they are deployed than cops would assume a requirement to remain at a crime scene for all eternity. All of these concepts are, of course, interrelated. Another variant on regime change is the decapitation strike, in which the ruling clique of a criminal government is eliminated without resort to a full-scale invasion bound to create collateral damage and punish the relatively innocent. Ethically and morally, decapitation strikes should appeal to us; however, we're trapped in traditional European thinking in which heads of state and senior officials are sacred beings, although the masses are disposable. And, as always, the well-meaning souls who do such terrible harm would cry, "Assassination!"

We have lost our grip on what is and is not moral. Would it have been immoral if we had possessed and employed the means to eliminate Hitler and his inner circle in 1942? Or in 1939, for that matter? In the twenty-first century, as various technologies coalesce to permit us to find and target individuals with standoff weapons, isn't it obviously more humane to target the lawless leader directly than to fight through the masses he has oppressed or conscripted? Yet every tinpot Hitler will have his defenders—especially among the Western intelligentsia.

We are not yet at a technological level that can guarantee success in decapitation strikes, but the day is coming. Tragically, though, our Air Force has already discredited this valuable concept. By flogging "shock and awe" as the answer to all our strategic needs, it oversold immature technologies and forgot human psychology. As Joint Forces Command Chief Gen. James Mattis, an exemplary Marine, grasped in his over-the-beach assault on "effects-based operations," we can't just impress a determined enemy into surrendering by breaking a few windows. In over-promising results from a succession of dismally ineffective shock-and-awe air campaigns, a procurement-driven Air Force refused to analyze the enemy: Why would someone in Saddam's position ever surrender, given his recognition that this was an all-or-nothing game? Saddam was perfectly willing to fight to the last Iraqi. Without killing him, his family, and his inner circle, you weren't going to get peace in our time. War isn't about show-and-tell. It's about killing.

As our capabilities are refined, we increasingly will have the ability to target the truly guilty—the leaders of hostile states or terrorist organizations. While war will remain a messy, ugly business overall, we occasionally will have the opportunity to strike and eliminate those who make the decisions, rather than those who have no choice but to carry out those decisions. This, rather than absurd and crippling rules of engagement, would introduce a new humanity to warfare. Eliminating hostile leaders and their cliques would not guarantee a perfect outcome, but it would increase the probability that the targeted regime's successors would behave more circumspectly.

Of course, academic theorists and activists in search of a cause will demand, "Who are we to decide to eliminate Dictator X?" The answer is "We're us. We represent freedom, decency, and civilization. In this world, force prevails. We're going to make sure it's our force."

GULLIVER'S TRAVAILS

We have the world's most capable military. And we're determined to cripple it. Splendid troops and cutting-edge weapons systems diminish precipitously in value when they are not employed with strategic insight, clear goals, sound planning—and courage. Since the end of the Vietnam War, successive administrations, Republican and Democrat, have deployed our troops simply because they couldn't think of anything else to do. Soldiers and Marines became the universal bandage, applied to unhappy patients by nearsighted physicians: Lebanon, Somalia, the Balkans, Afghanistan, Iraq—not one of these deployments began with a clear end-state in mind and a realistic plan for achieving it. The greatest "combat multiplier" we could acquire in the coming decades would be a new sense of realism about what war means and the necessity of clearly stated missions. Do the hard mental labor before pulling the trigger.

The ultimate military legacy of the administration of George W. Bush will not be the wars it fought but the future wars it made more difficult to fight effectively. We enter a new administration with a strategic arsenal emptied of sound ideas by disastrous performances.

COIN Lies We Love

Armed Forces Journal

May 2009

When it comes to fighting terrorists and counterinsurgency warfare, we have less intellectual integrity than Bernie Madoff had financial integrity. Priding ourselves on our educational credentials and career successes, we engage in comforting lies and bureaucratic superstitions so absurd that a shaman or witch doctor would only shake his head.

We believe what we choose to believe, not what the evidence tells us. We have no time for evidence, since facts confound us damnably.

A particularly destructive bit of nonsense that our military, diplomatic, and political establishments have embraced wholeheartedly and uncritically is the restatement by the French veteran of counterrevolutionary warfare, David Galula, of China's first Communist Party chairman Mao Zedong's proposition that "revolutionary war is 80 percent political action and only 20 percent military." We have embraced this slogan as if it were the Eleventh Commandment.

Worse, we misapply this wildly bogus statement. With our usual imprecision of language and slapdash pretense at analysis, we assume that Mao's and Galula's colorful proposition regarding "revolutionary war" applies equally to the very different phenomena of counterrevolutionary terrorist movements and insurgencies inspired or accelerated by a collapse into fundamentalist religion or a reawakened vision of ethnic supremacy. Mao exploited revolutionary conditions in China to impose an ideological transformation, while Galula observed attempts at ideological revolution in Algeria, Greece, and Indochina. None of their experiences involved mythologized religious or ethnic identities of the sort that lie at the heart of our current conflicts.

Revolutionary wars inspired by political credos are categorically different from rebellions galvanized by blood or belief. Revolutionary war, such as that in Mao's China or Galula's Algeria, seeks to overthrow the regime in power and replace it with a political innovation. Religious and ethnic insurgencies are counterrevolutionary, seeking to restore an idealized golden age or to assert exclusive supremacies. In Afghanistan and Iraq, we are the insurgents, the innovators, fighting for change. Our enemies, by contrast, apply the fundamental command "About face!" and seek to march into the past.

The revolutions that men such as Mao or Galula experienced sought to be inclusive. During the bygone era of these ideological revolutions, orators and authors rhapsodized about "the rights of man," not the rights of Shi'as or Serbs alone. Their ideological visions were vast, transcending religious affiliations (which were to wither away) or ethnic identities (which the new dispensation would cancel). Communism was for everybody, while the Algerian revolutionary vision was not only pan-Arab, but had room for Berbers and other minorities. The terrorist movements and insurgencies we face today are profoundly different, either demanding allegiance to a stern religious vision or asserting a blood-based nationalism (or both). We do not face enemies inspired by intellectual arguments, but ones driven by emotional needs and myths.

Not only have we conflated profoundly different challenges, but we've embraced a formula whose publicists, Mao and Galula, didn't themselves believe. With the proposition that revolutionary war is 80 percent political action and only 20 percent military, they were "firing for effect," exaggerating to make a point peculiar to their historical situations. Neither man offered any empirical data to support what was no more than a rhetorical device.

Adding confusion to error, we have inflated their adjective "political" to mean far more than they intended, from lavish aid programs to social engineering. If pressed, Mao and Galula would have offered narrower definitions of "political." Bureaucratically, we do to ideas what the Air Force does to combat aircraft and the Navy to new ships, adding on so many nice-to-haves that the initial concept disappears from view.

WHERE'S THE DATA?
But stick with the basic proposition: "Revolutionary war is 80 percent political action and only 20 percent military." Is it valid? No. And the corpse can be dissected with many different scalpels. Most obviously, where's the supporting data? Where are the historical facts to justify such a claim? Instead of dissembling by citing a few preferred case studies that we distort to our own ends, we should search for confirmatory evidence from three thousand years of history of revolutions, insurgencies, and terrorism.

That evidence overwhelmingly contradicts the 80:20 proposition. There is no statistically trustworthy accumulation of empirical data to substantiate the Mao-Galula maxim. On the contrary, the evidence of history is not only that insurgencies almost always have been defeated, but that they have been defeated through military means. History indicates that fighting insurgencies is at least 90 percent a military mission and often 100 percent a matter of arms. An objective evaluation of the historical evidence suggests that a blanket statement to the effect that defeating insurgencies is only 20 percent a military endeavor has all the intellectual heft of the claim that "life is just a bowl of cherries."

For those among us—and they are legion—who believe that we have transcended history and need pay it no mind (except when its selective exploitation gains us an advanced degree or a moment in the limelight), let us try a simple mental exercise to test the validity of the Mao-Galula proposition: Re-imagine Iraq during the surge. Now subtract the contributions of the State Department. Would the surge inevitably have failed? No. Some things might have been harder (and others easier), but the absence of diplomats would not have been decisive.

Now do the same drill with each other nonmilitary agency. You get the same answer: Their absence, singly or collectively, might have slowed or complicated specific aspects of progress in Iraq, but would not have altered the outcome.

Next, imagine the consequences if all of our military forces had been withdrawn, leaving the other agencies in place. Would Iraq have emerged from its fratricidal funk? Clearly, it's nonsense to suggest that the military role in Iraq was a mere 20 percent.

Cornered, the blithe spirits who toss around this beloved maxim respond that, "Well, it's not just about numbers. Of course, the military has more people on the ground." But if it's not about numbers, how can we measure it by percentiles? Employing such a metric implies a quantitative basis for the claim. But no one can supply one, because it doesn't exist. We just like to cite these percentages because they lend a pseudo-scientific authority to our prejudices.

MAO AND THE MILITARY

As for revering the maxim because it originated with Chairman Mao, why should we worship his sayings when the Chinese don't? Shall we also believe his claim that Communism was destined to master all the peoples of the earth? How about the statement in his *Little Red Book* that "the seizure of power by armed force, the settlement of the issue by war, is the central task and the highest form of revolution. This . . . principle of revolution holds good universally." Or, more pithily, "Political power grows out of the barrel of a gun." How do these maxims fit with the off-hand notion that revolutionary war is only 20 percent military? Are we to dismiss these more potent formulations, insisting that Mao didn't really mean them, but did mean the stuff we like?

With the 80:20 remark, Mao was making a point, not taking measurements, and exaggerating to make that point. Mao conquered China with vast armies. The great cities of the interior and coast were not subdued by unarmed commissars strolling in to debate the Nationalists and help the locals form sewing cooperatives. Mao's triumph was a military triumph.

Yet another in the long gray line of our intellectual evasions is the illogical assumption that if an insurgency is only 20 percent military for the insurgent, then it's inevitably only 20 percent military for us. Let us assume for the moment that Mao and Galula were correct in their formulation. It does not follow that the same percentages apply to both the insurgent and the counterinsurgent. Indeed, if the insurgency is 80 percent political for the rebel—who cannot hope to win militarily—the logical response might then be that the counterinsurgent's proportionality is the inverse, 20 percent political and 80 percent military.

We have the military strength to crush insurgencies and terrorist organizations. Instead of employing that power effectively, we have convinced ourselves that we should somehow react proportionately, that the rules governing the insurgent also apply to us. But this is asymmetrical warfare. The relative importance of the political and the military for the insurgent and the counterinsurgent is just one more asymmetry.

All artificial formulas are foolish and destructive when applied to war and conflict. There is no exact and universal mix of military and other factors that can be applied to every insurgency. If an insurgent movement is countered early on, a much lower level of military engagement may be required, while a greater commitment of diplomacy and aid might prove effective. If, however, an insurgency is already robust, there is no alternative—none—to the rigorous and determined application of military force. Other government institutions and even nongovernmental agencies may act as force-multipliers, but they will never be the force itself. If this is not so, let a statistically adequate, impartially selected collection of historical examples prove it wrong.

Well-meaning generals insist that "we can't kill our way out of an insurgency," even though, historically, success against insurgents—especially counterrevolutionaries seeking a religious restoration or ethnic supremacy—consistently required killing them in substantial numbers. Do we really believe that wishing will make it so? Perhaps "we" can't kill our way out of an insurgency, since we're afraid to do so, but our timidity does not invalidate history.

This is not to insist that only killing is required. Of course there's more to it, and all effective assistance is welcome. But beware of any doctrine that pleases Washington by offering politically correct prescriptions. Each insurgency has its unique qualities (a fact we acknowledge rhetorically, only to ignore in practice). Some have legitimate grievances that demand redress. Others are apocalyptic and must be countered with uncompromising violence. Nor is every insurgent alike in his level of commitment or brew of motivations. But we shall never progress in our attempts to understand our enemies if we blind ourselves with bumper-sticker nonsense.

To claim, as even some in uniform do, that the military has only a supporting role in defeating insurgencies is equivalent to claiming that an automobile's airbags are more important to its operation than its engine. Again, where is the empirical evidence? Where is the historical data to support so insidious and crippling a claim as the notion that the military is only a minor player in COIN? Think it's true? Just try it.

Of course, "interagency support for COIN" is just another urban legend: All of the players are full of fight in the locker room, but only the armed services show up on the field—and the State Department wants to call the plays from the skybox.

We don't deal in ideas. We deal in slogans masquerading as ideas. If we really loved and respected our troops, we wouldn't bow to political correctness. We'd fight for intellectual integrity in the analysis of the conflicts and enemies currently befuddling us.

The next time a general, diplomat, bureaucrat, "scholar," or pundit tells you that "fighting insurgents is only 20 percent military and 80 percent political," shock him. Demand the evidence. Tell him to break down the numbers on the spot. Insist on a statistically sound analysis based upon insurgencies across the last three millennia. I guarantee you he won't have a serious answer.

The No-Victory Lie

Armchair General

July 2009

Over the last half-century, leftist intellectuals have pounded into us the notion that "victory is no longer possible." We're told that "terrorists can't be defeated," that every crisis "requires a political solution," and always that "war doesn't solve anything."

Well, from the days of myth to the present, warfare has remained humanity's *primary* means of resolving great disputes. You don't have to like a fact for it to be factual. It's the political solutions that don't stick, and through the millennia, terrorists rarely won. As for the proposal that we can no longer win because the nature of war has somehow changed, it's utter nonsense.

But it's appealing nonsense to those who know nothing of history—and who don't want to know. The worst subversion against the American people in our time has been the radical degradation of history instruction in our schools and the elimination of military history in favor of politically correct fables.

For all the crocodile tears shed by activists over Americans killed in action in Afghanistan and Iraq during more than seven years of war, more Americans fell in a single *afternoon* at Cold Harbor. Our losses since 2001 are one bad week in Normandy. We've lost our grasp of the price of defending freedom.

Victory is always possible. But it isn't always cheap. If we're unwilling to fight to win—even in terms of the casualties inflicted on our enemies—then we lose and deserve it. The Unites States can't be defeated, unless we defeat ourselves. We've been doing just that since the Korean War.

The nature of warfare never changes. The outward trappings evolve, from weaponry and techniques to organizations. But the indispensable requirement for victory remains the same: strength of will. Ruthless determination doesn't guarantee a win, but it often enables the weaker side to prevail.

And strength of will is one asset that our terrorist foes don't lack. We have the might to triumph, but we talk ourselves out of using it, inventing scruples that make things worse in the long run. Our enemies will do anything to win.

Give them credit; religion-inspired terrorists live their cause. For all their hypocrisy and barbarism, the hardcore opponents we face today are not only willing but often eager to give their lives to defeat us.

We don't even like to be disturbed by gory pictures on the front page.

The fundamental demand of warfare is killing. You kill your enemies until they surrender or until they are all dead. That's what the history we no longer teach would teach us.

Even well-meaning military leaders have been infected by mindless political correctness. We hear it said, in all seriousness, that fighting this insurgency or that terrorist movement is "80 percent political and only 20 percent military." Yet none of those generals or colonels would dream of withdrawing our military from Afghanistan or Iraq and leaving behind only diplomats and aid workers (the diplomats and aid workers wouldn't hang around long, either). Military operations may not be the only requirement in irregular or asymmetrical warfare, but they remain the indispensable requirement.

It's true that fighting a terrorist movement doesn't always result in a clear-cut, permanent victory. But few human actions, including wars, yield perfect results. It's a fact that no matter how many casualties we inflict on al Qa'eda, Hezbollah, Hamas, or the Taliban, a residue of terrorists will remain. But the goal isn't to inaugurate the Age of Aquarius. It's to drive our enemies to the far fringes of their societies so that local governments can enforce the rule of law and terrorist sanctuaries can't spawn attacks against us.

If you want perfection, give a Zen monastery a try. Victory doesn't have to be flawless to be meaningful. The Second World War left half of Europe in Stalin's grip and China open to a communist takeover. Should we deny that victory's worth? A messy victory is always better than a clean defeat.

Watch: The continuing, unchallenged, and crippling assault on the study of serious history in our schools and universities.

Crisis Watch Bottom Line: Al -Qa'eda doesn't pose the greatest danger to our security. The greatest threat arises from historical amnesia among our population.

PART IV

Endless Wars

Where Are the Strategists?

Being Superb Operators Isn't Enough

Armchair General

November 2009

The difference between a politician and a strategist is that the former just wants the problem fixed now, while the latter has to judge the long-term costs and consequences of engagement. The politician wants to be able to say, "I did it!" The strategist has to weigh the costs, means, methods, and consequences of doing it.

Tactics is checkers, strategy is chess, and operations falls somewhere in the middle. A good tactician thinks a couple of battlefield moves ahead. A proficient operator thinks beyond a campaign's end. But a strategist has to deal with the big, ugly questions: What if the mission turns out to be impossible? If we fix this problem, what other problems do we create? What will be the third-, fourth-, and fifth-order effects across the theater of war and beyond?

There's currently no evidence of serious strategists at work in Washington. While the Army struggles to train top-performing officers as strategists, the institution remains trapped in an operational culture. And the Army's ahead of the pack. As for Washington beyond the Pentagon, no strategic culture exists. The State Department can't think beyond the next signing ceremony.

As a result, the president—any president—presides over a government without an integrated strategic vision, while the military contents itself with furious activity at the operational level. Our generals and admirals settle for doing what they do extremely well—making war at the tactical and operational levels—while avoiding the painful demands of strategic thought. When the Pentagon stages a "strategic review," it's just a game of musical chairs for defense contractors.

Our growing commitment to Afghanistan offers a classic example of the operational mentality eclipsing strategic thought. Afghanistan's no more than a big patch of worthless dirt, but we're obsessed with controlling terrain. Our true enemies, the terrorists of al Qa'eda, aren't even in Afghanistan anymore— they were merely transient tenants of a terrorist motel. As for the Taliban, it's a homegrown organization with genuine support among Pashtuns, Afghanistan's largest ethnic group. We can keep on defeating Taliban fighters forever, but their culture won't go away.

Meanwhile, extremists tear apart neighboring Pakistan, a state with nuclear weapons and five times Afghanistan's population. And there's nothing we can do to force Pakistan to save itself (strategy is also about recognizing what's achievable). So, in lieu of creative solutions, we default to sending more money to a corrupt government and handing over weapons that may soon be turned against us. And our appalling dependence on a single 1,500-mile supply line through Pakistan subjects us to Islamabad's blackmail. This is a strategic debacle in the making—all because we won't think beyond the immediate mission.

Plenty of alternatives are there to be grasped by no-nonsense strategists. Pakistan has been sponsoring terrorist attacks against India, relying on us to prevent New Delhi from retaliating. In effect, we're protecting terrorists. But what if we *reduced* our commitment in Afghanistan, concentrated strictly on destroying our enemies (rather than on nation-building where no nation exists), and told Pakistan it was on its own?

Without us to protect it from India, Pakistan would have to behave responsibly at last—or face a nuclear war it would lose catastrophically. And Pakistanis would have to decide how much their country is worth to them, whether to accept an extremist vision of religious rule or fight for the democracy foreseen at the country's founding. India could solve our Pakistan problem—but we just don't understand strategic leverage.

There are plenty of other examples of our lack of strategic grip, from our bumbling attempts to "solve" the Israeli-Palestinian problem, through our hesitation to contain Russia, to our enthusiasm for Saudi Arabia. But Afghanistan is the black hole of black holes, consuming forces, energy, and wealth for a trivial return. We're just not *thinking*.

Watch: Will military leaders involved in Afghanistan continue to ask for more troops—echoing Vietnam—without describing an attainable end-state in plain English?

Crisis Watch Bottom Line: Washington consistently chooses expedience over long-term advantage. The greatest power in history no longer even knows what strategy is.

12 Myths of
Twenty-First-Century War

The American Legion Magazine

November 2007

We're in trouble. We're in danger of losing more wars. Our troops haven't forgotten how to fight. We've never had better men and women in uniform. But our leaders and many of our fellow Americans no longer grasp what war means or what it takes to win.

Thanks to those who have served in uniform, we've lived in such safety and comfort for so long that for many Americans sacrifice means little more than skipping a second trip to the buffet table.

Two trends over the past four decades contributed to our national ignorance of the cost, and necessity, of victory. First, the most privileged Americans used the Vietnam War as an excuse to break their tradition of uniformed service. Ivy League universities once produced heroes. Now they resist Reserve Officer Training Corps representation on their campuses.

Yet our leading universities still produce a disproportionate number of U.S. political leaders. The men and women destined to lead us in wartime dismiss military service as a waste of their time and talents. Delighted to pose for campaign photos with our troops, elected officials in private disdain the military. Only one serious presidential aspirant in either party is a veteran, while another presidential hopeful pays as much for a single haircut as I took home in a month as an Army private.

Second, we've stripped in-depth U.S. history classes out of our schools. Since the 1960s, one history course after another has been cut, while the content of those remaining focuses on social issues and our alleged misdeeds. Dumbed-down textbooks minimize the wars that kept us free. As a result, ignorance of the terrible price our troops had to pay for freedom in the past creates absurd expectations about our present conflicts. When the media offer flawed or biased analyses, the public lacks the knowledge to make informed judgments.

This combination of national leadership with no military expertise and a population that hasn't been taught the cost of freedom leaves us with a government that does whatever seems expedient and a citizenry that believes whatever's comfortable. Thus, myths about war thrive.

Myth No. 1: War doesn't change anything. This campus slogan contradicts all of human history. Over thousands of years, war has been the last resort—and all too frequently the first resort—of tribes, religions, dynasties, empires, states, and demagogues driven by grievance, greed, or a heartless quest for glory. No one believes that war is a good thing, but it is sometimes necessary. We need not agree in our politics or on the manner in which a given war is prosecuted, but we can't pretend that if only we laid down our arms all others would do the same.

Wars, in fact, often change everything. Who would argue that the American Revolution, our Civil War, or World War II changed nothing? Would the world be better today if we had been pacifists in the face of Nazi Germany and imperial Japan?

Certainly, not all of the changes warfare has wrought through the centuries have been positive. Even a just war may generate undesirable results, such as Soviet tyranny over half of Europe after 1945. But of one thing we may be certain: a U.S.

defeat in any war is a defeat not only for freedom, but for civilization. Our enemies believe that war can change the world. And they won't be deterred by bumper stickers.

Myth No. 2: Victory is impossible today. Victory is always possible, if our nation is willing to do what it takes to win. But victory is, indeed, impossible if U.S. troops are placed under impossible restrictions, if their leaders refuse to act boldly, if every target must be approved by lawyers, and if the American people are disheartened by a constant barrage of negativity from the media. We don't need generals who pop up behind microphones to apologize for every mistake our soldiers make. We need generals who win.

And you can't win if you won't fight. We're at the start of a violent struggle that will ebb and flow for decades, yet our current generation of leaders, in and out of uniform, worries about hurting the enemy's feelings.

One of the tragedies of our involvement in Iraq is that while we did a great thing by removing Saddam Hussein, we tried to do it on the cheap. It's an iron law of warfare that those unwilling to pay the butcher's bill up front will pay it with compound interest in the end. We not only didn't want to pay that bill, but our leaders imagined that we could make friends with our enemies even before they were fully defeated. Killing a few hundred violent actors like Muqtada al Sadr in 2003 would have prevented thousands of subsequent American deaths and tens of thousands of Iraqi deaths. We started something our national leadership lacked the guts to finish.

Despite our missteps, victory looked a great deal less likely in the early months of 1942 than it does against our enemies today. Should we have surrendered after the fall of the Philippines? Today's opinionmakers and elected officials have lost their grip on what it takes to win. In the timeless words of Nathan Bedford Forrest, "War means fighting, and fighting means killing."

And in the words of Gen. Douglas MacArthur, "It is fatal to enter any war without the will to win it."

Myth No. 3: Insurgencies can never be defeated. Historically, fewer than one in twenty major insurgencies succeeded. Virtually no minor ones survived. In the mid-twentieth century, insurgencies scored more wins than previously had been the case, but that was because the European colonial powers against which they rebelled had already decided to rid themselves of their imperial possessions. Even so, more insurgencies were defeated than not, from the Philippines to Kenya to Greece. In the entire eighteenth century, our war of independence was the only insurgency that defeated a major foreign power and drove it out for good.

The insurgencies we face today are, in fact, more lethal than the insurrections of the past century. We now face an international terrorist insurgency as well as local rebellions, all motivated by religious passion or ethnicity or a fatal compound of both. The good news is that in over three thousand years of recorded history, insurgencies motivated by faith and blood overwhelmingly failed. The bad news is that they had to be put down with remorseless bloodshed.

Myth No. 4: There's no military solution; only negotiations can solve our problems. In most cases, the reverse is true. Negotiations solve nothing until a military decision has been reached and one side recognizes a peace agreement as its only hope of survival. It would be a welcome development if negotiations fixed the problems we face in Iraq, but we're the only side interested in a negotiated solution. Every other faction—the terrorists, Sunni insurgents, Shi'a militias, Iran, and Syria—is convinced it can win.

The only negotiations that produce lasting results are those conducted from positions of indisputable strength.

Myth No. 5: When we fight back, we only provoke our enemies. When dealing with bullies, either in the schoolyard or in a global war, the opposite is true: if you don't fight back, you encourage your enemy to behave more viciously.

Passive resistance only works when directed against rule-of-law states, such as the core English-speaking nations. It doesn't work where silent protest is answered with a bayonet in the belly or a one-way trip to a political prison. We've allowed far too many myths about the "innate goodness of humanity" to creep up on us. Certainly, many humans would rather be good than bad. But if we're unwilling to fight the fraction of humanity that's evil, armed, and determined to subjugate the rest, we'll face even grimmer conflicts.

Myth No. 6: Killing terrorists only turns them into martyrs. It's an anomaly of today's Western world that privileged individuals feel more sympathy for dictators, mass murderers, and terrorists—consider the irrational protests against Guantanamo—than they do for their victims. We were told, over and over, that killing Osama bin Laden or Abu Musab al Zarqawi, hanging Saddam Hussein or targeting the Taliban's Mullah Omar would only unite their followers. Well, we haven't yet gotten Osama or Omar, but Zarqawi's dead and forgotten by his own movement, whose members never invoke that butcher's memory. And no one is fighting to avenge Saddam. The harsh truth is that when faced with true fanatics, killing them is the only way to end their influence. Imprisoned, they galvanize protests, kidnappings, bombings, and attacks that seek to free them. Want to make a terrorist a martyr? Just lock him up. Attempts to try such monsters in a court of law turn into mockeries that only provide public platforms for their hate speech, which the global media is delighted to broadcast. Dead, they're dead. And killing them is the ultimate proof that they lack divine protection. Dead terrorists don't kill.

Myth No. 7: If we fight as fiercely as our enemies, we're no better than them. Did the bombing campaign against Germany turn us into Nazis? Did dropping atomic bombs on Japan to end the war and save hundreds of thousands of American lives, as well as millions of Japanese lives, turn us into the beasts who conducted the Bataan Death March?

The greatest immorality is for the United States to lose a war. While we seek to be as humane as the path to victory permits, we cannot shrink from doing what it takes to win. At present, the media and influential elements of our society are obsessed with the small immoralities that are inevitable in wartime. Soldiers are human, and no matter how rigorous their training, a miniscule fraction of our troops will do vicious things and must be punished as a consequence. Not everyone in uniform will turn out to be a saint, and not every chain of command will do its job with equal effectiveness. But obsessing on tragic incidents—of which there have been remarkably few in Iraq or Afghanistan—obscures the greater moral issue: the need to defeat enemies who revel in butchering the innocent, who celebrate atrocities, and who claim their god wants blood.

Myth No. 8: The United States is more hated today than ever before. Those who served in Europe during the Cold War remember enormous, often-violent protests against U.S. policy that dwarfed today's let's-have-fun-on-a-Sunday-afternoon rallies. Older readers recall the huge ban-the-bomb, pro-communist demonstrations of the 1950s and the vast seas of demonstrators filling the streets of Paris, Rome, and Berlin to protest our commitment to Vietnam. Imagine if we'd had 24/7 news coverage of those rallies. I well remember serving in Germany in the wake of our withdrawal from Saigon, when U.S. soldiers were despised by the locals—who nonetheless were willing to take our money—and terrorists tried to assassinate U.S. generals.

The fashionable anti-Americanism of the chattering classes hasn't stopped the world from seeking one big green card. As I've traveled around the globe since 9/11, I've found that below the government-spokesman/professional-radical level, the United States remains the great dream for university graduates from Berlin to Bangalore to Bogota.

On the domestic front, we hear ludicrous claims that our country has never been so divided. Well, that leaves out our Civil War. Our historical amnesia also erases the violent protests of the late 1960s and early 1970s, the mass confrontations, rioting, and deaths. Is today's America really more fractured than it was in 1968?

Myth No. 9: Our invasion of Iraq created our terrorist problems.
This claim rearranges the order of events, as if the attacks of
9/11 happened after Baghdad fell. Our terrorist problems have
been created by the catastrophic failure of Middle Eastern civilization to compete on any front and were exacerbated by the
determination of successive U.S. administrations, Democrat and
Republican, to pretend that Islamist terrorism was a brief aberration. Refusing to respond to attacks, from the bombings in
Beirut to Khobar Towers, from the first attack on the Twin Towers to the near-sinking of the USS *Cole*, we allowed our enemies
to believe that we were weak and cowardly. Their unchallenged
successes served as a powerful recruiting tool.

Did our mistakes on the ground in Iraq radicalize some new
recruits for terror? Yes. But imagine how many more recruits
there might have been and the damage they might have inflicted
on our homeland had we not responded militarily in Afghanistan
and then carried the fight to Iraq. Now Iraq is al Qa'eda's Vietnam, not ours.

*Myth No. 10: If we just leave, the Iraqis will patch up their differ-
ences on their own.* The point may come at which we have to
accept that Iraqis are so determined to destroy their own future
that there's nothing more we can do. But we're not there yet,
and leaving immediately would guarantee not just one massacre
but a series of slaughters and the delivery of a massive victory to
the forces of terrorism. We must be open-minded about practical measures, from changes in strategy to troop reductions, if
that's what the developing situation warrants. But it's grossly irre-
sponsible to claim that our presence is the primary cause of the
violence in Iraq—an allegation that ignores history.

*Myth No. 11: It's all Israel's fault. Or the popular Washington
corollary: "The Saudis are our friends."* Israel is the Muslim world's
excuse for failure, not a reason for it. Even if we didn't support
Israel, Islamist extremists would blame us for countless other
imagined wrongs, since they fear our freedoms and our culture
even more than they do our military. All men and women of

conscience must recognize the core difference between Israel and its neighbors: Israel genuinely wants to live in peace, while its genocidal neighbors want Israel erased from the map.

As for the mad belief that the Saudis are our friends, it endures only because the Saudis have spent so much money on both sides of the aisle in Washington. Saudi money continues to subsidize anti-Western extremism, to divide fragile societies, and encourage hatred between Muslims and all others. Saudi extremism has done far more damage to the Middle East than Israel ever did. The Saudis are our enemies.

Myth No. 12: The Middle East's problems are all America's fault. Muslim extremists would like everyone to believe this, but it just isn't true. The collapse of once-great Middle Eastern civilizations has been underway for more than five centuries, and the region became a backwater before the United States became a country. For the first century and a half of our national existence, our relations with the people of the Middle East were largely beneficent and protective, notwithstanding our conflict with the Barbary Pirates in North Africa. But Islamic civilization was on a downward trajectory that could not be arrested. Its social and economic structures, its values, its neglect of education, its lack of scientific curiosity, the indolence of its ruling classes, and its inability to produce a single modern state that served its people all guaranteed that, as the West's progress accelerated, the Middle East would fall ever farther behind. The Middle East has itself to blame for its problems.

None of us knows what our strategic future holds, but we have no excuse for not knowing our own past. We need to challenge inaccurate assertions about our policies, about our past, and about war itself. And we need to work within our community and state education systems to return balanced, comprehensive history programs to our schools. The unprecedented wealth and power of the United States allows us to afford many things denied to human beings throughout history. But we, the people, cannot afford ignorance.

Assessing the Surge

Armed Forces Journal

October 2007

U.S. commanders with whom I spoke in Anbar province in August were worried—worried that their Marines would get bored in the absence of combat action. Enlisted Marines on return tours of duty expressed surprise verging on bewilderment that cities such as Fallujah, long wracked by insurgent violence, were calm and open for business. Foreign terrorists who once ruled the streets still launched minor attacks, but had been marginalized across the province. And last year's Sunni-Arab enemies were busily scheming how to profit from the American presence.

Although a few portions of Anbar remain dangerous—not least, for Iraqis—the turnaround during the last six months has been remarkable, an illustration of the nonlinear developments in warfare that confound academic theorists. Numerous factors influenced the Sunni-Arab "flip," but, on the whole, it remains one of those events that analysts could not foresee and which was by no means inevitable. At a certain point, the chemistry was simply there and a few alert commanders recognized it and acted.

Now the crucial question is whether the shift in loyalties in Anbar can be replicated where the sectarian and political dynamics are different: Was this exclusively a Sunni-Arab phenomenon, or can truculent Shi'as be won over, as well? Eager commanders express optimism, but the truth is that we just don't know. The future of Iraq and of the U.S. presence will be shaped by the Shi'a response.

What happened in Anbar? Past a point, the emotional turns of identity groups, such as the province's Sunni Arabs, defy clinical analysis, but the evident factors are these: First, al Qa'eda behaved so barbarically and decreed forms of social discipline so alien to local norms that Anbar's Muslims rejected the terrorists who claimed to be their champions. With the murder of popular sheikhs, the kidnapping of daughters for forced marriages, the destruction of commerce, the suppression of everyday pleasures—including smoking, which may have been decisive—and the terrorists' sheer bloodlust, al Qa'eda in Iraq ultimately excited revulsion and outrage. While the American presence aimed at a political transformation, the foreign terrorists sought to regulate the intimate details of daily life. American troops may have been undesirable, but al Qa'eda was unbearable.

The second factor was the persistence of the U.S. effort. Sunni Arabs, who lost the most when Saddam Hussein's regime fell, didn't feel the immediate pain of war during our march to Baghdad. They had no real sense of having been defeated. It took years of fighting for them to accept their changed status, with the process of recognition hampered by the erratic nature of U.S. operations—fits of activity, such as the reduction of Fallujah in the autumn of 2004, interrupted by relative disengagement. (Green-Zone decisionmakers seem to have had an attention-span problem.) In this regard, the implementation of the troop surge in the first half of 2007 proved critical: The signal that we could not be driven out by violence, but were willing to raise the stakes, was at least as important psychologically as the additional boots on the ground were militarily.

We wore the Sunnis down, and al Qa'eda wore them out. Key tribal leaders and authority figures within the insurgency also realized, belatedly, that while the Americans intended to leave eventually, if on their own terms, al Qa'eda meant to stay forever. After that, the choice of allegiances wasn't difficult.

But the choice had to be offered, which was where experienced U.S. commanders came in. In Ramadi and elsewhere, they sensed that a window of opportunity had opened and took advantage of it to step inside the Sunni house. While it doesn't do to overstate the newfound affection the locals feel for things American, an undeniable commonality of interests has emerged. Complex emotional reactions also played an unacknowledged role. Speaking with Marine commanders on the ground, as well as with local security officials and sheikhs, one gets the sense that this alliance of convenience goes a bit beyond "the enemy of my enemy is my friend." While it's much too early for conclusive pronouncements, it appears that the longer-term outcome in Iraq may be just the opposite of the expectations held in 2003: We may find that it's the Sunni Arabs (as well as the largely Sunni Kurds), not the Shi'as, with whom we can achieve a useful accommodation.

And that's where the trouble starts.

THE SHI'A CURSE

The progress in Anbar province is undeniable. It may not be irreversible, but the sound money is on the intensification of the U.S.-Sunni rapprochement—not least because, for all the culture's endemic emotionalism, the Sunnis now demonstrate a higher degree of pragmatism than the country's majority Shi'as, whose penchant for oracular religion has spilled into the political arena. Long-suffering, the Shi'as are hypersensitive, distrustful of everyone, and expectant of persecution. In an office interview, Lt. Gen. Raymond Odierno, the Coalition's battle captain, put it this way: "The problem is that the Shi'a still haven't realized that they've won." The primary characteristic of the dysfunctional Shi'a-dominated government of Prime Minister Nouri al Maliki is paranoia.

Constituting 60 percent of Iraq's population, the Shi'as were long excluded from power. By and large, they are less-educated, more prone to obscurantism and occult beliefs, and particularly drawn to charismatic leadership (a political characteristic nurtured by Shi'a millenarianism). The Shi'a inability to govern well echoes the challenges faced by African states in the early years of independence, when the paucity of educated, experienced leaders left the stage vacant for demagogues, and elections became naked assertions of tribal power.

Nor is Shi'a anger entirely unjustified. Sunni-Arab repression of the Shi'as—and disdain for their ornate version of Islam—predated the Ba'athist era by many centuries. Contrary to the insistence of Western leaders and diplomats, it's by no means certain that Iraq's Shi'as, now empowered, can be cajoled or bullied into an equitable power-sharing arrangement with their historical enemies. To this community, democracy is a winner-take-all affair.

Iranian meddling exacerbates every problem the Shi'as pose, but, as deadly and destructive as Tehran's engagement may be, it's essential not to blame Iran for preexisting problems: Iranian agents aren't making trouble from scratch, but are simply encouraging and enabling the troublemakers in place. Nor is Iran likely to profit enduringly from even the most favorable short-term outcome in Iraq, since Persian racism toward Arabs is no secret to Iraq's Arab Shi'as. For now, though, Iranian mischief makes a bad situation worse.

And it could get much uglier. As the Sunni-insurgent threat dissolves and al Qa'eda is thrust onto the strategic defensive, a number of U.S. officers express the belief that we're moving beyond counterinsurgency operations toward peace-enforcement and, ultimately, a peacekeeping role, acting as the referee between Sunni-Arabs and Shi'as along the country's sectarian fault lines and in those urban neighborhoods that have not been ethnically cleansed. Others look beyond the current interconfessional violence to a possible showdown within the Shi'a community—pitting Muqtada al Sadr, who has positioned himself as a champion of the masses, against the (comparatively) moderate Shi'as, whose moral arbiter remains the Ayatollah Ali al Sistani.

In a conflict between al Sadr's Mahdi Army (the Jaish al Mahdi, or JAM) and the better-disciplined Badr Brigades and their allies, U.S. observers predict that Badr units would achieve initial victories against the more slapdash JAM, but that, as the struggle continued, the JAM's numbers and broad public support would begin to tell. And Iran would attempt to position itself so that it emerged behind the winning side—whichever side that might be.

In the lengthy chronicle of lost opportunities in Iraq, one of the sorriest now appears to be the feckless decision not to kill al Sadr in the summer of 2003, after he began his campaign to assassinate rivals for power. The legal justification was there, as was the operational necessity. But, in the classic postmodern American pattern, the decision was made to postpone the trip to the dentist in the hope that the cavity would get better on its own. In mid-2003, al Sadr had a bodyguard. Two years later, he had an army. Thousands of Iraqis and Americans have died because we failed to stop one man.

Of course, re-fighting the lost battles of 2003—or subsequent years—is an exercise for historians and a default stance for politicians. But the fact remains that those whom we expected to embrace as allies, the Shi'as, are increasingly hostile to our interests and hopes, while our initial enemies, the Sunni Arabs, are killing Muslim terrorists for us. The apocalyptic impulse and attendant paranoia within Shi'a Islam may be the greatest threat to a tolerable (if not quite tolerant) and equitable future for the population of Iraq.

AL QA'EDA'S HUMILIATION
If the paranoid, vengeful behavior of Iraq's Shi'as and the messianic pretensions of men such as al Sadr inhibit a bearable out-

come in Iraq, one great strategic triumph has been achieved: the Sunni-Arab repudiation and humiliation of al Qa'eda.

Although this Muslim rejection of al Qa'eda has been reported (if gingerly) in the Western media, few Americans sense the enormity of what's happened. For all of our inept efforts at "public diplomacy," our single public-relations triumph since the capture of Saddam Hussein—and a much greater one—has been handed to us by our former enemies. When Iraq's Sunni Arabs turned, violently and openly, against al Qa'eda, an organization which poses as the champion of Sunni Muslims, the strategic equation shifted. No matter how al Jazeera and other regional media may downplay this development, word gets out. Sunni Arabs fought beside al Qa'eda against the Great Satan—and ultimately found the Great Satan a preferable companion. This humiliation of al Qa'eda may prove, in retrospect, to have been the great turning point that led to the organization's long decline. Unfortunately, it will be a long, painful affair still. Future historians may even see this single result as having redeemed our entire Iraq experiment. Even if not a single al Qa'eda operative was in Iraq prior to 2003—a contention still in dispute—the terror organization made a colossal strategic error thereafter by declaring Iraq the central front in its struggle against America; al Qa'eda has now lost decisively on its "central front" and can only hope that America's domestic politics will rescue it.

CITY OF WONDERS
Baghdad plays a leading role in the Arab world's collective memory and myths. Sprawling and wretched, its glory days are a millennium behind it, yet, in the Arab imagination, it retains a charisma equal to the Western Protestant vision of "a city on a hill." Nor has it been only Arabs who romanticized Baghdad; industrial-age Westerners ascribed to it a greatness the city hadn't possessed since the Mongol conquest, from the dream of a Berlin-to-Baghdad railway to sanitized versions of "The Arabian Nights" and the pre-digital filmmaking feats of special-effects wizard Ray Harryhausen.

The city's apogee under Harun al Rashid predated the Christian conversion of most of northern Europe, and its destruction at the hands of the Mongols eight centuries ago haunts the Arab interpretation of history—which is little more than a search for excuses for centuries of ever-deepening failure. It's as if Westerners looked back to Charlemagne for routine encouragement—skipping everything in between—and bewailed the Fall of Constantinople as the cause of the subprime mortgage crisis.

"Baghdad" is an incantatory word for Arabs. As a consequence, the actual city's importance is exaggerated even beyond its notable size and strategic location. Westerners may never quite grasp the despair Arabs felt when American tanks reached the city with such ease in 2003; the brevity of the Iraqi defense of Baghdad shamed an entire civilization. As a result, Iraq's Sunni Arabs will never accept Shi'a domination of the city, no matter the argument of demographics. For their part, Iraq's Shi'as view Baghdad as the great prize that has fallen to them. On one level, the death-squad murders, terrorist bombings, and outright battles in the city have been about the concrete possession of turf, but, on another plane, this is a struggle for the ownership of a myth—in faux-academic terms, a contest to "dominate the narrative."

On the mundane side, where U.S. commanders have to operate, the city remains a crazy-quilt of neighborhoods foreign to one another. In classic third-world fashion, poverty often encroaches upon wealth and vice versa. Physically, some neighborhoods are relatively green and pleasant, while many others are fouled by ponds of sewage and poisoned by the stench of human waste. Many districts have been ethnically cleansed, while others remain mixed—the fault-line neighborhoods where the surge arrested ethnic cleansing, but which demand an enduring security presence.

Depending on where you look in Baghdad, you can find evidence for almost any political argument you wish to make. Sectarian and anti-Coalition violence remains endemic in some districts—most notably, in Shi'a neighborhoods loyal to Muqtada al Sadr—while other areas have come back to life under the enhanced security conditions the troop surge provided. Fault-line neighborhoods remain deadly for Iraqis and for us, while others, such as Haifa Street north of the Green Zone, which saw pitched battles as recently as last January, have begun to flourish again. Progress may be tenuous and security frail in the absence of U.S. forces, yet it's impossible to deny that the situation in the early autumn of 2007 is far better than it was one year ago.

The shift in political alignments is evident in Baghdad as well. Sunni neighborhoods, once bitterly hostile, increasingly welcome U.S. forces (and "welcome" is, indeed, the appropriate word—by providing dependable security at last, the U.S. military excited a fresh enthusiasm for our presence; Sunni Arabs do not want us to leave until a national settlement is in place and proven in practice). On the other hand, Sadr City, which I was not able to visit, remains volatile and embittered, its Lumpen-proletariat schooled by fanatics.

Of course, the reinvented American relationship with Iraq's Sunni Arabs, whether in Baghdad or in the provinces, fuels Shi'a paranoia, and the local passion for conspiracy theories is super-charged by the local passion for conspiracies. Viewing politics as a zero-sum game, Shi'a leaders view our new accommodation with the Sunnis and even the pacification of Sunni-Arab neigh-borhoods in Baghdad as a calculated diminution of their power and even as a betrayal. Our desire to build constructive relation-ships with both sides simply doesn't match the codes of the Shi'as' mental software and the program threatens to go haywire. In the country's Shi'a-heartland south, where the ballyhooed British "light touch" failed comprehensively, there is no longer any hope of an equitable, integrated society, and women's rights have been reversed by a century.

Yet, it would be strategically disastrous to write off the very real progress made this year as meaningless. We're recovering from nearly four years of appalling errors in Iraq. An objective observer, if one could be found these days, would be startled by how far we've come since January. Much of this progress is, of course, due to the fresh approach implemented by Gen. David Petraeus, but, as Petraeus himself stresses, many of the elements of the new strategy were already falling into place as local commanders explored their own initiatives for engaging and seducing former enemies. One quality of a first-rate commander that too often goes overlooked is the ability of a leader to recognize when his subordinates already have it right and either to build upon their success or get out of the way. While the return of Petraeus in his new role as our military commander had a decisive effect in Iraq, if not in Washington, our subsequent successes have been a collective achievement—which Petraeus is the first to point out. If our political leaders often seem to have learned little or nothing, our military, educated by six years of war in Afghanistan and Iraq, has learned a great deal.

QUO VADIS, BABY?

We don't know where Iraq is headed because the Iraqis don't know. No matter how well our military performs, the complex population of Iraq will determine their country's future in the end—if Iraq endures as a single entity. Yet I returned from this trip to Iraq guardedly optimistic. Success, which must now be defined down to a rational level, would be characterized by three achievements: al Qa'eda hammered down, Iran kept out, and sectarian violence reduced to a level that allows for general governance. On the first count, we're winning. On the second, we're holding the line. On the third, we're making progress, but the danger of an intra-Shi'a conflict is a wild card, while intransigent Shi'a solidarity vis-à-vis Iraq's minorities poses the greatest immediate obstacle to our strategic aspirations for the region.

Iraq isn't going to emerge as our dreamed-of model democracy in the Middle East. It may even end up in a hard partition. But there's a reasonable chance that a confederated Iraq will find its way to a more equitable form of government than any major state in the region (except for Israel) has achieved. Given how badly the occupation was botched early on, that would constitute a very big win for us. And even a stumbling democracy would be a great advance for the region.

The one thing we must avoid, whatever our individual political biases, is linear projections: If A and B, inevitably C. The Sunni Arab change of sides may only have been the first step in a complex series of internal realignments, and so much is in flux that we may find ourselves with unexpected allies of convenience—or new enemies—within the Shi'a community. But for all of the infernal complexity at work in Iraq today, we must bear in mind two fundamental points:

First, when all of the highfalutin' theories have been propounded and homage has been paid to every anthropological nuance, counterinsurgency warfare is about killing those who need killing, helping those who need help—and knowing the difference between the two. On that count, we've made enormous progress.

The second point has to do with loyalties and alliances, and it's ultimately clear-cut, as well: Those who help us kill our enemies are our allies, and those who continue to kill our troops are our enemies. For all their alarm over our new alliance with their country's Sunni Arabs, Iraq's Shi'as need to figure that one out.

What "Bomb Iran" Really Takes

The New York Post

July 17, 2008

My greatest worry on Iran's nuclear threat to civilization isn't the military option. It's trying that option on the cheap.

If there's any way to block Tehran's pursuit of nukes short of warfare, I'm all for it. Maybe yesterday's dispatch of the No. 3 U.S. diplomat to observe the European Union's talks with the mullahs about their nukes will work a miracle (don't hold your breath).

Military strikes must be the last resort. Even a successful attack would panic oil markets, interrupt supplies to an unknown degree, and make enemies of the Iranian people for another generation.

But the fanatics in Tehran may leave us no peaceful alternative. In that case, the most disastrous thing we could do would be to launch an economy-model attack.

If forced to strike, we have to do it right. When safe-at-home ideologues bluster, "Just bomb 'em," they haven't a clue how complex this problem is.

Nor is there any chance that the Israelis could handle Iran on their own (their recent air-force exercise was psychological warfare). As skilled as their pilots and planners may be, the Israelis lack the capacity to sustain a strategic offensive against

Iran—or to deal with the inevitable mess they'd leave behind in the Persian Gulf. Israel's aircraft could do serious damage to Iran's nuke program, but the U.S. military would face the potentially catastrophic aftermath.

Without compromising any secrets—the Iranians already know what we'd need to do—here are the basic requirements for smacking down Iran's nuke program:

- Take out Iran's air-defense and intelligence network to protect our attacking aircraft.
- Take down its national communications network to degrade its military reaction.
- Strike dozens of dispersed nuclear-related targets—some of them in hardened underground facilities, with others purposely placed in populated areas.
- Hit every anti-ship-missile installation along Iran's Persian Gulf coast and the Straits of Hormuz. The reflexive Iranian response to an attack would be to launch sea-skimmer missiles against oil tankers and Western warships. The Iranians know that oil's now the world's Achilles heel.
- Destroy Iran's naval capacity, including small craft, in the first twenty-four hours to prevent attacks on shipping (expect suicide attacks, too).
- Immediately take out all of Iran's long-range and intermediate-range missiles—not just those that could strike Israel, but those that could hit Saudi, gulf-state, or Iraqi oil refineries, pipelines, port facilities, and oil fields . . . or our installations in the region.
- Hit the military's key command centers in Tehran, as well as regional headquarters, with special attention to the Revolutionary Guards' infrastructure.
- Expect three to six weeks of intense air and naval fighting, followed by months of skirmishing and asymmetrical warfare. And Iraq will heat back up, too.

Screw up the effort, and today's oil prices will double or triple, with severe downstream shortages showing up in a matter of weeks—every oil tanker's insurance will be canceled immediately, even if the Straits of Hormuz remain open (unlikely).

And we'll be in the global doghouse.

Gimme-my-war chumps of the sort who believed "dissident" Ahmed Chalabi on Iraq insist that, if we weaken the Tehran regime by attacking, the Iranian people will overthrow it.

Utterly wrong.

Yes, many Iranians detest their killer-bumpkin president. But plenty of Americans despise our president—yet, if our homeland were attacked tomorrow, most would rally behind him. And we'd fight back. The Iranians would respond the same way.

If a war did spark regime change, the new government might well be even harder-line. Nobody likes to be bombed—and serious attacks on Iran's nuclear program would kill a lot of Iranians.

Yet it'd be even worse if we tried to hit Iran on the cheap, in some think-tank-concocted "shock and awe" part II. "Precision" attacks—limited to air-defense sites and nuclear facilities—would draw a swift and painful Iranian response against the gulf's oil exports.

And one last worry: If we decide we have no choice but to attack, we're so casualty-averse that our civilian leadership is apt to put critical targets off-limits to spare Iranian lives. We still want to win wars without hurting anybody, by just breaking the other guy's toys. And that's never going to happen.

If we have to fight, we have to fight to win.

Take down Iran's nuke program? I'm damned certain of one thing: If we start this one, we'd better get it right from the first shot.

War's Irrational Motivators

Armed Forces Journal

August 2008

The fundamental dictum guiding our diplomats and analysts has been that states and human collectives act in their own rational self-interest. This is utterly wrong, leading us to convoluted analyses that seek to justify our assumption, while guaranteeing diplomatic failure: It's difficult to defeat an enemy or even negotiate with a partner whose motivation you refuse to understand.

The fantasy claiming that states will act in their own rational self-interest is a product of late eighteenth- and nineteenth-century European self-delusion. Babble about enlightened self-interest made no sense when applied to a Promethean figure such as Napoleon—or to Britain's or the Iberian population's resistance to Napoleonic power. Accommodation, not confrontation, would have been the rational choice. The renowned nineteenth-century Austrian diplomat Prince Klemens Metternich was the exception, not the rule, and popular revolutions soon would shake the continent as states consistently failed to act in their own enlightened or rational self-interest. (We mistakenly equate reactionary politics with rational politics). The Prussian wars of aggression later in the nineteenth century masqueraded as Realpolitik but were, in fact, outbursts of nationalist fervor. Then came World War I, perhaps the most irrational major conflict in history.

Yet, the myth of rational self-interest as the motive factor in the behavior of states and peoples persisted. Mussolini launched wars of pride and Hitler indulged in grudge-fight wars of passion—of the Axis Powers, only Japan showed a glimmer of rational self-interest, although it expressed it in irrational acts. Nonetheless, the comforting delusion that human beings and their governments could, in the end, be counted upon to behave logically persisted. Nuclear arsenals expanded until they were capable of destroying life on earth many times over; their use has been prevented by fear, not reason.

The great decisions of our personal lives, too, are the products of emotion, not rational analysis (how many of us calmly choose a spouse according to a checklist?) Even academic disciplines increasingly accept the existence of irrationality in individual and collective decisionmaking. The great holdouts against the obvious are in the field of international relations, on campus, in think tanks, and in our State Department—although Pentagon and CIA analysts also contort themselves to fit acts of religious fervor or blood passion into a logical framework. From suicide bombers to the nationalist bumptiousness of today's Russia, analysts strive to construct rational models to explain emotion-driven behavior.

EMOTIONAL SELF-INTEREST
Instead of clinging to the failed model of rational self-interest as an analytical tool, substitute "emotional self-interest." It's akin to switching on a light. If, instead of fabricating logical sequences of calculation where none exist, we accept that individuals, peoples, and states act in ways that are emotionally satisfying, no end of knotty analytical problems dissolve. Whether we look at why we vote for the candidates we do, why a terrorist straps on a suicide belt, why Hutus massacred one million Tutsis with cold steel, or why states blunder into war, assessing the degree of emotional satisfaction gained from the act is as enlightening as seeking logic in such deeds is frustrating.

Consider a range of historical examples—chosen from many, many more—that snap into focus if we accept that emotion trumps reason in human affairs:

The Crusades. Since abandoning religious belief as beneath contempt, academic historians have struggled unconvincingly to explain why, over two centuries, hundreds of thousands of European dukes, knights, retainers, laborers, peasants, priests, mendicants, and not a few women left their homes to march east to free the Holy Land through force of arms without so much as reliable maps to guide them. Yes, younger sons were superfluous. But kings went, too. Yes, Europe had surplus labor. But why not let your neighbor risk his life? Yes, there was a chance of glory and wealth. But that was for the very few, not the masses, and even after riches proved illusory for most and tens of thousands perished miserably long before nearing the Holy Land, tens of thousands more knelt and took the cross.

Meta-Darwinism may one day offer a convincing explanation for this phenomenon, but for now the obvious answer is that a contagious, ecstatic vision of a divinely sanctioned mission, reinforced by the promise of eternal salvation, led vast columns of Europeans to brave hunger, thirst, plagues, betrayal, pirates, slavery, and battles against daunting odds in their determination to reach an envisioned Jerusalem of which they possessed not so much as a crude sketch. Few Crusaders survived to claim success of any kind, yet the emotional fervor believers felt was satisfying enough to justify unimaginable suffering. No Marxist explanation of the Crusades works. Emotional self-interest shaped by religious belief was the organizing factor.

The Holocaust. Fast forward to another historical enigma, in which Europe's German-speaking populations (abetted by others) systematically rooted out their Jewish minorities and did their best to exterminate them. In terms of rational self-interest, this was madness: Per capita, Jews made a disproportionate contribution to the modernization of Germany and Austria, leading developments in science, medicine, education, the arts, banking, and industrialization. German Jews, especially, saw themselves as every bit as patriotically German as any other citizen of the Reich (and proved it by winning an impressive number of awards for valor in World War I). The average German lost nothing because of his Jewish fellow citizens and gained a great deal. Yes, some Ostpreussische Junker had mortgaged their estates, while Christian academics sometimes felt envious of the success of their Jewish colleagues. But no explanation couched in terms of rational self-interest begins to offer a convincing explanation for the passion, energy, and commitment of resources in wartime that the German people applied to the destruction of European Jewry.

Instead, look at this monstrous frenzy in terms of the emotional satisfaction it provided. In "the Germanies," anti-Semitism enjoyed a popular appeal dating back to the Crusades and beyond—not only because Jews were different, but also because human beings need a malign force to blame for their self-wrought difficulties (or for acts of nature, such as epidemics). The factual innocence of the Jews was irrelevant. The cathartic satisfaction of taking revenge on a caricatured, dehumanized enemy, in nodding approvingly as thugs smashed shop windows and bellowed "Juden raus!" was enormous: Was anything pleasanter to a good German in 1938 than seeing a middle-class Jewish family reduced to a huddle of overcoats and suitcases? There was no German silent majority opposed to the Holocaust. If the German majority was silent, it was because they had no objections to what was happening and quite liked the whole business.

Enlightened self-interest? A dead end analytically. Emotional self-interest? There you have it. The satisfaction Germans derived from tormenting and murdering their Jewish neighbors was so great it drove them to act in a manner directly opposed to their rational self-interest.

At a minimum, analysts should supplement their standard queries as to which material or practical advantages a foreign power or hostile entity gains from a specific course of action with the question of what level of emotional satisfaction the opponent gains from the act itself. The attacks of September 11, 2001, did not deliver rational benefits to the realms of Sunni Islam, but the emotional high even Middle Eastern moderates felt in their immediate aftermath was unprecedented in recent generations.

Arab states, Palestinians, and Israel. According to rational-self-interest models of statecraft, Arab states and Palestinian leaders should have come to terms with reality and made peace with Israel after their defeat in 1967 or, at the latest, after the follow-up war in 1973. Yet only Egypt pursued a limited peace. For all of the other actors—as well as for many individual Egyptians—the emotional cost of making the best possible peace with Israel was unacceptably high. Although some heads of state reasoned that continuing their hostility through other means was necessary to ensure their personal survival, Arab populations, including the Palestinians, had far more to gain in practical terms through peace, trade, the reduction of military budgets, etc.

Pride trumped profit and progress. Telling themselves that, one day, the "Palestinian homelands" would be free once more—in fact, they were never free—Arab states and Palestinians alike continued to impoverish themselves for an odds-against-it dream. When Washington's emissaries touch down in the West Bank or Damascus with their carefully reasoned briefs as to who would gain what on a practical level, they're deaf and blind to the driving force behind the region's intractability: emotion.

Post-Soviet Russia. The collapse of the USSR resulted in a tremendous outburst of goodwill toward the new Russia. Indeed, it's hard to find another instance of the international community bringing such positive emotions to bear so swiftly on a recently threatening state that had oppressed hundreds of millions. Virtually everyone wanted to cooperate with, do business with, and invest in Russia. Western expectations soared extravagantly. Russia could write its own ticket.

Russia did. Unable to surmount its traditional paranoia, suspicious of the best intentions, humiliated by the loss of empire, and spiteful by character, Russia attempted to bully its former possessions, supplying arms to separatist groups and irredentist factions while invading one of its internal states—Chechnya—in a disastrous bloodbath. Instead of the rule of law, power brokers ruled. Business contracts were abrogated without regard to legality, starry-eyed foreign friends were rebuffed, and, by the time Vladimir Putin succeeded Boris Yeltsin as president, Russia had thrown away its chances for mutually beneficial cooperation with most of its former possessions and with all of its former satellites. Instead, the Kremlin re-embraced rogue regimes.

Rather than patiently developing a seductive energy strategy, in successive fits of pique, the Kremlin cut natural gas supplies to Ukraine and Georgia in the dead of winter, alerting Europe to the long-term dangers of an over-reliance on Russian gas. Instead of concealing its cyberattack capabilities until a real crisis arose, the Kremlin tipped its hands and attacked Estonia's infrastructure over the removal of a minor monument from one site to another. Aware on an intellectual level that a nuclear-armed Iran is a far greater threat to Russia and its interests than to Europe or North America, the Kremlin nonetheless sold dangerous technology to Tehran in deals whose profits were slight compared to the existential risks involved—helping Iran was another way to poke the West and, especially, Washington in the eye. Of late, Russia has been staging military provocations against Georgia, a tiny state that poses no threat to Moscow, but whose nascent democracy and rejection of Russian suzerainty is viewed as an affront by the Kremlin's masters.

Russia may produce brilliant mathematicians and chess masters, but its foreign policy has been driven by emotional self-interest, not rational calculation. The Schadenfreude Russians feel they are teaching the West a lesson. But how rational is it to scrape up spare parts to get two antique bombers into the air and fly them toward a U.S. Navy carrier? What does Russia gain in practical terms? We know their military is in a disastrous state, and they know that we know it. But such gestures make them feel good.

For our part, the U.S. Realpolitik quickly foundered on passionate national liberation movements then broke up on the rocks of reawakened religious fervor. Our diplomats are survivors clinging to rafts and driftwood. Our cherished explanations just don't work. And yet, we keep squeezing every new analytical problem into the old cookie press of material or political advantage. This is the behavior of the certifiably insane: the endless repetition of the same failed action in the expectation of a different outcome next time.

Suicide bombers. One of the most dismaying experiences I've had in Washington since September 11, 2001, (that's quite a standard) came a few years ago after a briefing at the National Counter-Terrorism Center. A senior analyst dismissively told me that Islamist suicide bombers were never motivated by religion. "Research has shown" that most had practical grievances, a mistreated relative, or personal reverses. And that was that. The point that many of us have personal grievances but that few Western Christians, Jews, or atheists become suicide bombers was lost on him. Nor did the logic faze him that taking revenge for a grievance need not involve suicide—why not just emplace a bomb and scram?

The analyst, who had little personal exposure to Muslim societies, could not grasp that religion isn't solely about personal faith, but also pervades the social environment, setting the parameters of acceptable behavior even for those who shrug at belief. The proud mother of the suicide bomber didn't factor into that analyst's equation, since she didn't fit. Yet it has been the atmosphere of encouragement and approval, of admiration for the sacrifice of self-immolation, that has fostered the cult of the suicide bomber. While offense given to a sister or the imprisonment of a cousin might have awakened the impulse, it was ultimately the sense of emotional satisfaction, of anticipated catharsis and the admiration of others that compelled the suicide bomber to walk into a marketplace or a clinic and detonate himself.

Logic doesn't work here. Suicide bombing is an emotional act. The puppet masters above the bomber may have cynical goals (along with their religious zeal), but suicide bombing doesn't make sense in a Cartesian universe—the obvious point being that human beings don't operate according to strict Cartesian logic even in the West, and when we expect them to do so, we call it wrong.

Suicide bombing isn't a logical act. It's a selfish one.

The bring-the-troops-home-now movement. If you need an example closer to home of how emotional satisfaction trumps rational self-interest in human affairs, you need look no further than the current mindset of the leave-Iraq-now advocates in the United States.

Over the past eighteen months, the situation in Iraq has turned around remarkably, and, while challenges remain, every major indicator has turned positive. A strictly logical analysis would suggest that, at this point, a premature withdrawal of our forces would pose enormous risks to Iraq, to the region, and to our own security. Furthermore, with casualties down and "peace breaking out," there are no compelling logical arguments for a swift retreat. According to the rational-self-interest model, activist politicians and voters should have changed their positions. Yet there has been no shift at all in the position of antiwar activists in the face of the evidence that the surge succeeded, that Iraqis are making rapid progress, that al Qa'eda has suffered a catastrophic defeat, while Iranian designs have been frustrated, and that an objective assessment suggests that the odds now favor a reasonably positive outcome. Given the proven threat that al Qa'eda has posed to our citizens and our interests, the terrorist organization's loss of potency and status alone would argue that our efforts are not wasted, while a premature evacuation would allow al Qa'eda to claim victory and recover. In terms of rational self-interest, we should stay—hands down.

But rational self-interest was never in play for most of the activists. Empirical data are irrelevant. The movement was always about emotional satisfaction, about acting out, about an emotional rejection of our involvement in Iraq as a symbol of their perceived political and social nemeses. One only has to turn on the television to hear yet another political activist deny that the surge has made any difference. The behavior is that of a child shutting his eyes and clamping his hands over his ears to make reality go away.

This isn't a matter of whether we should or should not have gone into Iraq. Responsible citizens can disagree about that. The point is that emotional self-interest, the need to be right at all costs, trumps both reason and our collective self-interest—and we're supposed to be the rational actors on the world stage.

The closest thing we have witnessed in our own country to rational self-interest in the behavior of individuals has been the drop in sales of SUVs during the current fuel-cost crisis. On the other hand, it wasn't rational calculation that drove the huge sales of SUVs over the past decade but emotional self-interest, the satisfaction of projecting a certain image in the dangerous wilds of suburbia.

The purpose of this essay is not to argue against objective analysis but to expand the scope of our analysis to include a consideration of our opposite number's emotional needs. Identifying an enemy's emotional composition is essential to predicting his strategic course: In the ineffectual shock-and-awe campaign against Saddam Hussein's regime, we expected him to respond according to our desires and we ignored his own emotional makeup; the result was that our "rational analysis" proved to be irrational, a case of wishful thinking carried to a strategic extreme. It was a repetition of our analysis in 1990, when our diplomats and their advisers reasoned that Saddam would not be irrational enough to invade Kuwait—we looked at the dictator's world through Western lenses and failed to see what was happening, literally, before our eyes in Iraqi divisional assembly areas on the border.

We rely on analytical methodology that fits our own prejudices comfortably, rather than on techniques suited to the strategic climate. That, too, is an emotional choice.

We need not totally discard rational analytical models, but we must stop relying on them exclusively. In Iraq, Afghanistan, Pakistan, Sudan, the West Bank, Russia, and on, ad infinitum, we can witness, on any given day, how powerful emotion can be as a galvanizing factor, how dominant emotional self-interest is in human affairs, and how passion trumps practicality, while pride overrules rational self-interest.

It isn't the human mind that's the killer. It's the human heart.

Wishful Thinking and Indecisive Wars

The Journal of National Security Affairs

Spring 2009

The most troubling aspect of international security for the United States is not the killing power of our immediate enemies, which remains modest in historical terms, but our increasingly effete view of warfare. The greatest advantage our opponents enjoy is an uncompromising strength of will, their readiness to "pay any price and bear any burden" to hurt and humble us. As our enemies' view of what is permissible in war expands apocalyptically, our self-limiting definitions of allowable targets and acceptable casualties—hostile, civilian, and our own—continue to narrow fatefully. Our enemies cannot defeat us in direct confrontations, but we appear determined to defeat ourselves.

Much has been made over the past two decades of the emergence of "asymmetric warfare," in which the ill-equipped confront the superbly armed by changing the rules of the battlefield. Yet such irregular warfare is not new—it is warfare's oldest form, the stone against the bronze-tipped spear—and the crucial asymmetry does not lie in weaponry, but in moral courage. While our most resolute current enemies—Islamist extremists—may violate our conceptions of morality and ethics, they also are willing to sacrifice more, suffer more, and kill more (even among their own kind) than we are. We become mired in the details of minor missteps, while fanatical holy warriors consecrate their lives to their ultimate vision. They live their cause, but we do not live ours. We have forgotten what warfare means and what it takes to win.

There are multiple reasons for this American amnesia about the cost of victory. First, we, the people, have lived in unprecedented safety for so long (despite the now-faded shock of September 11, 2001) that we simply do not feel endangered; rather, we sense that what nastiness there may be in the world will always occur elsewhere and need not disturb our lifestyles. We like the *frisson* of feeling a little guilt, but resent all calls to action that require sacrifice.

Second, collective memory has effectively erased the European-sponsored horrors of the last century; yesteryear's "unthinkable" events have become, well, unthinkable. As someone born only seven years after the ovens of Auschwitz stopped smoking, I am stunned by the common notion, which prevails despite ample evidence to the contrary, that such horrors are impossible today.

Third, ending the draft resulted in a superb military, but an unknowing, detached population. The higher you go in our social caste system, the less grasp you find of the military's complexity and the greater the expectation that, when employed, our armed forces should be able to fix things promptly and politely.

Fourth, an unholy alliance between the defense industry and academic theorists seduced decisionmakers with a false-messiah catechism of bloodless war. In pursuit of billions in profits, defense contractors made promises impossible to fulfill, while think-tank scholars sought acclaim by designing warfare models that excited political leaders anxious to get off cheaply, but which left out factors such as the enemy, human psychology, and five thousand years of precedents.

Fifth, we have become largely a white-collar, suburban society in which a child's bloody nose is no longer a routine part of growing up, but grounds for a lawsuit; the privileged among us have lost the sense of grit in daily life. We grow up believing that safety from harm is a right that others are bound to respect as we do. Our rising generation of political leaders assumes that, if anyone wishes to do us harm, it must be the result of a misunderstanding that can be resolved by that lethal narcotic of the chattering classes, dialogue.

Last, but not least, history is no longer taught as a serious subject in America's schools. As a result, politicians lack perspective; journalists lack meaningful touchstones; and the average person's sense of warfare has been redefined by media entertainments in which misery, if introduced, is brief.

By 1965, we had already forgotten what it took to defeat Nazi Germany and Imperial Japan, and the degeneration of our historical sense has continued to accelerate since then. More Americans died in one afternoon at Cold Harbor during our Civil War than died in six years in Iraq. Three times as many American troops fell during the morning of June 6, 1944, as have been lost in combat in over seven years in Afghanistan. Nonetheless, prize-hunting reporters insist that our losses in Iraq have been catastrophic, while those in Afghanistan are unreasonably high.

We have cheapened the idea of war. We have had wars on poverty, wars on drugs, wars on crime, economic warfare, ratings wars, campaign war chests, bride wars, and price wars in the retail sector. The problem, of course, is that none of these "wars" has anything to do with warfare as soldiers know it. Careless of language and anxious to dramatize our lives and careers, we have elevated policy initiatives, commercial spats, and social rivalries to the level of humanity's most complex, decisive, and vital endeavor.

One of the many disheartening results of our willful ignorance has been well-intentioned, inane claims to the effect that "war doesn't change anything" and that "war isn't the answer," that we all need to "give peace a chance." Who among us would not love to live in such a splendid world? Unfortunately, the world in which we do live remains one in which war is the primary means of resolving humanity's grandest disagreements, as well as supplying the answer to plenty of questions. As for giving peace a chance, the sentiment is nice, but it does not work when your self-appointed enemy wants to kill you. Gandhi's campaign of nonviolence (often quite violent in its reality) only worked because his opponent was willing to play along. Gandhi would not have survived very long in Nazi Germany, Stalin's Russia, Mao's (or today's) China, Pol Pot's Cambodia, or Saddam Hussein's Iraq. Effective nonviolence is contractual. Where the contract does not exist, Gandhi dies.

Furthermore, our expectations of war's results have become absurd. Even the best wars do not yield perfect aftermaths. World War II changed the planet for the better, yet left the eastern half of Europe under Stalin's yoke and opened the door for the Maoist takeover in China. Should we then declare it a failure and not worth fighting? Our Civil War preserved the Union and abolished slavery—worthy results, surely. Still, it took over a century for equality of opportunity for minorities to gain a firm footing. Should Lincoln have let the Confederacy go with slavery untouched, rather than choosing to fight? Expecting Iraq, Afghanistan, or the conflict of tomorrow to end quickly, cleanly, and neatly belongs to the realm of childhood fantasy, not human reality. Even the most successful war yields imperfect results. An insistence on prompt, ideal outcomes as the measure of victory guarantees the perception of defeat.

Consider the current bemoaning of a perceived "lack of progress" and "setbacks" in Afghanistan. A largely pre-medieval, ferociously xenophobic country that never enjoyed good government or a central power able to control all of its territory had become the hostage of a monstrous regime and a haven for terrorists. Today, Afghanistan has an elected government, feeble though it may be; for the first time in the region's history, some of the local people welcome, and most tolerate, the presence of foreign troops; women are no longer stoned to death in sports stadiums for the edification of the masses; and the most inventive terrorists of our time have been driven into remote compounds and caves. We agonize (at least in the media) over the persistence of the Taliban, unwilling to recognize that the Taliban or a similar organization will always find a constituency in remote tribal valleys and among fanatics. If we set ourselves the goal of wiping out the Taliban, we will fail.

Given a realistic mission of thrusting the Islamists to the extreme margins of society over decades, however, we can effect meaningful change (much as the Ku Klux Klan, whose following once numbered in the millions across our nation, has been reduced to a tiny club of grumps). Even now, we have already won in terms of the crucial question: Is Afghanistan a better place today for most Afghans, for the world, and for us than it was on September 10, 2001? Why must we talk ourselves into defeat?

We have the power to win any war. Victory remains possible in every conflict we face today or that looms on the horizon. But, for now, we are unwilling to accept that war not only is, but must be, hell. Sadly, our enemies do not share our scruples.

THE PRESENT FOE

The willful ignorance within the American intelligentsia and in Washington, D.C., does not stop with the mechanics and costs of warfare, but extends to a denial of the essential qualities of our most determined enemies. While narco-guerrillas, tribal rebels, or pirates may vex us, Islamist terrorists are opponents of a far more frightening quality. These fanatics do not yet pose an existential threat to the United States, but we must recognize the profound difference between secular groups fighting for power or wealth and men whose galvanizing dream is to destroy the West. When forced to assess the latter, we take the easy way out and focus on their current capabilities, although the key to understanding them is to study their ultimate goals—no matter how absurd and unrealistic their ambitions may seem to us.

The problem is religion. Our Islamist enemies are inspired by it, while we are terrified even to talk about it. We are in the unique position of denying that our enemies know what they themselves are up to. They insist, publicly, that their goal is our destruction (or, in their mildest moods, our conversion) in their god's name. We contort ourselves to insist that their religious rhetoric is all a sham, that they are merely cynics exploiting the superstitions of the masses. Setting aside the point that a devout believer can behave cynically in his mundane actions, our phony, one-dimensional analysis of al Qa'eda and its ilk has precious little to do with the nature of our enemies—which we are desperate to deny—and everything to do with us.

We have so oversold ourselves on the notion of respect for all religions (except, of course, Christianity and Judaism) that we insist that faith cannot be a cause of atrocious violence. The notion of killing to please a deity and further his perceived agenda is so unpleasant to us that we simply pretend it away. U.S. intelligence agencies and government departments go to absurd lengths, even in classified analyses, to avoid such basic terms as "Islamist terrorist." Well, if your enemy is a terrorist and he professes to be an Islamist, it may be wise to take him at his word.

A paralyzing problem "inside the Beltway" is that our ruling class has been educated out of religious fervor. Even officials and bureaucrats who attend a church or synagogue each week no longer comprehend the life-shaking power of revelation, the transformative ecstasy of glimpsing the divine, or the exonerating communalism of living faith. Emotional displays of belief make the functional agnostic or social atheist nervous; he or she reacts with elitist disdain. Thus we insist, for our own comfort, that our enemies do not really mean what they profess, that they are as devoid of a transcendental sense of the universe as we are.

History parades no end of killers-for-god in front of us. The procession has lasted at least five thousand years. At various times, each major faith—especially our inherently violent monotheist faiths—has engaged in religious warfare and religious terrorism. When a struggling faith finds itself under the assault of a more powerful foreign belief system, it fights: Jews against Romans, Christians against Muslims, Muslims against Christians and Jews. When faiths feel threatened, externally or internally, they fight as long as they retain critical mass. Today the Judeo-Christian/post-belief world occupies the dominant strategic position, as it has, increasingly, for the last five centuries, its rise coinciding with Islam's long descent into cultural darkness and civilizational impotence. Behind all its entertaining bravado, Islam is fighting for its life, for validation.

Islam, in other words, is on the ropes, despite no end of nonsense heralding "Eurabia" or other Muslim demographic conquests. If demography were all there was to it, China and India long since would have divided the world between them. Islam today is composed of over a billion essentially powerless human beings, many of them humiliated and furiously jealous. So Islam fights and will fight, within its meager-but-pesky capabilities. Operationally, it matters little that the failures of the Middle Eastern Islamic world are self-wrought, the disastrous results of the deterioration of a once-triumphant faith into a web of static cultures obsessed with behavior at the expense of achievement. The core world of Islam, stretching from Casablanca to the Hindu Kush, is not competitive in a single significant sphere of human endeavor (not even terrorism since, at present, we are terrorizing the terrorists). We are confronted with a historical anomaly, the public collapse of a once-great, still-proud civilization that, in the age of supercomputers, cannot build a reliable automobile: enormous wealth has been squandered; human capital goes wasted; economies are dysfunctional; and the quality of life is barbaric. Those who once cowered at Islam's greatness now rule the world. The roughly one-fifth of humanity that makes up the Muslim world lacks a single world-class university of its own. The resultant rage is immeasurable; jealousy may be the greatest unacknowledged strategic factor in the world today.

Embattled cultures dependably experience religious revivals: What does not work in this life will work in the next. All the deity in question asks is submission, sacrifice—and action to validate faith. Unlike the terrorists of yesteryear, who sought to change the world and hoped to live to see it changed, today's terrorists focus on god's kingdom and regard death as a promotion. We struggle to explain suicide bombers in sociological terms, deciding that they are malleable and unhappy young people, psychologically vulnerable. But plenty of individuals in our own society are malleable, unhappy, and unstable. Where are the Western atheist suicide bombers?

To make enduring progress against Islamist terrorists, we must begin by accepting that the terrorists are Islamists. And the use of the term "Islamist," rather than "Islamic," is vital—not for reasons of political correctness, but because it connotes a severe deviation from what remains, for now, mainstream Islam. We face enemies who celebrate death and who revel in bloodshed. Islamist terrorists have a closer kinship with the blood cults of the pre-Islamic Middle East—or even with the Aztecs—than they do with the *ghazis* who exploded out of the Arabian desert, ablaze with a new faith. At a time when we should be asking painful questions about why the belief persists that gods want human blood, we insist on downplaying religion's power and insisting that our new enemies are much the same as the old ones. It is as if we sought to analyze Hitler's Germany without mentioning Nazis.

We will not even accept that the struggle between Islam and the West never ceased. Even after Islam's superpower status collapsed, the European imperial era was bloodied by countless Muslim insurrections, and even the Cold War was punctuated with Islamist revivals and calls for jihad. The difference down through the centuries was that, until recently, the West understood that this was a survival struggle and did what had to be done (the myth that insurgents of any kind usually win has no historical basis). Unfortunately for our delicate sensibilities, the age-old lesson of religion-fueled rebellions is that they must be put down with unsparing bloodshed—the fanatic's god is not interested in compromise solutions. The leading rebels or terrorists must be killed. We, on the contrary, want to make them our friends.

The paradox is that our humane approach to warfare results in unnecessary bloodshed. Had we been ruthless in the use of our overwhelming power in the early days of conflict in both Afghanistan and Iraq, the ultimate human toll—on all sides—would have been far lower. In warfare of every kind, there is an immutable law: If you are unwilling to pay the butcher's bill up front, you will pay it with compound interest in the end. Iraq was not hard; we made it so. Likewise, had we not tried to do Afghanistan on the cheap, Osama bin Laden would be dead and al Qa'eda even weaker than it is today.

When the United States is forced to go to war—or decides to go to war—it must intend to win. That means that rather than setting civilian apparatchiks to calculate minimum force levels, we need to bring every possible resource to bear from the outset—an approach that saves blood and treasure in the long run. And we must stop obsessing about our minor sins. Warfare will never be clean, soldiers will always make mistakes, and rounds will always go astray, despite our conscientious safeguards and best intentions. Instead of agonizing over a fatal mistake made by a young Marine at a roadblock, we must return to the fundamental recognition that the greatest "war crime" the United States can commit is to lose.

OTHER THREATS, NEW DIMENSIONS

Within the defense community, another danger looms: the risk of preparing to re-fight the last war, or, in other words, assuming that our present struggles are the prototypes of our future ones. As someone who spent much of the 1990s arguing that the U.S. armed forces needed to prepare for irregular warfare and urban combat, I now find myself required to remind my former peers in the military that we must remain reasonably prepared for traditional threats from states.

Yet another counter-historical assumption is that states have matured beyond fighting wars with each other, that everyone would have too much to lose, that the interconnected nature of trade makes full-scale conventional wars impossible. That is precisely the view that educated Europeans held in the first decade of the twentieth century. Even the youngish Winston Churchill, a veteran of multiple colonial conflicts, believed that general war between civilized states had become unthinkable. It had not.

Bearing in mind that, while neither party desires war, we could find ourselves tumbling, à la 1914, into a conflict with China, we need to remember that the apparent threat of the moment is not necessarily the deadly menace of tomorrow. It may not be China that challenges us, after all, but the unexpected rise of a dormant power. The precedent is there: in 1929, Germany had a playground military limited to a hundred thousand men. Ten years later, a rearmed Germany had embarked on the most destructive campaign of aggression in history, its killing power and savagery exceeding that of the Mongols. Without militarizing our economy (or indulging our unscrupulous defense industry), we must carry out rational modernization efforts within our conventional forces—even as we march through a series of special-operations-intensive fights for which there is no end in sight. We do not need to bankrupt ourselves to do so, but must accept an era of hard choices, asking ourselves not which weapons we would like to have, but which are truly necessary.

Still, even should we make perfect acquisition decisions (an unlikely prospect, given the power of lobbyists and public relations firms serving the defense industry), that would not guarantee us victory or even a solid initial performance in a future conventional war. As with the struggle to drive terrorists into remote corners, we are limited less by our military capabilities than by our determination to pretend that war can be made innocently.

Whether faced with conventional or unconventional threats, the same deadly impulse is at work in our government and among the think-tank astrologers who serve as its courtiers: An insistence on constantly narrowing the parameters of what is permissible in warfare. We are attempting to impose ever sterner restrictions on the conduct of war even as our enemies, immediate and potential, are exploring every possible means of expanding their conduct of conflicts into new realms of total war.

What is stunning about the United States is the fragility of our system. To strategically immobilize our military, you have only to successfully attack one link in the chain, our satellites. Our homeland's complex infrastructure offers ever-increasing opportunities for disruption to enemies well aware that they cannot defeat our military head-on, but who hope to wage total war asymmetrically, leapfrogging over our ships and armored divisions to make daily life so miserable for Americans that we would quit the fight. No matter that even the gravest attacks upon our homeland might, instead, re-arouse the killer spirit among Americans—our enemies view the home front as our weak flank.

From what we know of emerging Chinese and Russian warfighting doctrine, both from their writings and their actions against third parties, their concept of the future battlefield is all-inclusive, even as we, for our part, long to isolate combatants in a postmodern version of a medieval joust. As just a few minor examples, consider Russia's and China's use of cyber-attacks to punish and even paralyze other states. We are afraid to post dummy websites for information-warfare purposes, since we have talked ourselves into warfare-by-lawyers. Meanwhile, the Chinese routinely seek to infiltrate or attack Pentagon computer networks, while Russia paralyzed Estonia through a massive cyber-blitzkrieg just a couple of years ago. Our potential enemies believe that anything that might lead to victory is permissible. We are afraid that we might get sued.

Yet, even the Chinese and Russians do not have an apocalyptic vision of warfare. They want to survive and they would be willing to let us survive, if only on their terms. But religion-driven terrorists care not for this world and its glories. If the right Islamist terrorists acquired a usable nuclear weapon, they would not hesitate to employ it (the most bewildering security analysts are those who minimize the danger should Iran acquire nuclear weapons). The most impassioned extremists among our enemies not only have no qualms about the mass extermination of unbelievers, but would be delighted to offer their god rivers of the blood of less-devout Muslims. Our fiercest enemies are in love with death.

For our part, we truly think that our enemies are kidding, that we can negotiate with them, after all, if only we could figure out which toys they really want. They pray to their god for help in cutting our throats, and we want to chat.

THE KILLERS WITHOUT GUNS

While the essence of warfare never changes—it will always be about killing the enemy until he acquiesces in our desires or is exterminated—its topical manifestations evolve and its dimensions expand. Today, the United States and its allies will never face a lone enemy on the battlefield. There will always be a hostile third party in the fight, but one which we not only refrain from attacking but are hesitant to annoy: the media.

While this brief essay cannot undertake to analyze the psychological dysfunctions that lead many among the most privileged Westerners to attack their own civilization and those who defend it, we can acknowledge the overwhelming evidence that, to most media practitioners, our troops are always guilty (even if proven innocent), while our barbaric enemies are innocent (even if proven guilty). The phenomenon of Western and world journalists championing the "rights" and causes of blood-drenched butchers who, given the opportunity, would torture and slaughter them, disproves the notion—were any additional proof required—that human beings are rational creatures. Indeed, the passionate belief of so much of the intelligentsia that our civilization is evil and only the savage is noble looks rather like an anemic version of the self-delusions of the terrorists themselves. And, of course, there is a penalty for the intellectual's dismissal of religion: humans need to believe in something greater than themselves, even if they have a degree from Harvard. Rejecting the god of their fathers, the neo-pagans who dominate the media serve as lackeys at the terrorists' bloody altar.

Of course, the media have shaped the outcome of conflicts for centuries, from the European wars of religion through Vietnam. More recently, though, the media have *determined* the outcomes of conflicts. While journalists and editors ultimately failed to defeat the U.S. government in Iraq, video cameras and biased reporting guaranteed that Hezbollah would survive the 2006 war with Israel, and, as of this writing, they appear to have saved Hamas from destruction in Gaza.

Pretending to be impartial, the self-segregating personalities drawn to media careers overwhelmingly take a side, and that side is rarely ours. Although it seems unthinkable now, future wars may require censorship, news blackouts, and, ultimately, military attacks on the partisan media. Perceiving themselves as superior beings, journalists have positioned themselves as protected-species combatants. But freedom of the press stops when its abuse kills our soldiers and strengthens our enemies. Such a view arouses disdain today, but a media establishment that has forgotten any sense of sober patriotism may find that it has become tomorrow's conventional wisdom.

The point of all this is simple: *Win.* In warfare, nothing else matters. If you cannot win clean, win dirty. But *win.* Our victories are ultimately in humanity's interests, while our failures nourish monsters.

In closing, we must dispose of one last mantra that has been too broadly and uncritically accepted: the nonsense that, if we win by fighting as fiercely as our enemies, we will "become just like them." To convince Imperial Japan of its defeat, we not only had to fire-bomb Japanese cities, but drop two atomic bombs. Did we then become like the Japanese of the Greater East Asia Co-Prosperity Sphere? Did we subsequently invade other lands with the goal of permanent conquest, enslaving their populations? Did our destruction of German cities—also necessary for victory—turn us into Nazis? Of course, you can find a few campus leftists who think so, but they have yet to reveal the location of our death camps.

We may wish reality to be otherwise, but we must deal with it as we find it. And the reality of warfare is that it is the organized endeavor at which human beings excel. Only our ability to develop and maintain cities approaches warfare in its complexity. There is simply nothing that human collectives do better (or with more enthusiasm) than fight each other. Whether we seek explanations for human bloodlust in Darwin, in our religious texts (start with the Book of Joshua), or among the sociologists who have done irreparable damage to the poor, we finally must accept empirical reality: at least a small minority of humanity longs to harm others. The violent, like the poor, will always be with us, and we must be willing to kill those who would kill others. At present, the American view of warfare has degenerated from science to a superstition in which we try to propitiate the gods with chants and dances. We need to regain a sense of the world's reality.

Of all the enemies we face today and may face tomorrow, the most dangerous is our own wishful thinking.

Trapping Ourselves
in Afghanistan

and Losing Focus on the Essential Mission

Joint Forces Quarterly

3rd Quarter 2009

Afghanistan doesn't matter. Afghanistan's just a worthless piece of dirt. Al Qa'eda matters. To a lesser degree, the hardline elements within the Taliban matter. Pakistan matters, although there is nothing we can do to arrest its self-wrought decay. But our grand ambition to build an ideal Afghanistan dilutes our efforts to strike our mortal enemies, mires our forces in a vain mission civilatrice, and leaves our troops hostage to the whims of venomous regimes.

Afghanistan is the strategic booby prize. Even a perfect success in Kabul (which we shall not achieve) influences nothing beyond the country's largely imaginary borders. No other state looks to Afghanistan—a historical black hole—as an example. Political partisanship blinded many Americans to the importance of Iraq in our effort to get at the roots of terror. Addressing topical symptoms rather than deep causes, we decided that Afghanistan was vital because our enemies, al Qa'eda's lethal gypsies, had based themselves there when they wore out their welcome elsewhere. The more important issue was the "why?" behind al Qa'eda. That *why* leads to the Arab Middle East, not Afghanistan, and the emotional heart of the Arab world lies in Baghdad. While Saddam Hussein's Iraq was not a safe haven for al Qa'eda, its archetypal problems formed the foundation for Islamist terror: the comprehensive failure of Arab attempts at political modernity, resulting in the estrangement of frustrated individuals who turned to stern Islam as an alternative to secular strongmen and preyed-upon societies. Positive changes in Iraq, however imperfect, will resonate throughout the Middle East (if not as swiftly as the neoconservatives hoped). Progress in Afghanistan is a strategic dead end.

Even the assumption that, if we do not "fix" it to Western specifications, Afghanistan will become a terrorist base again misreads the past. Afghanistan became a terrorist haven because we refused to attack the terrorists we knew were there. Osama bin Laden could have been killed. Al Qa'eda training camps could have been destroyed. The Taliban could have been punished. Instead, the Clinton administration simply hoped the threat would fade away. Our problem was fecklessness, not the neomedieval lifestyle of villagers in remote valleys. We have embraced a challenge of marginal relevance, forgetting that al Qa'eda was a parasite on the Afghan body and choosing to address an Arab-fathered crisis by teaching our values to illiterate tribesmen who do not speak Arabic.

Even if we could persuade Afghan villagers that our values and behaviors are superior, if we could reduce state corruption to a manageable level, if we built thousands of miles of roads, eliminated opium growing, and persuaded Afghans that women are fully human, it would have no effect on al Qa'eda. The terrorists who attacked our homeland were not Afghans. Afghanistan was just a cheap motel that was not particular about asking for identification. Even a return to power of the Taliban—certainly undesirable in human-rights terms—does not mean that September 11, Part Two, then becomes inevitable. The next terror attack on the West will not be launched from Afghanistan.

Pause to consider how lockstep what passes for analysis in Washington has become. The Taliban's asymmetric strategy is not to defeat us militarily, but to make Afghanistan ungovernable. But what if our strategy, instead of seeking to transform the country into a model state, were simply to make it ungovernable for the Taliban? Our chances of success would soar while our costs would plummet. But such a commonsense approach is unthinkable. We think in terms of Westphalian states even where none exist.

We buy into so many unjustified-but-comfortable assumptions that it is bewildering. There is no law, neither our own nor among international statutes, that commands us to rescue every region whence attacks against us originate. Our impulse to lavish aid on former enemies was already a joke in the 1950s. By the 1960s, our "send money" impulse had grown so wanton that it began to destroy allies. In Vietnam, our largesse corrupted our local partners. For their part, the North Vietnamese enjoyed the strength of their poverty: As South Vietnamese officials and officers grabbed everything they could, North Vietnam concentrated on grabbing South Vietnam. Today, we are repeating that strategic decadence, deluging an ethically inept government with so much aid that we only anger the frustrated population while enriching those in power. And, of course, we hardly give a thought to what the Afghan people truly want or do not want.

Nor are we willing to recognize that the Taliban, or something like it, will always exist in those forbidding valleys. Unlike al Qa'eda in Iraq, the Taliban is an indigenous movement (its rise accelerated by aid from Pakistan's Inter-Services Intelligence). The hold of religion—and the paralyzing social customs upon which faith insists—is powerful beyond our ken. We wish it away, pointing out the corruption among mullahs or the hypocrisy of believers willing to stone women to death for human foibles while enjoying the forbidden delights of pederasty themselves. But if hypocrisy negated the power of religion, there would be no religion anywhere. The human mind grows supple when self-interest and power come into play—even the mind chock full of religious doctrine. *Do as I say, not as I do* is an appropriate motto for faiths of all complexions—but that does not make religion any less potent. A "holy man" can rationalize personal monkey business in any number of ways but still believe implacably in the destiny of his faith. The Taliban's rank and file are not draftees, after all. Yes, social pressures exist, and, for some, fighting is a job (and not an unwelcome one). But subtract religion from the equation and we have no Taliban (or al Qa'eda).

A modern state as we wish to see it rise cannot coexist with Afghanistan's traditional values. The distance between Afghanistan and Iraq is not twelve hundred miles, but twelve hundred years—give or take a few modern weapons.

This circles back to the prime thesis of this essay: even if everything broke our way in Afghanistan, so what? Afghanistan is a sideshow to its eastern neighbor, Pakistan, and to its western neighbor, Iran. We are renovating, at great cost, the outhouse between two blazing strategic mansions.

When Washington dramatically increases aid to a troubled country—as we are doing with Pakistan—we might as well put the death notice on the international obituary page. Pakistan, which has well over five times Afghanistan's population and a nuclear arsenal, cannot be rescued by American efforts. Why? Because Pakistan does not *want* to be rescued. A succession of demagogues (including the late Benazir Bhutto) turned the country into an anti-American bastion by blaming Washington for every jot of suffering in Sindh and each increase in poverty in the Punjab. Pakistan cannot serve up its favored elements within the Taliban (although the military is willing to take on other elements of that complex network of fundamentalist organizations). Ever obsessed with India, Pakistan views Afghanistan as providing strategic depth and sees "its" Taliban as a useful auxiliary force. Now, having underestimated the power and will of Islamists, Pakistan's government and military watch helplessly as terror groups gnaw into the country's vitals. Pakistan is the new ground zero of terror.

And it is our lifeline.

CRIMINAL IRRESPONSIBILITY

Even if Afghanistan were important to our security, we would still be foolish to deploy ever more troops in the nebulous hope that things will somehow break our way. We have reached—indeed, passed—a point where our military's can-do attitude and our government's nice-to-do impulses have put our troops in the worst position they have faced since the autumn of 1950 in Korea, if not since December 1941 in the Philippines.

While I recognize that, given the time and resources, our troops can defeat (although not destroy) the Taliban and keep a Kabul government in office indefinitely, the problem is not the quality or even the quantity of our Armed Forces, but the vagueness and relative pointlessness of the tasks assigned: our men and women in uniform will do what they are asked and do it well, but decisionmakers should ask them to do sensible, useful things.

As I write, we are sending twenty-one thousand additional American troops to Afghanistan, with the prospect that more will follow. It is appalling—and a gross dereliction of duty—that no senior officers have spoken out against the violation of fundamental military principles involved in this troop increase.

In order to roll more Afghan rocks uphill, we are ignoring the *essential* requirement to secure supply lines adequate to the mission. Even if Afghanistan were worth an increased effort, the lack of reliable, redundant lines of communication to support our forces would argue against piling on. In the wake of 9/11, it was vital to send Special Operations Forces and limited conventional elements to Afghanistan to *punish* al Qa'eda and its hosts despite the risks. Indeed, we might usefully have sent more soldiers in those early months. But instead of striking hard, shattering our enemies, then withdrawing—the one military approach that historically worked in Afghanistan—we put down roots, allowing ourselves to become reliant upon a tortuous fifteen-hundred-mile lifeline from the Pakistani port of Karachi northward through the Khyber Pass to various parts of Afghanistan.

We have put ourselves at the mercy of a corrupt government of dubious stability with an agenda discordant with ours. Strategically, our troops are Pakistan's hostages.

And Islamabad already has taken advantage of our foolishness. While milking us for all the military and economic aid it can extract, Pakistan's security services recently demonstrated just how reliant we are on their good will. In the wake of the Mumbai bombings—sponsored by a terror organization tacitly supported by Pakistan's government—attacks on our convoys transiting the Khyber Pass, as well as raids on supply yards in Peshawar, swelled in number and soared in their success rate. This could not have occurred had the Pakistanis not given the green light to the attacks. Pakistan was strong-arming us into getting an angry India under control. And we did.

Serious strategy requires balancing potential rewards with inherent risks. Above all, it demands a clear recognition of what is doable and what is not, as well as the ability to differentiate between what is merely nice to do and what is essential. A strategic goal may be desirable in itself but not worth the probable cost. To put fifty thousand or more U.S. troops at risk demands a no-nonsense analysis of the dangers weighted against the potential strategic return. That analysis has not been done. We are arguing over tactics and thinking, at most, in terms of operations, while missing the critical strategic context.

Meanwhile, the belated awareness that our troops are de facto prisoners of war to Pakistan has led to the even greater folly of contemplating a four-thousand-mile supply line from the Baltic Sea through Russia and various Central Asian states to provide nonlethal goods to our troops and those of the North Atlantic Treaty Organization (NATO). Even though the evidence is irrefutable that Moscow bribed Kyrgyzstan to deny our continued access to Manas Air Base—a critical support node—elements within the U.S. administration actually argue that, in the interests of "resetting" our relationship with Russia, it is essential to "expose" ourselves to risk to show the Russians that we trust them. These are serious arguments made by American officials. One suspects they do not have children serving in our military.

Few strategic calculations are more obvious than Prime Minister Vladimir Putin's ploy to addict us to a Russian-controlled supply line. With a domestic economic crisis on his hands (during which he still managed to promise Kyrgyzstan $2.5 billion to close Manas to us), he senses that he will need to create foreign diversions and that the time is right to back an electoral *putsch* in Ukraine and to force regime change in Georgia. Putin calculates that we would accept these moves (protesting vigorously and briefly) in order to keep the supply line open. We are walking into *this* trap with our eyes willfully shut to the obvious peril.

Other voices have suggested bargaining for an ambitious supply route across China into the Afghan panhandle, crossing some of the roughest country on Earth. There are even whispers about opening a line of communication through Iran, an exemplary case of leaping out of the frying pan into the fire.

The logistics problem should have shaped our strategy in Afghanistan. After the late spring of 2002—when we had done what *needed* doing in Afghanistan—our further goals and the means allocated to achieve them should have been determined by one ironclad criterion: What size force could be deployed, sustained, and, if need be, evacuated *in its entirety* by airlift? One vehicle beyond that calculation is one vehicle too many.

Even beyond the logistics debacle, we lack an integrated strategy, either specific to Afghanistan or regional. We have picked the wrong country to "save." We are sending more troops, without clearly defining the endstate they are to achieve (echoes of Vietnam there). And the problem is where we *are not*—in Pakistan and, to an even greater extent, on the Arabian Peninsula. Indeed, there are serious opportunity costs worldwide, including in our own hemisphere, that are bewilderingly absent from the national debate—to the extent Washington allows a serious debate.

Yes, we *can* make Afghanistan a better place, for us and for the Afghans, if we are willing to remain for a full generation while immobilizing a substantial slice of our battle-worn Armed Forces (it is astonishing that, as Mexico degenerates under the impact of a savage narco-insurgency, our military officers are agonizing over the moods of toothless village elders on the other side of the world; the crisis is on our border here and now, and it is fueled by an array of other drugs, not opium).

Even if we hang on in Afghanistan, giving our all as we bribe cynical foreign powers to let us feed our troops, what ultimate benefit will make the mission worthwhile? Be *specific*: What do we get out of it?

Can we even define the mission in plain English?

WHAT MAKES SENSE

Historically, our military has taken risks with its logistics under three types of circumstances: when we had no choice, as in the desperate efforts in the North Atlantic or the Pacific in the first years of our involvement in World War II; when the gamble was carefully calculated to achieve a clearly defined end *and* was of limited duration, as in Winfield Scott's march on Mexico City or the culminating maneuvers of Ulysses Grant's Vicksburg campaign; or when we grew overconfident and careless, which led to the Bataan Death March and the collapse of the thrust toward the Yalu in Korea. The fragile lines of communication supporting our forces and those of our allies in Afghanistan do not fit the first two models.

Any serious strategic analysis would recognize that Pakistan is the problem, not part of the solution. Our natural ally in the subcontinent is India, but developing a closer relationship with New Delhi will be strained by our need to warn India off from retaliating after Pakistani-sponsored or Islamabad-condoned provocations. Pakistan has no incentive to stop its rabble-rousing efforts to embarrass India over Kashmir or other matters, since Islamabad is convinced that we will keep an angry India in check. (Were we completely honest with ourselves, we would recognize that a nuclear exchange between India and Pakistan, however grim in human terms, would not only leave India the clear victor, but might solve quite a number of strategic problems.) Under the current conditions, Pakistan, a state that cannot control its own territory, is our regional boss.

And every troop increase in Afghanistan strengthens Pakistan's grip on us. Or, God help us, Russia's hold, if we really get it wrong.

Another obstacle to a more rational approach to Afghanistan is the difficulty that U.S. officers, once given responsibility for a problem, have in admitting that there may be no solution. Our military is not good at cutting its losses. So now we have flag officers who, protesting all the while that Afghanistan is not Iraq, appear intent on applying the techniques that worked in Iraq to Afghanistan: troop surges, security for the population, train up the local security forces, and so forth. While the situational differences are so great that it would require another article of this length to enumerate them, the basic proposition is that Iraq is a semimodern society that wants to get better, while Afghanistan is a feudal society content with its ways and impatient with our presence (in large part thanks to the cynical populism of President Hamid Karzai). In Iraq, religious extremism was imported. In Afghanistan, it sprouts from the soil with the ease of poppies.

And, decisively, Iraq matters.

To determine which strategy makes sense going forward, we need to have the mental discipline to distinguish between what we need to do for our own security and what merely appears desirable to idealists. We *do* need to continue to hunt al Qa'eda and to prevent Afghanistan from becoming a safe haven for global-reach Islamist terrorists again. We do *not* need to pursue the disproportionately expensive and probably futile mission of creating a modern state in the Hindu Kush. Indeed, a fundamental problem we face is that Afghanistan was never an integrated state in which a central government's writ ran to each remote valley. Afghanistan has always meant the city-state of Kabul, with tributary cities along caravan routes and tribal regions that coexisted under various terms of compromise with the government and their neighbors. Iraq at least has a nascent, if not yet robust, sense of national identity. Beyond a few Western-educated figures, Afghanistan does not and will not.

If we accept the need to continue the pursuit of our sworn enemies, but abandon the self-imposed requirement to build a modern state where none existed, the dimensions of the problem shrink and our requirements become sustainable. A sound strategy with realistic goals would look different from our present approach, though. Roughly outlined, the strategic goals and means from which we might choose are these:

Enemy-focused Approach #1. Concentrate on the continued attrition of al Qa'eda and the prevention of an outright Taliban takeover. Cease development efforts. Turn domestic security requirements over to "our" Afghans, reversing our hapless attempt at being an honest broker in favor of supporting those figures and groups willing to fight against the radical Islamists. Reduce our footprint to a force that can, if necessary, be sustained entirely by air (fifteen thousand troops or less). Establish a mothership base at Bagram, with a few subsidiary bases distributed around the country. Design our residual force around special operations capabilities reinforced by drones, conventional attack, and rotary wing aircraft, and sufficient conventional forces for local defense and punitive raids. Ask all NATO forces that do not contribute directly to the core mission of destroying our mutual enemies to leave the country. Ignore the opium issue. Instead of attempting to foster governance, concentrate on rendering provinces ungovernable for the most extreme Taliban elements, striking fiercely whenever they come out in the open to exercise control of the population.

Enemy-focused Approach #2. While less desirable than the first approach, a complete withdrawal of our forces from Afghanistan—while continuing to strike our enemies with over-the-horizon weapons and supporting anti-Taliban Afghan factions to keep the Pashtun provinces ungovernable by our enemies—

would still be preferable to an increase in our present forces. Allow Afghanistan to further disintegrate if that is its fate. Let an unfettered India deal with Pakistan.

The past and persistent tragedy of our involvement in Afghanistan began with our unwillingness to accept that punishing our enemies is a legitimate military mission and need not be followed by reconstruction largesse. We never sense when it is time to leave the party, so we wind up drunk on mission creep. At home, a polarized electorate defined our simultaneous commitments solely in domestic political terms: For the left, Iraq was Bush's war and, therefore, bad. But those on the political left felt the need to demonstrate that they, too, could be strong on national security, so Afghanistan became the good war by default. It has been impossible to have an objective discussion of the relative merits, genuine errors, appropriate lessons, and potential returns of each of these endeavors.

In this long struggle with Islamist terrorists, our focus should not be on holding territory, but on the destruction of our enemies. That is a lesson we should have taken from al Qa'eda's disastrous engagement in Iraq. Thanks to its own grave miscalculations, al Qa'eda suffered a colossal strategic defeat as millions of Sunni Muslims turned against it. Its error was to believe that a terrorist organization could and should hold ground. Al Qa'eda immobilized itself by seeking prematurely to administer cities and districts, forsaking its flexibility and losing the war of popular perceptions. In Afghanistan, we are in danger of making a parallel mistake as we assume that physical terrain still matters.

Throw away the traditional maps. Chart the enemy. Our focus should be exclusively on his destruction.

As the Obama administration attempts to come to grips with the Afghan morass, it must begin with the strategist's fundamental question: "What's in it for *us*?"